From "ma" – may, 1998

Our Kind of People

Helen and Bill Yardley at Chatham Hall in the early 1950s

Our Kind of People

THE STORY OF

AN AMERICAN FAMILY

Jonathan Yardley

WEIDENFELD & NICOLSON

NEW YORK

Published by Weidenfeld & Nicolson, New York
A Division of Wheatland Corporation
841 Broadway
New York, New York 10003-4793

Published in Canada by General Publishing Company, Ltd.

Grateful acknowledgment is made to Little, Brown and Company for
permission to quote from Verses from 1929 On by Ogden Nash: "Song
of the Open Road," copyright 1932 by Ogden Nash, first appeared in
The New Yorker; and "The Hippopotamus," copyright 1935 by The Curtis
Publishing Co., first appeared in The Saturday Evening Post.

Wickford Point by John P. Marquand copyright © 1975 by John P.
Marquand is used by permission of Peter Smith Publisher, Inc., Gloucester, MA.

Library of Congress Cataloging-in-Publication Data

Yardley, Jonathan.
    Our kind of people: the story of an American family / Jonathan
Yardley.—1st ed.
        p.   cm.
    ISBN 1-55584-174-0
    1. Yardley family. 2. Yardley, Jonathan—Family. 3. United
States—Biography. I. Title.
CT274.Y37Y37   1989   88-30531
929'.2'0973—dc 19   CIP

Manufactured in the United States of America

This book is printed on acid-free paper

Designed by Irving Perkins Associates

First Edition

1   3   5   7   9   10   8   6   4   2

FOR JANE, SARAH AND BEN

Contents

These matters are of no importance except for the light which they may throw upon strange vanished days which no one living can understand. . . . All those stiff-necked figures in the picture album, with their heads supported by invisible brackets—all their likes and dislikes—all the endless anecdotes about them which have died into a strange hushed silence—have given Wickford Point its quality. As one tries to piece them all together, the responsibility becomes enormous, for one is speculating about history and toying rudely with the springs of change. We can interpret, but we can never know. All that is certain—and this is as sure as fate—is that these vanished people made things what they are.

John P. Marquand
Wickford Point

Behold the hippopotamus!
We laugh at how he looks to us,
And yet in moments dank and grim
I wonder how we look to him.
Peace, peace, thou hippopotamus!
We really look all right to us,
As you no doubt delight the eye
Of other hippopotami.

Ogden Nash
"The Hippopotamus"

Prologue

For NEARLY forty years the secrets of my parents were kept in a wooden cabinet that stood next to the small desk at which my mother conducted her correspondence and paid the family bills. The cabinet had been built for them in 1947 by Toimi Paarsinen, a refugee from Finland who had been hired to teach woodworking at the private school where my father was then headmaster. It was made of mahogany and other old woods and consisted of a single box, fourteen inches wide, twelve high and twelve deep, that could be separated—but in my memory never had been—from the four-legged platform on which it stood. Upon its lid, which lifted toward the rear, was a brass plate on which my parents' names had been engraved:

WILLIAM W. YARDLEY
HELEN G. YARDLEY

I was seven years old when the cabinet was placed in the house we occupied in Tuxedo Park, New York, and forty-seven years old when I opened it for the first time, at the house in Middletown, Rhode Island, where my parents' half-century together ended. In all those intervening years I had no notion, and surprisingly little curiosity, about its contents. The little chest was kept locked when

3

I was a boy, and when I became an adult I lost whatever interest I may once have had in it; I was a man now, with my own life to lead and my own secrets to keep.

Then, on the evening of November 2, 1986, I was in Middletown visiting my father, who had become a widower two months earlier. His poor health had not been improved by his grief and bewilderment at my mother's death; he was in the care of an attendant who lived upstairs in the small bedroom that had once been my sisters'. Dinner was over and she was putting him through his prolonged and elaborate preparations for bed. I had cleared the table and done the dishes, and was sitting near the desk in the old New England corner chair my mother had used throughout her married life. Idly, I brushed my hand upward against the lid of the cabinet. Quite to my astonishment, it opened; as it did, I entered for the first time the world of my parents.

What I found in there startled me; quite literally, it took my breath away. This was not because I found, in the cabinet, amazing surprises about my parents' lives—their lives were quiet, and contained no great surprises—but because I found two adults named Bill and Helen Yardley. Here at last was concrete evidence that they had lived existences quite apart from their roles as parents, that in fact parenthood—however important it may have been to me—had been only one of many interests they followed. They loved their four children deeply and well, but as I read through their old letters and documents and financial statements I understood, more immediately and intimately than I ever before had, that we children had been only part of the picture: and not, in truth, an unduly large part. A few weeks earlier I had read *A Summons to Memphis*, in which Peter Taylor wisely remarks that parents must be "whole human beings and not become merely guardian robots of the young." Here, in that small cabinet, was all the evidence I could ask for of the wholeness of my parents' lives.

Thus, for example, in a file called "H.G.Y.: Personal" I found a collection of letters written in the fall of 1935 to Helen Gregory by a man named J. J. Lankes. My immediate reaction was puzzlement that my mother-to-be should have received flirtatious letters from a strange man only a few months after her engagement, but gradually the purpose of the correspondence became clear. J. J. Lankes, I learned, was a well-known woodcutter, a member of the American Artists Group along with Rockwell Kent, José Orozco, Diego Rivera and others. Helen had written to ask what he would charge for a bookplate—a "B/P," Lankes called it—to be given to her fiancé as a Christmas present. Only Lankes's side of the correspondence survives, but the tone of his letters suggests that she entered enthusiastically into the bantering game he had begun, and that she did nothing to discourage his avuncular, if goatish, interest. As "supplementary compensation" in addition to his $10 fee, he hoped to exact from her a kiss, but that was not to be:

> Yes, I realized immediately on getting your commission to do the Yardley B/P that Yardley stood in the way of getting supplementary compensation. It is my usual luck. I am too early, when not too late, in all things. There is this about the matter that should reconcile you to the loss: You will have a happy life with Yardley. In all cases where one of my bookplates has been used to cement a relation the relation has always been of the sweetest.

Reading those words, I could see Helen Gregory reading them too. She had turned twenty-two and was entering the final months of college. In June of the next year she would be married to a man she scarcely knew and would begin a life the shape of which she could not hope to imagine. For now, though, all was excitement and promise, and to cap it off she was exchanging teasing letters with a woodcutter of sufficient renown to be associated with Kent, Orozco and Rivera. His letters must have thrilled her as much as they amused her, suggesting as they did that she was now sufficiently mature to engage the interest of a proven man of art.

But the man foremost on her mind was Bill Yardley. She gave him the bookplate at Christmas, and it pleased him hugely. It showed a tree bending in the wind, with "YARDLEY" carved below, and it was printed in a mellow shade of green. Then and for the rest of his life he pasted it to the endpapers of every book in a library that over the years grew in size and diversity: Trollope and Faulkner, biblical concordances and encyclopedias of old silver, histories of England and accounts of seafaring heroics, Thackeray and

Marquand. Eventually the bookplate became a totem of my parents' marriage and the family it produced: a flourishing tree that, even without the word below, was the expression and embodiment of "Yardley."

The tree accompanied them to Bedford Village, in Westchester County, and then to Pittsburgh, as my father began his career as a teacher in private schools. The next step was to Tuxedo Park. In a file called "W.W.Y.: Professional" I found an envelope addressed to Mr. and Mrs. William W. Yardley, Tuxedo Park, New York, which contained, on the letterhead of the Tuxedo Park Country Day School, Anthony V. Barber, Headmaster, this brief invitation:

> The Board of Trustees of the Tuxedo Park Country Day School request the pleasure of your company Saturday, the Third of July, at the swimming pool of the Tuxedo Club to meet Mr. and Mrs. William W. Yardley.
>
> From 5:30 P.M. to 7 o'clock

What an evening that must have been! Anthony V. Barber was leaving his post at Tuxedo to assume the headmastership of the Lawrence School, and William W. Yardley, late of the English Department at Shady Side Academy in Pittsburgh, had been chosen to succeed him. All those summers at Harvard, where he had studied "Philosophy of Education" and "Principles of Teaching" and "Educational Measurement," at last were paying off. The school at Tuxedo was small and in difficult times, but it was now *his* school, and at 5:30 on the evening of July 3, 1943, he was to meet for the first time the men and women whose children he had been charged with educating.

That would have been reason enough for excitement and apprehension, but there was more to the occasion than the initial encounter between an educator and his new clients, more even than the moment of passage from the ranks of teachers into those of administrators. Tuxedo Park was a private town, Pierre Lorillard's Beulah Land for the rich and privileged, "a restricted private preserve of over one thousand acres"; my parents had been granted admission to it not as equals—though that is how the best of their new friends would treat them—but as members of the servant class: as providers of a service, in their case education, that the rich and privileged required. It was a role they performed for the rest of their working lives, always with consummate dignity and self-respect, but a role all the same, one that demanded they stand forever poised between the inside and the outside, their circumstances defined by the implacable reality of the money they did not have.

On that afternoon at the Tuxedo Club the presence of money—other people's money—must have been overwhelming. In the clubby little world of northeastern society Tuxedo's club was in that day the ultimate one; not merely was it there that the celebrated Autumn Ball was held—debutantes from the Main Line to the North Shore would happily have killed for invitations to the Autumn Ball—but it was at this club that Lorillard had been seen wearing a formal jacket without tails: the tuxedo, as it came to be known. No doubt my parents carried the day with their customary savoir-faire, but as the afternoon began their nerves must have been taut and at its end their relief must have been inexpressible; they had been placed under the microscope, had been found acceptable, and could now get about the business for which they had been engaged.

Money: they never could get away from it. They rarely had quite enough, and they were forever at the bidding of people who had too much. They always managed to meet their obligations, largely because my mother had a passion for figures and the wit to make them come out right, but it was not until they entered a genteel retirement that they could set financial cares aside; even then, a watchful eye was necessary. There was ample evidence of this in the file cabinet, in the carefully preserved income-tax returns and Medicare forms and merchants' receipts. There was also evidence of it in my mother's personal file:

To Helen, on her 36th Birthday

How soon hath time, upon fast-flying wing,
Stolen away my Helen's six-and-thirtieth year!
May He, in flying, richest blessings bring
And scatter treasures on my never-fading Dear:

7

Diamonds and rubies, otter, mink and fox,
Rosewood, teak, ivory, castle with a moat,
Satin, sapphires, rubies, pearls in silken box—
In lieu of these, accept

> *this plated gravy boat.*

W. W. Y.

11/22/49

That verse was written on the letterhead of Chatham Hall, Office of the Rector, Chatham, Virginia. My father had assumed the position in the summer of 1949, and in so doing had moved into the front rank of private education. Chatham Hall was a school for girls and was regarded by many college admissions directors as the best such school in academic if not social terms. But then as now schools for girls had considerably less éclat than did those for boys; the rector of Chatham Hall might be on speaking terms with the rector of Justin but he spoke from a position of inferiority. This was borne in upon my parents with particular force during the 1950s, as I was painfully reminded by the contents of a file called "Jonathan." My parents had enrolled me in Groton, the preparatory school in Massachusetts upon which Louis Auchincloss's fictional Justin Martyr is based. Just as they had been admitted to Tuxedo Park on sufferance, so I had been allowed to enter Groton on scholarship, a condition I found inherently distasteful. My rebellion against Groton lasted three years and brought me again and again to the edge of dismissal, only to be rescued again and again by my father's pleas. Here is one of them, in a letter to John Crocker, the headmaster of Groton, dated January 2, 1956:

> It is easy to see what sort of boy Johnny must be at school. We have girls of that sort at Chatham Hall. They may not actually commit open crimes, but they nibble at the foundations of what the school is supposed to do. I am mortified that my son finds himself in this undistinguished company and pays back for his scholarship by unconstructive attitudes. . . .
>
> Helen and I think that your talk with him was wonderful and that he is really determined to do well for the rest of the year. If you feel that he would be detrimental as a senior and does not deserve the

chance, by all means act according to your best judgment. Do let me beg of you, however, to let us know as early as possible if you decide he should not return. It is very hard to get a boy into a half-way decent school for his final year, especially if he has been dropped by a first class one.

Let me beg of you too to follow him along a little bit and to lay it on the line in no uncertain terms. He has personally great respect for you, a respect colored by affection and a respect heightened by your conversation of December. It seems to me that education is a redemptive as well as a condemning process and that we school people do not always solve our problems just by getting rid of them. I have got rid of many by the process you suggest for Johnny and these children that I dropped have stayed much longer on my conscience than the problems we kept and continued to work on.

My pain at reading this letter was intense, but it can have been nothing by comparison with my father's at writing it. Not merely were his words abject—"I am mortified"! "Let me beg of you"!— but they were addressed to a man whom he did not like, whom he regarded as overbearing, humorless and self-satisfied. By my childish if explicable behavior I had forced him to address an importuning entreaty to a man whom he saw—whether fairly or not is quite beside the point—as his natural if not titular inferior. That these words were first dictated to his secretary must have been galling; that they were directed to Jack Crocker can only have been unbearable.

Yet if you read these words closely, you will see that Bill Yardley the parent, pleading for his prodigal son, is not the only person speaking here. Bill Yardley the headmaster is also in this letter, and he gives it more dignity than at first it appears to possess. Beneath the words of supplication and abasement lie words of instruction and admonition; the soft glove of humility disguises a mailed fist of conviction about the duties that a school owes to its students. Though Crocker probably was too obtuse to recognize it as such, the final paragraph of that letter is a forthright and uncompromising lecture: "Education is a redemptive as well as a condemning process," and Groton would be a far better place if it did more of the former and less the latter. This, beyond a doubt, is the real message of my father's letter; the message was written man to man, with no subservience or self-abnegation.

But then lecturing was something he did habitually, as a matter of reflex. He was a man of decided and emphatic opinions, and nothing gave him greater pleasure than the expression of them. His correspondence was Menckenian in both vigor and volume, and it was never more splenetic than when he believed himself to have been wronged, especially if the culprit was an institution with which he had regular dealings. He regarded institutions as sentient beings blessed, or cursed, with distinct personalities, and he addressed them accordingly. Consider, for example, a document that I came upon in "W.W.Y.: Personal." It is a letter written on August 28, 1967, to an employee of Brooks Brothers, a haberdasher for which my father nursed a lifelong passion: "Mr. Brooks," he customarily called it. This employee had called my father's attention to a balance overdue on his account and had written—quite politely, as I interpret it—that "if you have no special reason for withholding payment, we would appreciate your cheque within the next few days." My father's reply began with a rather unconvincing defense of his delinquency, then launched into the real business at hand:

> My Brooks Brothers account dates back to my sophomore year in college in the early '30s. Perhaps when Brooks Brothers was really Brooks Brothers things were easier. Most certainly when my account was overdue back in those gentle old, old days I received a very courteous reminder and eventually paid up. If I was slow in paying it was my own extravagance. . . .
>
> I remember my father's saying that if a firm tried to make collections in under a year it was a sign that the firm is financially shaky. I hope certainly that this is not the case with Brooks Brothers. This has been a landmark of mine for nearly all my life. I had been under the delusion that Brooks treated its old customers like human beings, not like IBM cards. I have always hoped that I would be a name, not a number at Brooks.
>
> Perhaps the days when one kept his tailor waiting longest are over.

Ah, yes, "those gentle old, old days": my father pined for them all his life, and the older he got the harder he pined. While my

mother accepted the coming of the new world with good humor
and resignation, my father railed mightily against it. He despised
Mother's Day and television and Muzak and other odious inven-
tions of the age of technology, but his greatest anger was directed at
what he regarded as the loss of old-fashioned civility. His own
manners were ostentatiously impeccable, and he expected the
same in others. When, as was usually the case, he did not receive it,
he reacted either with scorn and ridicule, at both of which he was
astonishingly adept, or with wistful longing. I found an example of
the latter in a file called "Sarah." The younger of my two sisters
had graduated from Chatham Hall in the spring of 1966 and now,
two years later, was at college in Canada. The rebellious urges that
had been suppressed in Chatham were beginning to find expression in the northern air, and her letters home were taking on a
querulous, if not impertinent, air. Here is how our father
responded to one of them:

> I am glad that they call you Miss Yardley at McGill. It is rather
> nice to be given the full stature of adulthood. I have never forgotten
> being called Mr. Yardley as a freshman at the Johns Hopkins, and I
> wonder whether the good old JHU has stuck with this ancient and
> honorable custom: it is an outward and audible sign that the student
> is now an adult, or is at least trying to be one.

But it is a tradition long since abandoned by "the good old JHU"
and every other institution of higher education. The world in
which my father came to maturity, the world he believed to be the
only one worth living in, was near extinction as he wrote those
words, and none of his railings or lamentations could bring it back.
It was in fact his recognition of this unpleasant but inescapable
reality that had much to do with his decision to retire from
Chatham Hall well before his time. The actual date of his departure was June 30, 1971, two months before his sixtieth birthday,
but it had been announced a year earlier, affording him the opportunity for one final hurrah. He had been the rector of Chatham
Hall for more than two decades, and in that time had assembled a
large and loyal constituency. Its members—alumnae, friends of
the school, students, active and former faculty, trustees—greeted

the news of his resignation with dismay that clearly was genuine, and swamped him with letters expressing their admiration and regret. He answered each with a personal note, but in all there was a common theme. It is succinctly expressed in this letter, from a file called "Retirement":

And now let me chide you very gently: Chatham Hall is much more than one family or one person. It is a school. It will endure. Its motto is ESTO PERPETUA. Please renew your loyalty to the school and your total enthusiasm for it because the incoming man will need all the help he can get. He needs loyal old girls like you to support him and be enthusiastic about the school. Most of all new girls come to us through someone else's enthusiasm. Don't you dare go around with a long face about Chatham Hall and the Yardleys! Just be glad that the school has a chance to get fresh new blood and to move on into a new and exciting era.

Thus his career ended, on a note of fealty to the school and its people that may have been as deeply felt as anything he ever said or wrote. Thus, too, my trip through the little cabinet ended. I was exhausted. I closed the file and went to my father's study. I opened the foldaway bed he had often used as refuge from my mother's nocturnal noises and lay down to sleep, but sleep was slow in coming. My head was filled with the images the files had brought to mind, and my heart overflowed with a new, wholly unexpected awareness of my parents. It came to me as I lay in the darkness that at the age of forty-seven I was as old as my father had been when he was at the height of his powers at Chatham Hall, and that I might at last be in a position to understand what life really had been like for him and my mother: to see them not as my parents, but as people. It was a comforting thought, and after a while I slept on it.

But it did not go away. Driving home to Baltimore a couple of days later, I remembered a remark I had noticed in my father's notes for a speech he once gave. "I had been born for the age of steam," he wrote, "and was plunged into the age of electricity which I did not want and still don't particularly like even today." My father was born in 1911, my mother in 1913. Has any generation, in any time or place, ever undergone greater or more traumatic change than that of which my parents were beneficiaries, victims and witnesses? Theirs was the last generation to have seen and known America before its despoliation by the quintuple pestilence of overpopulation, the automobile, the developers, the industrial polluters and television; in the more than three score years and ten of their lives the entire world changed, at a rate so rapid as to be dizzying and disorienting. Yet somehow they not merely survived it but, my father's rumblings and protestations to the contrary notwithstanding, adjusted to it; they absorbed the blows of progress as steadily as they were delivered, and with remarkable equanimity.

But if they managed to cope with change, they did not acquiesce in it. They both honored, in their different ways, the traditions and beliefs—the "values," as our corrupted vocabulary now has it—of that vanished world into which they had been born. Whatever their faults, and certainly both of my parents had faults, they were people of principle and conviction, who had been reared in families and communities that held these qualities in high regard. They believed in loyalty to family both as a particular group and as a general idea; in religious faith, even if they did not always practice it; in patriotism, but devoid of chauvinism or flag-waving; in thrift, both in the expenditure of money and in the exercise of one's energies and talents; in education and knowledge, which were far more to be valued than money and prominence; in skepticism about the fruits of "progress" and willy-nilly growth; in reticence and restraint in personal behavior; in respect for the past and dutiful attention to the lessons it teaches; in the permanence of institutions and the insubstantiality of those who serve them; and in well-rounded, productive lives in which family is as important as work and individual accomplishment. From time to time they strayed from these beliefs, but not far and not for long; whatever else may be said of them, they were good people.

They were also entirely unknown, except within their small circle of friends and professional relationships; my father once remarked, when he was relatively young, that he hoped to have "a niche as a minor character in educational drama"—but his role was indeed minor, and the drama was played out on a small stage. Yet though my parents were anything except famous, their lives and those of their forebears touched in glancing but interesting ways on the country's history. Whether by marriage or by distant relationship or by mere passing acquaintance, the Yardleys and the Gregorys were connected to people who made contributions—in a few instances noteworthy and important ones—to the evolution of American life. These connections meant a great deal to my father, who was prone to exaggerating them, and rather less to my mother, who was not given to flights of fancy; but both of them were pleased to be descendants of men and women who had come to the newfound land in the seventeenth century and who had served, first the colonies and then the country, honorably and well. This sense of personal identification with American history was a central part of their heritage, and they passed it along to their children with the insistence that it be cherished.

Theirs was as well the heritage of those who are white, Anglo-Saxon and Protestant. That meant something quite different at the end of their lives from what it had at the beginning. Though the great wave of immigration from Europe had passed its crest by the time of their birth, the United States was still very much a nation in which white Anglo-Saxon Protestants controlled every significant aspect of public life; as the children of families that had been in the country since its earliest years they had, in Kenneth Rexroth's phrase, "the sense that the country is really theirs," and the knowledge that their birthright was the possibility, if not the eventuality, of successful and prosperous lives. In the circumstance it is hardly surprising that they spent those lives almost entirely in the company of people just like themselves, and that the relatively few hyphenated Americans with whom they came into contact were, with infrequent exceptions, servants and tradespeople.

But though they went quite unaffected by it, the country was changing demographically as well as technologically during these seven traumatic decades. The hyphenated Americans were either abandoning their hyphens or becoming assertively proud of them, and people whose roots lay elsewhere than Mother England and her isles were moving into positions of power and influence. The acronym WASP came into being, and soon evolved into a term of derision, one meant to describe a class of people notable only for their adherence to disagreeable prejudices, their clannish perpetuation of anachronistic totems and taboos, their peculiarly unstylish taste in food and clothing, and their rampant snobbery. This may be an age in which slavish imitation of all things British is a ticket to social success, but that is mere window dressing; as a ruling class, the WASPs are dead.

Perhaps this is all to the good; as a white Anglo-Saxon Protestant who has spent nearly half a century witnessing his fellows at work and play, I can testify to the need of the species for new blood. Yet I am also proud of who I am, proud of those from whom I am descended, and reluctant to see our kind of people reduced to mere caricature. So it is that the more I thought about my parents' lives the more I became convinced that they represented traditions and beliefs deserving praise rather than censure, that their lives were in fact emblematic of those traditions and beliefs.

Reflecting on these matters over a period of months, I slowly concluded that I wanted to write about their lives, and the lives of those Yardleys and Gregorys—and Thornes and Ingersolls and MacNeills and Woolseys—who came before them. I decided this not merely because I saw my parents' lives as representative of a certain time and place in American history, but because it seemed to me that my father's correspondence should not be allowed to waste away in unopened file cabinets. For twenty-two years, from the summer of 1949 until the summer of 1971, my father had the services of a secretary; he used these services with what football coaches call reckless abandon, compiling in that time a correspondence as notable for its wit and elegance as for its copiousness. Every letter he wrote—with one startling exception, to which in time we shall come—was dictated to his secretary: business letters, notes to my mother, a family "round-robin" to his own mother and his children, memoranda to himself, bulletins for faculty and staff, comments on applicants and students. Carbons of all these documents were made, and duly filed away; as eventually I learned, the letters in the little cabinet in Middletown were only a hint of what was to be found in other files and other places.

What I came upon in my father's files is the bedrock upon which this chronicle is constructed; it could not have been written without them. My mother, by unfortunate contrast, did not have so high an opinion of her epistolary efforts and for that matter did not have a secretary to assist her with them. She wrote either by hand or at a portable typewriter at which she was not especially adroit; her letters were so perfunctory and routine that few people to whom they were addressed bothered to save them. Thus there are moments in my story when my father and his bulging files barge their way into the limelight and my mother retreats into the wings; this is regrettable, but it cannot be helped.

In any event I had other ways to discover and understand her. From the oral testimony of family and friends I learned enough about my mother that, when combined with my own memories, gave me evidence to place her in something approximating her proper position in her marriage and in family mythology. Obtaining this testimony was itself an education, one that showed me how much the experience of my family in recent decades has mirrored that of the nation itself. Before the Second World War, I could have found all the Yardleys and Gregorys I needed for my research within two hundred miles of New York City; but in the 1980s I had to travel as far east as Truro, on Cape Cod, and as far west as Kauai, in Hawaii, in order to find my family in situ, and I found more members of it in California than in any other state. I further learned that it is now as difficult to maintain ties in my family as in any other; not merely are we separated by great physical distances, but divorce—anathema within both families at the time my parents were married—is now pandemic, among my parents' children and their brothers' as well. The more I traveled, the more I came to realize that much though the four children of Bill and Helen Yardley cherish them and the traditions they sought to pass down, our record in maintaining and honoring those traditions has been spotty at best. Soon enough I found myself asking, Is it the Yardleys who have changed, or the country? The answer, I fear, is both.

So my tribute to my parents is also a farewell: to them, and to the age to which they belonged. It is written not as child to parent, but as adult to adult. On that November evening in Middletown I saw them for the first time as the people they really were, and that is how I see them now. Thus it is that henceforth in this chronicle they shall be called not my mother and father, but Helen and Bill. In my family it would have been unthinkable for any of their children to call them by their first names, but this is not a child's book. It is their book, and they weren't "my mother and father"; they were Helen and Bill.

Their story is of two lives lived together: of the forces that strengthen and divide a marriage, of work and pleasures both shared and separate, of the growth of a nuclear family and the shaping of its character. But before those lives were together they were apart, in the two families—themselves the offspring of countless other families—that gave birth to and nurtured them. My own interest in genealogy is decidedly limited, and I shall inflict no more of it upon you than seems necessary to the telling of the tale, but this we must remember: "These vanished people made things what they are."

PART ONE

Two Families

EARLY IN the century a son was born to Alfred and Helen Gregory in their floor-through apartment at 230 St. James Place in Brooklyn. He was their first child, and they had awaited his arrival for what must have seemed an eternity; Alfred was thirty-two years old at the time of the child's birth, Helen thirty-one, and their wedding two years earlier had followed a courtship of nearly a decade's duration. So after all this time they rejoiced in the birth of their son, whom they named George in honor of his paternal grandfather, but they understood that his prospects were uncertain, for his delivery had been difficult and he had been injured in the course of it. Still, even the knowledge that his life was frail did not prepare them for the full burden of his death only a few weeks later. Both parents were shattered; they put George's bassinet in the attic and rarely spoke of him again, though Alfred did once say that the day of his firstborn's death was "the blackest of my life."

Understandably, then, the Gregorys greeted Helen's second pregnancy with apprehension. They had given one hostage to fortune, and the thought of losing another must have been nightmarish. This time, though, there was no cause for alarm. On November 22, 1913, Helen Ingersoll Gregory gave birth in the front chamber of the St. James Place flat to a seven-and-one-half-pound girl, whom Alfred insisted upon naming in his wife's honor: Helen Marie Gregory. As he often did in the years to come, Alfred quoted Poe in celebration of his daughter:

> *Helen, thy beauty is to me*
> *Like those Nicean barks of yore,*
> *That gently, o'er a perfumed sea,*
> *The weary, wayworn wanderer bore*
> *To his own native shore.*
>
> *On desperate seas long wont to roam,*
> *Thy hyacinth hair, thy classic face,*
> *Thy Naiad airs have brought me home*
> *To the glory that was Greece*
> *And the grandeur that was Rome.*

How they loved her! "I was received with great joy," Helen said years later, "and probably spoiled badly." Thus began a girlhood that seems to have been as happy as any child could hope for. The Gregory family grew rapidly—a daughter, Marianne, in 1915; a son, Alfred, in 1917; another son, Arthur, in 1919—and its prospects waxed ever brighter. Alfred Gregory was a man of intelligence, determination and character whose qualities were recognized and rewarded by the partners in his law firm, where his rise was rapid; before the birth of his second child he was sufficiently prosperous to vacate the apartment in Brooklyn and join the tide of middle-class migration from the cities to the new suburbs. The one the Gregorys chose was called Maplewood, formerly Jefferson Village, in New Jersey; they took a house there, at 24 Mountain Avenue, that had been built for them by Helen's father.

For Alfred Gregory the move to Maplewood was both fulfillment of the dream of success and confirmation of his faith in it. He was a self-made man, a third-generation American whose gaze was fixed not on the past but on the future. His grandfather, George Gibson Gregory, came to the United States from England or Scotland— family mythology is unclear on this point—in the early 1840s, but

Alfred was not given to dwelling on matters genealogical. "I just had Scots ancestors who came over and that's all that I know about them," he used to say, and he had scant interest in pursuing the subject further.

George Gregory and his wife, Ellen, had one son, George Warlow Gregory, born in North Carolina in 1844, who became a traveling salesman. With his Scots bride, Marianne MacNeill, this George had four children: three girls and a son, Alfred. He was born on August 26, 1878, in Jersey City, the base from which his father traveled on his rounds. George Warlow Gregory was as a consequence of his employment an irregular presence in his son's life, but in no way did that diminish the lasting devotion the two felt for each other.

Young Alfred repaid his father's love and confidence. He did well at the public schools of Jersey City, then went directly from high school to a law school in New York that offered a two-year course for the state bar; to help support himself he worked as office boy in a Jersey City firm. It was while discharging these obligations that he attended the twenty-first birthday party of a high-school classmate, William Harrison Ingersoll, whose family had moved from Jersey City to Bedford Avenue in Brooklyn. There, on March 22, 1899, Alfred Gregory was introduced to Will's eighteen-year-old sister, Helen Marie Ingersoll. Soon Alfred—by now a young man of medium height, sturdy build and purposeful disposition—came calling, and in time he and Helen began going out with each other. "Perhaps it wasn't 'love at first sight,'" she observed a half-century later, "but it was almost and we encouraged the inclination."

She was a small girl, cute and pert if given somewhat to plumpness, whose joyful response to life reflected that of the family into which she had been born. By contrast with the dogged, determined Gregorys, the Ingersolls were eccentrics who paused to smell the flowers whenever the opportunity presented itself, as often it did in the course of their irregular wanderings through the New World.

They got here early: sometime in 1629 the three Ingersoll brothers—Richard, Thomas and John—left England and settled in the Massachusetts communities of Lee and Westfield. They were farmers and like innumerable other farming families in Colonial times they gradually scattered in search of fresh, arable land. Helen's branch of the family, which descended from John, lived for a few generations in the Berkshires, then in the early eighteenth century decided to try its luck farther to the west. Erastus Ingersoll, Helen Ingersoll's great-grandfather, had fallen under the somewhat peculiar spell of Sylvester Graham, a zealot on matters of health and diet whose self-righteous, humorless manner disguised a fair degree of common sense; he advocated the use of whole-wheat rather than white flour, for which, in tribute to him, graham flour and graham crackers were named.

Evidently Erastus Ingersoll and his brood saw their salvation in whole wheat, for they hitched up a team of oxen and followed the Grahamite rainbow, how slowly and with what difficulty we can now scarcely imagine, to a place in Michigan called Delta, a crossroads near the settlement of Olivet. As they traversed these hundreds of miles Erastus's seven-year-old son, Orville, encouraged the oxen with occasional flicks of a switch cut from a willow. When at last they reached Delta and his father said, "We stop here," Orville stuck the switch into the ground. According to one of the enduring legends of the Ingersoll family, it took root and became a mighty tree, a great willow that Helen gazed on as a girl in the 1880s. Whether the legend is in fact true is quite impossible to demonstrate—it seems, at the least, botanically improbable—but it has been treasured by generations of Orville's descendants. Whether true or not is in fact quite beside the point; if you are a descendant of Orville Ingersoll, you believe it, as I most assuredly do.

Orville grew to manhood in Michigan; somewhere along the way he met, and later married, a young woman from Connecticut named Elizabeth Beers. They had nine children, the second of whom was a boy named Arthur Nichols Ingersoll, born on August 31, 1844. On that same day in that same year, some three hundred miles to the east, a girl was born near Toronto named Nancy Agnes

Wright; thirty-one years later she became Arthur Ingersoll's wife and, on July 14, 1880, the mother of Helen Marie Ingersoll, who as a girl was firmly convinced that, because her parents shared the same birthday, they were twins.

Arthur Ingersoll had studied the Grahamite gospel for two years at Olivet College, but his attachment to the whole-wheat crusade was less impassioned than his yearning for adventure. A pioneer at heart, he ventured to the Dakotas two or three years after Helen's birth and took a homestead there, to which he intended to move his wife, son and daughter. But a gentleman from Canada sang the praises of Huntsville, a town of two or three hundred people on the Muskoka River. A grist mill was for sale there, which Arthur Ingersoll promptly arranged to purchase; thus it was that his family was headed not west but north.

For little Helen it proved to be a move into the Canadian equivalent of the little house on the prairie. The Ingersolls had a real pioneers' cabin, which they made snug with laths and plaster and a sturdy wood stove in the kitchen, supplemented by another in the modest front room, which they immodestly called the parlor. They supplemented Arthur's erratic income from the mill by taking in summer boarders; they fed themselves from a thriving garden and a small collection of livestock. Once one of the cows got into Arthur's supply of bran, ate its fill, and wandered to the nearby lake to wash down this hearty repast. But the combination of bran and water proved combustible, with the unhappy if spectacular result that the cow swelled and burst. Two generations later that story, told with much dramatic emphasis—"And then the cow went *boom!*, and exploded all over the place!"—over and over reduced Helen Ingersoll's grandchildren to helpless laughter.

For all her life Helen remembered Huntsville with deep pleasure: her father walking across the frozen lake from the mill to his house, the ice cracking ominously under his feet; her first piano lessons, under the tutelage of the parson's daughter; her mother's hospitable welcome to the summer boarders, a welcome so genuine that Helen believed she was taking them in for the pure pleasure of it; "tea meetings" at the church, held after members of the congregation built new houses or barns; "agricultural concerts" at the church hall, "under the auspices of the East Muskoka Agricultural Society"; stupendous dinners, also served at the church hall, to mark the "Huntsville Friendly Reunion."

Then one winter day in 1891 her father came in from milking the cow and announced, "Rob is here." This was his younger brother, Robert H. Ingersoll, who with his brother Charles had established a firm at 45 Fulton Street in New York, dealing in mail-order "Novelties & Specialties": rubber stamps, key rings, stencils, dog leashes, pencil compasses, pocket hat brushes, whisk and toy brooms, toy sewing machines—you name it, Ingersoll & Brother was likely to sell it. Rob urged Arthur to find his fortune in Manhattan and offered him a job. The peripatetic Arthur could hardly refuse, so in the spring he packed up his family and headed for New York.

Helen hated to leave her friends in Huntsville, but she loved the city from the moment she saw it: crossing to New York on the ferry, gasping with astonishment at the World Building—*"twenty-three stories high!"*—and the mad clutter of human activity. After boarding briefly in Brooklyn near Rob and Charles, the Ingersolls found a house at 80 Danforth Avenue in Jersey City and moved in. It was brand-new and offered delights they had not before experienced: running water and a bathroom, gaslights instead of kerosene lamps, a furnace in place of heated stones.

Helen excelled at music lessons, studying piano under an accomplished teacher who annually gave a scholarship to the pupil who had progressed most satisfactorily during that year; Helen won the award in 1896. She was now sixteen "and full of ambition," but she was unable to establish herself as a piano teacher and succumbed to the wishes of her mother, who sent her to a finishing school and then to Pratt Institute, where she studied domestic science and was awarded a degree in 1906. After that she was an instructor in homemaking at a women's college in Ohio for one year and then taught the same subject in the public schools of South Orange and Maplewood.

At this point, we must remind ourselves, her meeting with Alfred Gregory was many years in the past, and romance certainly had flowered. But there were difficulties. The first, and most easily surmounted, was that Alfred believed he should be financially secure before he married. The second, far more vexing, was opposition to the engagement in both families. Agnes Ingersoll felt that her daughter was too good for Alfred Gregory, whose family for some reason she regarded as beneath her own and whose heavy smoking of Fatima cigarettes she found thoroughly offensive. On the other side the three Gregory sisters, two of whom were well along the road to spinsterhood, considered it their brother's paramount obligation to support them as grandly as he could and resisted the marriage vigorously.

In the end love won out, though no one in the family now knows exactly why or how. Perhaps it finally dawned on Agnes Ingersoll that her only daughter was in serious danger of becoming an old maid; perhaps the Gregory sisters were finally persuaded that Alfred was doing well enough to provide for both his own family and his sisters—as in fact he did for years to come. Whatever the case, justice was done, and in 1908 Alfred Gregory at last took Helen Ingersoll as his bride.

Alfred Gregory and Helen Ingersoll, circa 1908

When, seven years later, he transported her and their eighteen-month-old daughter from Brooklyn to Maplewood, they were a well-established young couple. Between their first meeting and their marriage Alfred had completed his legal education and then had done his apprenticeship in the legal department of the United States Fidelity and Guaranty Company. Now, in the late spring of 1915, he was with the Wall Street firm of Hawkins & Delafield, specializing in corporate law and refining the skills that in time permitted him to assume the senior partnership. He was making a generous income, and he was looking to spend it: Alfred Gregory liked a good suit of clothes and an ample meal and a handsome carpet on the floor, and now he was in position to have all of that and more.

If anything he had the inside track, for in moving to Maplewood he was settling his family in Ingersoll territory. Some years before, Arthur Nichols Ingersoll had purchased a large piece of land on Mountain Avenue, beginning at Lot Number 2 and continuing up the hillside to Number 70, and he was turning it to profitable use. Maplewood was then gradually undergoing the transformation from rural to suburban life; it was about four miles due west of Newark and was accessible to Manhattan by way of the Lackawanna Railroad, with connections at Hoboken.

In his quiet way Arthur Ingersoll was one of Maplewood's principal developers, though the word in its modern definition—with its connotations of venal profiteering and environmental despoliation—is anything but appropriate to this gentle, nature-loving man. At first he farmed the land, but step by step he divided it into lots of perhaps a half-acre each and built houses on them: unpretentious clapboard structures, roomy but not opulent, in the Dutch Colonial and Queen Anne styles. By doing this he was able to earn enough money to live comfortably, though far from lavishly, and to indulge himself in the quiet familial pleasures he cherished.

Of these, few if any meant more than his granddaughter Helen, who by the summer of 1915 was beginning to speak and was pronouncing her own name as "Hon." This soon became "Honey," and so, too, did she; she was Honey to her family and friends, and she remained Honey to her two brothers until the last day of her life. It was not a nickname that, as she grew older, she much appreciated, and she shed it as soon as she could—just as, years later, her own first child eagerly shed "Johnny" for "Jon"—but the nickname spoke the truth. It may have been an accidental result of childish mispronunciation, but it was also an accurate expression of the abiding love in which she was wreathed.

Both parents loved her; her father adored her. This was a central fact of her childhood, one that colored her adult life in numerous ways. After all four of his children had been born and the family character had begun to take definable shape, Alfred used to shake his head and say, "I just don't understand my three younger children, I only understand my oldest daughter." If later Honey thought that she had been spoiled, the facts suggest otherwise; what Alfred's great love gave her was a sense not of entitlement but of responsibility. As a child and a teenager she had all the material goods she wished for, but her wishes were not unreasonable and her treasure trove was therefore relatively modest for a girl whose circumstances were, in truth, quite privileged. She acquired, by example as well as inheritance, Alfred's purposefulness and self-discipline, and his fatalistic belief in each individual soul's inherent and inescapable loneliness. Because she was Alfred Gregory's favorite girl, she grew up faster than most children do, and matured earlier.

In no sense, though, was she a humorless or priggish child. When she talked to her own children about her girlhood, it was always about the laughter and happiness of those days. Unlike many children of that era, she was resolutely healthy except for a case of diphtheria when she was about six. She was the center of adoring attention not merely in her own household but also in that of her Ingersoll grandparents, who lived just around the corner from 24 Mountain Avenue, on Ridgewood Road.

Honey was so at home in the Ingersolls' house that she occasionally wandered over there for weeks at a time, sleeping in a guest room and going to her own house only for brief visits; this caused no offense to any of the Gregorys, no doubt because the two families were so attached to each other, and later Honey felt it probably was a convenience to her mother, who had three younger children to care for. No matter where she was staying, on Saturday mornings she was regularly in attendance at Grandma Ingersoll's weekly bread-baking sessions. Each child was given a lump of dough with which to work; after rolling the dough around on the floor for a while the children presented the results of their labors to Agnes Ingersoll, who solemnly baked them along with the loaves of bread. Grandpa popped in as the bread was coming out of the oven, and he was always game for a bite of the children's grimy lumps. "Mmmmmm," he said. "That sure tastes good to me!"

The Ingersolls were the family connection with which the Gregory children were most familiar, but the connection on their father's side was important too. George Warlow Gregory died when Honey was four, and she remembered little of him except that he came from Jersey City to Maplewood each week for a Sunday visit; Marianne MacNeill Gregory, who died when Honey was ten, she recalled as "white-haired, dignified and rather awe-

42 Mountain Avenue

some." The Gregory aunts—Maude, Minnie and Lillie—were present only on special occasions but they were steady, if not always visible, presences in the children's lives.

Still, the Ingersolls unquestionably came first, and the Ingersoll household became even more convenient in Honey's first-grade year, for it was then that her grandfather built a larger house at 42 Mountain Avenue; the Gregorys moved into that one, and the Ingersolls succeeded them in Number 24. Now, as she walked up the hill from school, Honey could stop off and have cambric tea with her grandmother, a treat in which she often indulged herself.

Moving to 42 Mountain Avenue was the crowning moment in Alfred Gregory's progress; it also provided his children with a house and yard that all of them loved passionately, a place they spoke of for the rest of their lives as "home." It was larger than their first house, and on a considerably more spacious lot, but as was true of all the houses Arthur Ingersoll built—as in fact was true of Maplewood itself—it was devoid of ostentation or grandiosity; it meant a great deal to Alfred, though, that the house had cost him the considerable sum of $12,000, and he was immensely proud that he had no difficulty paying it. On its central staircase was a landing with a large window looking out to the rear yard; it had a comfortable little window seat on which Honey loved to snuggle with a book and where she spent many of her happiest childhood hours.

She was an ardent reader, as a child and to the last day of her life. Her parents had given her many gifts, but somehow self-confidence was not among them, and she found that escape into the world of books was a way of fending off a real world in which, outside the loving embrace of her family, she sometimes felt uncertain and unconfident. This shyness manifested itself from time to time within the family. She adored her father but she was also slightly afraid of him; he could be distant, aloof and abrupt as well as loving, and as she grew older he found it ever more difficult, as fathers often do with daughters, to express his affection in a satisfactory fashion.

The Gregorys did things *en famille*. Eventually the Studebaker—the model was the President, with a rear compartment large enough to include folding seats for the boys—yielded to a Model A Ford, for Honey and Minnie to drive to school, and a lavish LaSalle touring car, for Alfred and Helen. Oddly enough, Alfred himself declined to drive his elegant auto or any other vehicle; early in the marriage, when Helen had expressed nervousness about his driving, he said, "Well then, you do the driving," and that was that. She proved a capable motorist, so Alfred was happy to relax in the passenger's seat and try, as best he could, to close his ears to the childish din behind him.

The children got on well together. Al and Art looked up to Honey with admiration, and she regarded them with amused affection. They were scalawags, Ingersolls to the bone, who held no mortal in abject reverence, not even their formidable father. Al, a lifelong iconoclast, was especially adept at getting his father's goat. He infuriated Alfred Sr., who loved Shakespeare, by marching around the house reciting a mock-Shakespearean verse: "If life were life and life were life then what is life and why is life if life were life then who is life. . . ." He persisted merrily in this witticism, knowing full well that he was driving his father crazy.

Honey delighted, if at times silently, in her brothers' irreverence, and when she reminisced about them years later it was always with laughter and genuine affection. Her feelings about Marianne—called Minnie—were rather more complicated. They shared the same room for two decades, with no more than the usual sisterly rancor, but there was an underlying tension that others in the family—and, later, Honey's own children—occasionally felt in the air. Minnie resented Honey's closeness to their father, her superior position as "assistant mother," and her occasional condescension toward Minnie. As children and as teenagers they were markedly dissimilar; Minnie was outgoing, fun-loving and companionable, while Honey was sometimes lonely, often shy and selective about her friends. Minnie was also full-figured and sexy, while Helen, at five feet five, was slender and given to hiding her quiet, freckled prettiness under unflattering hairdos; the two looked just enough alike to be identifiable as sisters, but in appearance and manner they were quite different.

It was not until they had grown and left Maplewood, though, that the tensions came into the open. Unlike Al and Art, who went

The young Gregorys: Art, Al, Minnie and Helen

on to have families and interesting careers, Minnie was dealt a bad hand. During her senior year at Wheaton College she was driving a car with four young people in the front compartment and three in the rumble seat when another car crossed the road and rammed head-on into theirs. Three girls were killed, two were severely injured but recovered, and Minnie lost her right leg, which was amputated at mid-thigh. She was not at fault in the accident, but an action for damages was taken against Alfred and a settlement was made.

The accident was a ghastly experience for both father and daughter, but it did not unite them in suffering as strongly as one might expect. Alfred's remorse was for his daughter's shattered life rather than for any losses of his own, and he attempted to treat her with great tenderness, but Minnie turned bitter for a long time: against fate, mostly, but also against what she imagined as her unjustly inferior position within her own family. Her brothers were startled to hear her speak of resentments against Honey that they had only dimly perceived theretofore, and for a while her relations with her sister were cool. Over time, as Minnie healed and adjusted to her altered lot, the sisters became affectionate again; Honey asked Minnie to serve as godmother when I was born in 1939, and a quarter-century later I asked her to perform the same honor for my own first son, Jim.

It was hard not to love Minnie, even when she lapsed into petulance. She was smart, funny and iconoclastic: like her brothers, she was all Ingersoll. She could have let her handicap control her life—and at the time it was incurred Alfred had enough money to set her up in a life of indolent self-pity—but she declined the opportunity. She got a wooden leg, taught herself to walk again, and became a normal person. In my mind's eye I see her limping sturdily down the long, steep wooden steps to the beach at Cape Cod, tossing her leg into the little bathing house that had been built for her at the bottom of the stairs, then taking herself into the chilly bay water on crutches, her stump swinging uselessly in the air.

The house on Cape Cod, which was built in the early 1920s, was the family's retreat from the world and Alfred's retreat from the family. It stood on a bluff overlooking Cape Cod Bay at Brewster, a village on the Lower Cape that had been discovered by several of the Gregorys' friends in New Jersey. Like Maplewood, it was a place without pretense. The houses were built for the beach, not for luxury; a half-century later, when my first wife and I rented one of them for a couple of weeks, we found ourselves in a primitive if charming prefab that had no insulation or interior paneling to keep the brisk night air from seeping in through the exterior walls. The Gregory house was fancier than that, but not by much. It was made of shingles, with bedrooms around a balcony that looked down to the living room in which the family's summer life was centered; immediately outside was a deck that faced the bay, and atop the roof was a tall chimney that routinely collapsed whenever even the feeblest hurricane passed over the Cape.

Helen and the children went to the house as soon as school was out and left it just before school opened. At first, before the roads through New England improved, they drove to New York and took the celebrated Fall River Line; the children rushed to the boat's top deck to snap pictures of the Manhattan skyline and Long Island Sound, then went below to eat in the stately dining room where lumps of sugar came wrapped in paper. Later, Helen drove all the way, stopping on demand to permit one child or the other to be carsick behind cover of a tree—a family tradition that has continued uninterrupted through the generations.

The Cape was heaven for the children but purgatory for their mother. Alfred came up only about three weeks each summer; the rest of the time Helen was on her own, with limited adult companionship and limitless maternal obligations. The boys often terrified her, going out into the bay on their sailboat in the morning and not returning until the supper hour was near. Honey and Minnie gave her less to fret over, but as they grew older they began to have social lives—or lack of social lives—and that was something else to worry about.

Meantime there was Alfred, back in his usual routine at 42 Mountain Avenue and 49 Wall Street. There was a side of him that felt he'd done his duty to his children by buying them boats and building them a summer house. "I took care of those boys," he'd say to Helen, "I got them a sailboat, and I've done all of these things for them so now they're not going to get into any mischief." Thus satisfied by his paternal munificence, he could turn his attention to his business at what was now called Hawkins, Delafield & Longfellow; so far as he was concerned it was woman's work to take care of the children with their insistent demands, and though he missed Helen he was glad to have a quiet house in those months of school vacation.

Each morning he rose at about seven, put on the dark suit and tie that were his daily uniform, ate the substantial breakfast prepared for him by the cook, and was picked up by a cab for the ride to the Lackawanna Railroad's Maplewood depot; the station was only three-quarters of a mile away, and the walk was lovely, but Alfred Gregory always took a taxi, to and from the station. Usually he rode the 8:33 train to Hoboken, where a ferry took him across the Hudson to Lower Manhattan. At day's end he reversed the process, though he stopped in Hoboken long enough to have a couple of drinks at a tavern—a speakeasy, during the twenties—and then took train and cab home to the bland meat-and-potatoes fare that was the family's year-round diet.

When Alfred was at work, home was far from his mind; he

35

separated the two to a degree that relatively few successful men are able to achieve. His practice was primarily corporate, of the sort that rarely makes headlines but requires intense concentration and a deeply sophisticated knowledge of the law. In the view of one of his colleagues, E. J. Dimock, who eventually went on to a distinguished judicial career, his great knack as a lawyer was to cut through all the verbiage in which legal matters are smothered and get right to the heart of the issue; Dimock, who had dealt with innumerable lawyers, said that Alfred was the best he had known.

He was a man of a certain style. His hero was William Pitt, the Earl of Chatham, whom he admired for his way of doing things; he used to say that he respected Pitt for presenting himself "as a picture, as an act," as if he were always conscious of the persona he presented and the effect it had on others. Alfred liked to go first-class; he and Helen had their photographs taken by Fabian Bachrach, he bought his boring gray suits at Rogers Peet, he shelled out $5,000 ($50,000 in late-1980s dollars) for Helen's Steinway—yet he wouldn't let her teach piano, much though she wanted to, because he thought this unsuitable, not to mention unnecessary, for the wife of a successful man. He sent his children to Sunday school at St. George's Episcopal Church, though he and Helen didn't go to church themselves, because it seemed to him the proper thing for them to do, a way to acquire the style that society would expect of them.

In this respect as in many others he ran, with Helen's full complicity, a stern and conservative household. Breakfast and dinner were at set hours, everyone was expected to be on time and dressed appropriately, and conversation was conducted—unless Al and Art could lead it in more amusing directions—in an orderly, instructive way. The open display of emotion, sorrow especially, was frowned upon; when Helen's beloved brother Will died prematurely, in 1946, she shed no public tears for him, because to do so would have been a violation of the Gregory code. It was a pattern that later was repeated in Honey's family: everyone loved everyone else, and everyone was loyal to the collective idea of "family," but each member kept his feelings pretty much to himself.

36

Yet there is an odd contradiction here. Though Alfred clearly was the dominant figure within his family, the influence that most shaped its true character was Ingersoll rather than Gregory. One reason may be that the proximity of the Ingersoll grandparents heightened the Ingersoll role in family life; another may be that Alfred's absences, in the long workday and then the summer holiday, similarly reduced the Gregory role. But whatever the explanation, the fact is that for all their pro forma obeisance to the Scots taciturnity and reticence with which Alfred was most comfortable, all but one of his children remained Ingersolls at heart and ultimately became, once released from the confines of the parental household, Ingersolls in fact as well. In their different ways, Minnie and Al and Art all were, as adults, blithe spirits. Only Honey, Alfred Gregory's favorite child, remained a true Gregory.

But even Honey had her Ingersoll side. It showed in the self-sufficient, independent streak that was her strongest characteristic, and as she emerged from childhood it showed in some of the interests she pursued. Though never a brilliant student, she worked with great diligence on her studies and she followed extracurricular activities that were not always just what one might have expected from the attorney's daughter.

Throughout elementary, secondary and high school she was in the public-school system of Maplewood. Its capstone was Columbia High School, which Honey entered in the fall of 1928—except that by then she was no longer Honey. By the time she reached high school she had gotten that particular monkey off her back and, for the first time since infancy, was Helen once again. It was a sign of her coming maturity, of her emergence into the world not as agent and creation of her family but as her own self; if she regretted the loss of her old childhood nickname, she never said a word about it.

Columbia was a big school, with some twenty-three hundred students enrolled. Its principal, Curtis H. Threlkeld, was a bright man who took a strong interest in his students' individual as well as collective lives and who encouraged them to follow whatever paths

Helen in her high school years, circa 1928

aroused their curiosity. Thus Helen discovered a strong interest in clothes design and in developing the artistic skills it requires. She drew posters and maps and charts for her history class; joined the Art Club, the Parnassus Dramatic Club and the French Club; and, at home, took lessons in music and dancing. Her marks were in the mid-80s and upper 70s and she achieved them through hard work; her guidance counselors reported that "she has stability, is independent and self-reliant, and takes responsibility."

Outside the classroom her life was rather less successful, or so at least it seemed to her. She fretted that "my social life in school has been very limited," and in truth she did not hang out with the football players and cheerleaders; for company she preferred to be "with congenial friends or else reading or drawing by myself." She had no serious high-school romances, and never mentioned any crushes to any of her children. She didn't do much dating, but then neither did anyone else; boys and girls in suburban New Jersey traveled in packs in those days, so a girl who didn't go out regularly with a particular fellow was not regarded as unusual.

Her mind in any case was far less on social matters than on

academic ones. She was to graduate from Columbia High School in June, 1932, and what came next was uncertain. Were she to follow the example of women of earlier generations on both sides of the family, she would marry, enter a school of domestic science or some other polite field of vocational study, or go to work. But that was not in Helen's plans; she wanted to go to college—the first in her family to do so—and both of her parents were solidly support-ive. Alfred in fact "entered her at Vassar years ago when she was a kid and personally I hope that she will go to Vassar," but Helen herself was less sure that one of the staid Seven Sisters would be the right place for her. She was worried about whether her marks were good enough to gain her admission to Vassar, but there was more to it than that. The Ingersoll in her was coming to the fore. She had been reading, in newspapers and magazines, about plans to establish an experimental, progressive school for women outside an isolated Vermont town called Bennington, so Alfred wrote to one of its founders about her:

> My daughter for years has indicated a desire to be a dress designer or illustrator. While she is not a budding genius, she has a slight bent towards using a lead pencil but has had no special training at all. I have rather seriously thought of suggesting to her when she left high school the possibility of going direct to an art school, such as Yale Art School. I want her educated to make her own living as she will have to do unless she finds some young man to support her, but I would like her to be trained for marriage as well as for making a living and I, therefore, would like her to get a good general educa-tion before she specializes. If you can give me any information which you think will be of use to me, I will be glad to get it.

That Alfred Gregory should so enthusiastically have supported his daughter's interest in a progressive if not radical college may seem out of character, but it points to a quality that was at times difficult to discern behind his lawyerly façade. It is true that he was a Wall Street attorney, and a most prominent if unpublicized one, but it is also true that he lived on Mountain Avenue, not Fifth Avenue, and that he was close enough to his roots to be fully conscious of their humble nature. He was not in actuality a member of the upper class and he shared few of its pretensions or prejudices; if a new school with wild ideas about educational techniques and policy was where his daughter wanted to go, then that was fine with him. He loved her deeply, and he wanted her to be happy.

Then too it was quite obvious to him that if the college was supported by the likes of his old friend James Colby Colgate, of the Colgates whose ample donations had persuaded a university to name itself in their honor, its radicalism was likely to be tempered by the conventions of polite society. Bennington may have been progressive and experimental by the standards of its day, but at $1,675 a year plus travel and expenses it was going to be an expensive place to attend and as a result its clientele mostly would be people who, like Alfred and Helen Gregory, could afford it. There might be longhairs on the faculty and visionaries in the administration, but Alfred could be serenely confident that his beloved Honey would be, in the company of her fellow students, among her kind of people.

So she applied, with the enthusiastic endorsement of her principal and teachers. The admissions packet from the college included a confidential "Personal History" that her mother filled out. It is a remarkable and touching document, for what it tells us about mother and daughter alike. Asked to list Helen's "outstanding personal traits," her mother wrote: "Helen is a rather modest girl, her ideals are high and her judgment rather severe. She appeals more to older people than to her contemporaries unless they know her well." Then, under "Supplementary Information," she wrote:

> I hope that College may supply to Helen what we have not been able to give her at home, or rather what she has not had by social contacts. Mr. Gregory and I were both reared in modest circumstances—in my case we changed residences a great many times and drifted away from friends so that our home and family life became more than outside interests to us. Mr. Gregory's family was similar and we have a small circle of friends and it so happens that they have not families like ours and do not naturally form a social group for our young people. I am not a club woman and not socially ambitious—my home life has been so satisfying to me and my few

friends have given me so much that I have only recently realized that I should have been building for this side of the children's life. Helen misses this more than the others for she is timid and shy, probably self-conscious and sensitive too, but she longs to be "popular" socially and will not attempt to for fear of making herself conspicuous. She is lovely and loveable, unselfish and kind.

Helen was accepted. In September of 1932 she packed her bags and went to the place that gave her four of the happiest years of her life.

Before she left, her mother had reminded her that apart from being the location of her college education, Bennington had played an important role in Ingersoll family history. Helen Ingersoll Gregory's great-great-grandfather, David Ingersoll, marched to the Battle of Bennington in August, 1777, with the Berkshire militia, where he served for several days before mustering out as expeditiously as possible; he also answered the alarm at Berkshire on October 14, 1780, served in Captain Amos Porter's company for three days, and then answered a second alarm on October 18, this time serving four days. Deacon Ingersoll's military career may not have been exactly distinguished, but it certainly was authentic, and it gave his great-great-granddaughter sufficient ammunition to fill out, but never mail, an application for membership in the National Society of the Daughters of the American Revolution.

This was a piece of family lore that pleased Helen, who liked to tell her own children the story of Deacon David, and perhaps it gave her a sense of personal identification with the hilly, verdant countryside in which her new college was situated. But she needed no family ties to arouse her enthusiasm for the experiment that officially began with the opening of Bennington's first semester at nine o'clock on the morning of Tuesday, September 6, 1932. The atmosphere was filled with excitement and high anticipation; a new day in the education of American women had arrived, and the eighty-seven members of Bennington's first class, the Class of '36—the "Pioneers," as in time they came to be known—were at center stage.

What Helen found when she arrived that September was a campus of great beauty, with views of the Green Mountains to all sides; she was assigned to Kilpatrick House, in a four-bedroom grouping that was to be her home until graduation. To the nineteen faculty members of the college and their administrative colleges, she was introduced, as was each of her classmates, in a one-page mimeographed summary of her high-school record and her interests. "Helen has traveled very little except in a few of the eastern states," they were told, "and her reading seems to have been rather superficial. Among the better books which she has read recently are *Anna Karenina* and *Vanity Fair*. Her favorite authors are Galsworthy, Maurois, Deeping and Thackeray. Her main interest is in art, especially design. She thinks that she might make the designing of clothes her future vocation. She wishes to take various art courses at Bennington and in addition study English, literature and history."

When she looked back on it in later years, nothing pleased Helen more about her Bennington years than her exposure to the avantgarde. She was introduced to Joyce, whom she read with delight, and Lawrence as well; she came back from a winter trip to Mexico with an illicit copy of *Lady Chatterley's Lover*. A teacher of poetry named Genevieve Taggard, hugely popular among literature students, sponsored poetry evenings that drew students, faculty and townspeople. The most celebrated visitor was Robert Frost, but the one who drew the most comment was e. e. cummings. He entered the auditorium to find the students chanting his poetry, and after his reading he attended a party at Miss Taggard's. Helen was at both the reading and the party, and was thrilled; it was an evening she often told me about, after I came to share her affection for cummings's work. While at Bennington she assiduously collected first editions of his books; forty years later she presented all of them to me, a quiet gift of love that pleased me more than I can say.

Helen's life in Kilpatrick was immensely important to her. For four years her closest friend was Edith Noyes, a New Yorker a couple of years younger than she; they were suite-mates the first three years, and in their senior year they shared a bedroom, using the second bedroom as their private living room. They had been drawn together initially because the two other women in the suite

Modernism comes to Bennington: Helen in the art studio, 1937

were considerably older and shocked Helen and Edie, who were shy and innocent, with their vivid language. The friendship deepened over their undergraduate years as the two became powerfully involved in their educations and in the growth of the college; both Helen and Edie were active in regular community meetings, and each served a term as president of the house.

It was, to a degree remarkable even among academic communities, an isolated and hermetic existence. New York was three or four hours away by train or car and the nearest boys' college, Williams, was fifteen miles to the south; Bennington students were thrown on their own resources most of the time, with the happy result that they developed an intimate communal life from which students and faculty alike drew strength. But Bennington's physical isolation, and the prosperity of its student body, kept the hard realities of the Depression away from the door; it was an oasis of privilege in a hard-pressed land, so its students learned less than they might have about what their fellow Americans were undergoing in those painful years.

This sense of privilege was heightened all the more for Helen because of the presence, only a few miles away, of her father's friends the Colgates; they had a large Victorian house with a swimming pool, and in warm weather—such of it as there was during the academic year in that climate—they invited Helen and her friends over to picnic and swim. Her social life also included boys from Williams, occasionally from more distant schools such as Dartmouth and Wesleyan. A roadhouse near the Vermont–Massachusetts border was a popular dancing spot, and there were various movie theaters; fraternity parties at Williams were especially popular with Bennington girls.

Once again Helen had no serious romances, but she was far more popular with the boys than she'd been at Columbia High School. She was pretty, with a small but pleasing figure, fine features, and lively, candid eyes; she had a ready, irreverent sense of humor and a quick, contagious laugh. She went out on dates often, all the more so as she became ever more successful at college and her self-confidence steadily increased. By the end of her junior year, at the age of twenty-one, she was no longer a girl but a young woman, poised at the entrance to adulthood.

Not surprisingly, at this point life in the Gregory household had begun to pall for her; she had discovered the world and her parents' house—even one so loving and comfortable as the Gregorys'— now seemed confining to her. Even worse was the prospect of another summer at Brewster, a place of which she was fond but where she had few friends and almost nothing to do. So in 1935 she asked her mother and father if she could spend a few weeks at one session of the Harvard Summer School. She wanted to take Knox Chandler's course, "The Age of Dryden: English Literature from 1660 to 1700," and to see what the classroom experience was like at a more traditional college than Bennington.

Off she went. She lived in Chestnut Hill, presumably with friends, and commuted to Cambridge by day. Possibly it was in her English class that she made the acquaintance of a fellow named E. Trudeau Thomas. He was several years her senior, outgoing and personable, the headmaster of a small private day school in Westchester County called Bedford-Rippowam. One day they ran into each other in Harvard Yard, and stopped to chat.

"Say, Helen," Thomas said, "there's a fellow I'd like you to meet. . . ."

Early in the century a son was born to Tom and Louise Yardley in the house on Gowen Avenue in Mount Airy, Pennsylvania, in which much of Louise's childhood had been spent. He was their first child, and they had awaited his arrival for many years; Tom was thirty-six years old at the time of the child's birth, Louise twenty-eight, and their marriage a year earlier had followed a courtship of five years' duration. So after all this time they rejoiced in the birth of their son, whom they named Thomas Henry Yardley, Jr., in honor of his father, and gave him the nickname Harry.

But here the parallels with the story of the Gregory family quickly and abruptly end. Poor George Gregory died within weeks of his birth; Harry Yardley, born on June 18, 1906, lives as these words are written, in a nursing home in California, his vital organs somehow functioning after decades of punishment by alcohol, his health frail but his spirit sturdy. What a sad fate for the favored child whose mother cherished him, to the last day of her own long life, as a blessing above all others: who loved him not wisely but well, providing a maternal refuge to which, even as an old man, he could retreat from the vicissitudes of a world that persistently refused to accept him on his own terms. Born a dreamer, Harry never came to grips with the world, always believed that it owed him and his genius a living; and Louise, in whose eyes Harry quite literally could do no wrong, out of the goodness of her heart never permitted her first son to reach full independence.

Harry was not alone in paying the toll for his mother's abiding, greathearted and debilitating love. Five years after his birth, a second child was delivered to Tom and Louise Yardley, a son for whom the relationship between his mother and his elder brother became a controlling element in a life of internal and external conflict. He was born on September 7, 1911, in the parental double bed at the rectory of St. Paul's Church in Stockbridge, Massachusetts. In honor of his great-great-grandfather, William Walton Woolsey, his parents named him William Woolsey Yardley; they called him, to what eventually was his considerable discomfort, Billy.

Six years later, on June 15, 1917, the last of the Yardleys' three sons, Paul Thorne Yardley, was born in Catonsville, Maryland. If Harry was Louise's quite obvious favorite among the boys, Paul—bright, kind, handsome, commonsensical—soon became Tom's.

Louise, Bill and Harry, probably 1912

That left Bill in the middle; he was loved by his parents, and he loved them, but he was nobody's favorite. This was by no means a cruel fate, but it was a decisive one. Bill tried over the years to disguise his resentment of Harry—a resentment that at moments slipped into hatred—with wit; he once described Harry as "the extreme non-conformist of a somewhat non-conforming family," and to Harry himself he said, "You, my boy, are included in that fortunate company of perpetual Peter Pans." But his wife and his children knew better; Bill could hardly speak of Harry without either ridicule or rage, or a particularly volatile combination of the two.

Bill liked to believe that Harry was "born rotten." This was a mockery of the truth—if Harry was selfish he was also generous, and he possessed a genuine sweetness that endeared him to many who found him otherwise infuriating—and it was also a convenient way of shifting blame for Harry's irresponsibility away from their mother. Louise Yardley was a strong, demanding, indomitable woman who often tried Bill's patience but for whom he had great respect and love; he wanted more of her love than she was able or willing to give him, and as a result spent much of his adult life trying to win the unsparing approval that she never wholly proffered. How revealing it is that, more than half a century after his birth, in an unguarded moment he said to a friend, "Whenever I go back to see my mother, I feel like a little boy in knickers again."

She was a Thorne of Philadelphia and, by ancestry, a Hart and a Lippincott and a Badger and a Worrell, connections of which she was fiercely proud and of which she made her sons intimately aware. The first of those in her direct line of descent to cross the Atlantic, William Thorne, sailed in or about 1635 and three years later "was made a freeman at Lynn, Massachusetts," which suggests that he had come over as an indentured servant and had earned his freedom. In the ensuing generations his descendants scattered in various directions just as the Ingersolls had: in search of fresh land and new opportunities. By the nineteenth century another William Thorne and his wife, Rebecca Lippincott, had reached Pennsylvania; it was there that their only son, William Henry Thorne, was born on January 28, 1847, into a family that, like virtually all Thornes before it, was "moderately well-to-do and very upright."

It was an Orthodox Quaker family, but that did not prevent William from joining the Union Army, at the age of fourteen, as a drummer boy; his parents, offended at this violation of Quaker principles, sought him out and obtained his release, but had to go through the entire business all over again when he later fled and joined the Navy as a paymaster. He wasn't warlike, merely patriotic and adventuresome, and when he was brought back to Philadelphia for the second time he began to prepare for the career in mechanical drawing at which he was to distinguish himself; he also made the acquaintance of Eva Hart, a young woman of position in Philadelphia society, whom he married in 1873. Together they had six children, of whom four lived to maturity.

Eva Louise was born on January 27, 1878. She was diminutive, lively and, as she grew out of childhood, most becoming if in a somewhat sharp-featured way. She had, as did so many in this chronicle, a happy childhood, one lived in the last years of the Victorian era. In stormy weather she and her sister Kitty were taken to the Friends School by cab, which both found "so humiliating!" They owned "watchman's rattles," wooden contraptions that, when vigorously shaken, emitted a great noise calculated to scare off burglars, and they spied on their neighbors through a Philadelphia peculiarity known as a "busybody," a Y-shaped double mirror that was screwed outside a second-floor window: "One could sit comfortably in an armchair by the window, and see everyone that went up or down the street!"

The last of the children, Margaret Lamphier Thorne, was born on August 21, 1890. Her older sisters thought Margaret "a darling little creature," and after their mother's death the next year the baby was a great comfort to the bereaved William Henry Thorne, but her life ended early and terribly. As a young woman she eloped, to her father's fury, with a Navy man with whom she moved to Virginia and had two children. Then, around 1920, she was found murdered, her head bashed in by the butt end of an oar. The two children were sent to live with Louise and Tom Yardley, but the father was acquitted of murder and the children—whose "sad and frightened little faces" Harry never forgot—were returned to him by court order. For Louise it was a shattering event that caused her grief both unknowable and incalculable; Margaret's calamitous end was something she never talked about, and pointedly excluded from her memoirs.

Nor did she talk, or write, about another familial event that gave her unhappiness. Some years after her mother's death William Henry Thorne was quite unexpectedly remarried, to a woman evidently a good reach below his own station who turned out to be a drunkard. William was shocked by this unanticipated turn of events; he separated from his second wife but, true to his honor, supported her for the rest of her life. This marriage was kept so secret for so long that it was not until the Yardley boys were into their teens that they, to their own considerable shock, learned about it, long after their grandfather's death, in 1926, at the age of seventy-nine.

It must have been just about the only indiscretion of William Henry Thorne's admirable life. Born into a plain family, he married into a wealthy and socially prominent one but declined to be swept into society. He "had little or no use for organized religion," Harry recalled, "but I never knew a more ethical or kindlier person"; Bill described him as "gentle, modest, with white mustachios permanently stained yellow by the fine Havana cigars he smoked continuously." His daughters remembered him with utter devotion, especially when they recalled their summer excursions to a place in Rhode Island called Saunderstown.

This tiny settlement on the west bank of the Mettatuxet River lay several miles and two ferry rides from Newport. At the turn of the century it was a summer colony for a few families from the Philadelphia area and for a handful of permanent Newport residents who fled their own houses when the gaudy newly rich opened their Bellevue and Ocean Drive "cottages" for the Season. It was a shingle seaside community of the old style. Its rocky beaches made swimming uninviting, so there wasn't much to do except sail, socialize and watch the ferry go back and forth between

Saunderstown and Conanicut Island. The first Thorne sojourn there was in the summer of 1899; Louise stayed behind in Pennsylvania, lodging with friends in the Poconos. But her curiosity about the Rhode Island resort was piqued when, at summer's end, Kitty returned to give it a glowing account. She said, "Oh, Louise, we met a family there you'd really love—just your kind of people!"

And so, at last, here come the Yardleys. What a strange lot they are, with their overdeveloped sense of familial identity, their ambivalence toward power and status, their longing for the past, their passionate regard for books and words, their oddly mingled principles and affectations, their loving attachment to pictures and chairs and silverware and *things*, their obsessive fascination with ancestry. What are they but characters from a Marquand novel, flashbacks to a world gone by? "I guess we're a queer family," Mary Brill says to her cousin Jim Calder in *Wickford Point*. "Do you think we're crazy?" "Well," Jim replies, "every family is. That's the trouble with a family."

Ah, families! My distant cousin Yardley Beers, to whose exquisite name I at times raise a silent cocktail-hour toast, informs me that "our family derived its name from the Manor and Parish of Yardley, which is now incorporated into Greater Birmingham, England." The name began in the Old English *Gyrdaleah*, which means a woodland from which yards or spars are taken, and over the centuries evolved to its present shape: from *Gyrdaleah* to *Gerdeslai* to *Jerdelai* to *Jeardelegh* to *Yerdele* to *Yardeley* to—ruffles and flourishes!—*Yardley*.

The first record we have of it, as an ancient family genealogy notes, is the name "William Yardley, L.M.," signed as a witness to "the first Magna Charta given by John I to England, dated June 15th, 1215"—a momentous piece of history, the evidence of his family's participation in which was to provide pleasure beyond measure to yet another William Yardley, this one born seven centuries later in Stockbridge, Massachusetts. In the *Patronymica Britannica*, according to one family history, "we find the family is spoken of as an ancient one, with residence in Staffordshire, England, and whose heads were called 'lords of Yardley.' " Thus it is that on the wall of Bill Yardley's study in Middletown, Rhode Island, a map of Staffordshire was prominently displayed. "I can trace my ancestry back to a protoplasmal primordial atomic globule," W. S. Gilbert wrote in *The Mikado*, an operetta Bill loved. "Consequently, my family pride is something *in*-conceivable. I can't help it. I was born sneering."

Between William the Signer and William the Emigrant, the centuries race past in a blur, the family's comings and goings lost in the mists of history. Then, in March of 1681, a devout Quaker named William Yardley obtained from his friend and coreligionist William Penn, for the sum of ten pounds sterling, a grant of five hundred nineteen acres on the Delaware River. The Yardley grant had approximately one-third of a mile of frontage on what was, at that point in its meanderings, a snug little river, and extended three miles deep. Of this William Yardley we shall have more to say later; for now let it suffice that on July 28, 1682, he arrived at Penn's colony aboard the *Friend's Adventure*, with his wife, Jane; their children, Enoch, Thomas and William; and their servant, Andrew Heath.

They cleared a piece of land and built a house, a substantial edifice that they called "Prospect Farm." They worked the land and participated in the affairs of the community, and won the respect of all. Then, quite suddenly, they died: in 1693 in an epidemic of smallpox. There being no survivors, the estate reverted to William's brothers in England. None exercised the right to take control of the property, so eleven years after William's death it fell to his nephew, Thomas, to cross the Atlantic and assume ownership of the estate; with his arrival, the American family Yardley began.

This Thomas Yardley took over "Prospect Farm" and in 1706 married a neighbor, Ann Biles, with whom he had ten children, all but one of whom lived to maturity. He was a man of energy, ambition and principle who was elected to the provincial assembly in 1715 and 1722, served as justice of the Bucks County courts from 1725 until 1741, established Yardley's Ferry on the Delaware, and developed a sophisticated water-management system to power the settlement's grist and saw mills. Long before his death in 1756 Thomas Yardley's holdings had grown so vast—more than fifteen hundred acres—that they became known first as Yardley's Ferry, then as Yardleyville, finally as Yardley. That it is today: a suburb about thirty miles northwest of Philadelphia, population 2,533 but growing rapidly as tract houses rise on Thomas's once-beautiful land.

The family has long since withered away in Yardley, yet Thomas is still a vivid, powerful presence, for there in the heart of town is his house, "Lakeside," a magnificent stone structure across the street from a serene little lake; he built the house in 1728 and lived in it for the remaining three decades of his life. He was succeeded at "Lakeside" by several generations of Yardleys, but by early in the nineteenth century one branch of the family had left the ancestral village and pressed on to Philadelphia.

Thomas Howe Yardley, born December 3, 1800, became a prominent physician of that city and in so doing brought the family from rural to urban life. This estimable gentleman's life was a high moment of the family's history in the United States. A graduate of the University of Pennsylvania's medical school in 1825, he established a flourishing practice among his fellow Quakers and, according to a contemporary, "enjoyed in a high degree the esteem of his professional brethren."

He was as devout a family man as he was physician and Quaker. Before his twenty-ninth year had elapsed he became engaged to Sarah Warner Johnson, a fellow Friend whose mother had built for her, as a wedding gift, a house on Fourth Street near the corner of Greene; faithful to Quaker tradition, Sarah did not once cross the threshold of her new residence until March 11, 1830, the day she walked out of the meetinghouse next door as Thomas Howe Yardley's wife. The certificate of their marriage can only be described as an extraordinary document. Measuring approximately twenty-six by twenty-four inches, it is on parchment of the finest imaginable strength and quality. Across the top, in large and elegant script, are the details of the marriage; below are the signatures, numbering more than one hundred fifty, of those pious Friends who bore witness to the matrimonial rites. On the reverse are inscribed, in Thomas's hand, the records of his family. Here is one of them:

> Jane Johnson Yardley, 2nd child of Tho. H. & Sarah W. Yardley, died at 9½ o'clock A.M. on this day the 26th of second month A.D. 1836. She was attacked with Scarlet Fever at 4 o'clock P.M. on the 20th and suffered severely the whole 5 days. She was attended by Dr. Wood of the Parish, but the disease bid defiance to Medicine.— She was a child of whose beauty and intelligence any parent might be proud. A truly lovely girl.

Only two of Thomas and Sarah's four children lived to adulthood, and Sarah herself was taken by consumption in the fall of 1842, a loss that wounded her husband and children grievously. Eventually Thomas recovered and married a distant cousin with whom he lived in a mansion on Arch Street. More children were born to them, and reared in the faith. As a descendant wrote of one of them: "Nobody can know the good that Aunty Jane did. But Quakerism takes much joy from life when strictly followed. Aunty never had gone to a picture gallery, never had heard a concert, nor would she even go to the Exposition in 1876. She never went to a wedding, though always to funerals!"

Thomas Howe Yardley's life ended in the early morning of January 4, 1860. He had been roused from a troubled sleep by news of a sick patient, and left to attend him over his wife's objection that he was himself too ill to be about. He had gotten only part of the way when he returned home and collapsed in his office. "All is not right here," he said, tapping his chest, and then he died. His son Henry was now the head of the family.

Henry Albert Yardley: born in Philadelphia to Thomas Howe and Sarah Johnson Yardley on December 30, 1834, the first of their children to survive after the deaths of a son and daughter. Henry was a gentle fellow of sturdy character but sickly nature who, after graduation from Yale in 1855, spent two years in Europe and read for, but decided against pursuing, the law. Instead he tutored students in Latin at Yale for a time, then answered his call and studied theology; he was ordained a deacon of the Protestant Episcopal Church at New Haven in 1860, and a priest at Lenox, Massachusetts, the following year.

It was while he was a deacon in Lenox that he married Jane Andrews Woolsey, and it was there also that he fell grievously ill. He was diagnosed as suffering from locomotor ataxia, a grim disease of the nerves; "it is excessively painful," his widow wrote years later, "with sciatic pangs and a gradual failure of the power of balance and walking." He was ordered to refrain from work for a full year, after which, in 1864, he began his career as Professor of Homiletics and Christian Evidence at the Berkeley Divinity School, in Middletown, Connecticut. During this year he made a European trip for which he obtained a passport, an ample document on which he was described as five feet, five inches in height, blue-eyed and brown-haired, with a "high" forehead, "ordinary size" nose, "medium" mouth, "round" chin, "sallow" complexion and "long & oval" face. How small the country was then: the passport, filled out by an anonymous clerical hand, was signed by the secretary of state, William H. Seward.

Upon his return Henry and Jane—whom he called Jenny—settled in a cottage near the divinity school, a cottage where two children died in infancy and four survived: Tom, Isabel, Elizabeth and Laura. Henry had, in his wife's recollection, "a great power and influence over his students at Berkeley," whom to the end of his life he taught regularly and conscientiously. By the spring of 1882 his condition was desperate, yet he insisted on meeting his students in his study, where he sat in a wheelchair and wrote with a typewriter, no longer able to hold a pen. On the evening of April 1 a student rang his doorbell and asked to see him. Henry cordially called out, "Certainly, I will be there in a minute!" The student spent a quarter-hour with him; then after the youth's departure Tom, eleven years old, ran to his father's room with his Latin grammar.

"Oh, Papa, are you going to bed?" the boy asked. "Well, never mind."

"What is it, my darling?" his father replied. "Something puzzles you? Oh, I can wait long enough for that."

So father and son huddled together under the lamplight, and when the lesson had been thoroughly examined Henry asked, "Do you quite understand now?"

"Yes, quite."

"Then kiss me good night, my darling little boy!"

Tom never saw his father again. The following day Henry's condition was so dire that he begged Jenny not to let the children see him, and before dawn the next morning he died. A few hours earlier he had sat up in bed and slowly recited, in whole, this hymn:

> *Father! Whate'er of earthly bliss*
>   *Thy sovereign hand denies,*
> *Accepted at Thy throne of grace*
>   *Let this petition rise;—*
> *Give me a calm, a thankful heart,*
>   *From every murmur free;*
> *The blessings of Thy grace impart,*
>   *And make me live to Thee.*
> *Let the sweet hope that Thou art mine*
>   *My life and death attend;*
> *Thy presence through my journey shine,*
>   *And crown my journey's end.*

For Henry's small family it was a terrible blow; "we had many dark days." Jenny decided that she would be most comfortable near her mother, who had built a house, known as "The Jungle," at 93 Rhode Island Avenue in Newport, and determined to construct her own residence on part of the lot—"Brown Beeches," as it became known—at 91 Rhode Island Avenue. To finance this she signed a five-year promissory note, for $5,000 "without interest," which note in fact she repaid in full before the year was out. The payment was acknowledged, on the stationery of the New York

Central & Hudson River Railroad Co., Grand Central Depot, and signed by the chairman of the board of directors:

Dec. 26, 1884

Dear Mrs. Yardley,

Yours of 24th inst. enclosing check for $5,000 to pay note, received this morning, and I herewith return the note. Please accept my sincere thanks.

With my best wishes to you & yours for a Merry Xmas & Happy New Year, I am

Yrs faithfully,
C. Vanderbilt

Alice would join me in good wishes if she knew I was writing you.

Cornelius Vanderbilt: how on earth or heaven did modest Jenny Yardley know him, much less know him well enough to ask for and be granted an interest-free loan of $5,000? The Yardleys and Woolseys most certainly were not participants in the social ramble of Bellevue and Ocean Drive and the Casino, and possessed no ambitions to join it; but the promissory note was written in Newport, so presumably the transaction was carried out there. Perhaps Henry and Jane had known Vanderbilt through Berkeley Divinity School, since the second Cornelius Vanderbilt was a person of great religious and philanthropic enthusiasms as well as legendary business acumen. He took a particular interest in Yale University, the divinity school of which eventually brought Berkeley under its wing; possibly Henry's association there, combined with the family's connection to the well-placed Woolseys, is the key to the puzzle.

Whatever the explanation, the loan enabled Jenny to build a house in which the family was able to recover its equilibrium and enter into a new, happy life. Tom, who had been born on July 8, 1869, was the only male in two households of Woolsey aunts and his own mother and sisters, but in this great female company he thrived. He was so universally loved and treasured that he grew, like his father, into the gentlest of men. He was educated in

57

Newport's public schools before following Henry to Yale, but he stayed there only a year; Uncle Theodore Dwight Woolsey was no longer president but remained a formidable presence on campus and embarrassed Tom to the quick one day when, seeing the youth with a group of his friends, he loudly asked, "Tom, have you written home to your mother this week?"

From Yale, Tom went to M.I.T., where he studied architecture, which he practiced for a time but abandoned for the ministry; he studied for it at Trinity College and then at the General Theological Seminary in New York, where he lived in a handsome but poorly heated building in the company of other seminarians. It was here that his intellectual life really began to unfold and his faith acquired greater discipline and depth. Upon graduation and ordination he took a succession of assignments, as deacon or vicar, at churches in New Haven and East Providence and elsewhere. He also—and this I dearly wish we knew more about—did missionary work in Nebraska, under one Bishop Worthington; all we have been told is that there were a number of young priests and deacons in this mission, working in what was still primitive country, and we must assume it was a challenge to Tom's health, which like his father's was never robust.

By this time Tom and Louise had met at Saunderstown, but betrothal and marriage were still some years away. He assumed the "Chair of English" at St. Stephen's College, Annandale-on-the-Hudson, and found his resources daily challenged; he was expected to teach Anglo-Saxon, about which he knew nothing, and was hard-pressed to keep one page ahead of his students in the textbook. Then it was back to Trinity, as assistant to a cousin who was chairman of the English department; Tom was lonely here, especially as he and Louise now were beginning to make plans for a future together, but he whiled the time away by making a blanket box for her and carving her initials on the front—a box she used for the rest of her life. Tom seems to have been a good teacher, but in his heart he yearned for the ministry and, in time, a church of his own. The latter was too much to hope for at first, but he gained the former in the fall of 1904, when he agreed to become vicar at Old St. Peter's in Philadelphia. Only half a year later, on June 1, 1905, he and Louise at last were married, at Grace Church in Mount Airy, with a reception afterward on William Henry Thorne's ample suburban lawn.

Tom and Louise moved into St. Peter's House, 100 Pine Street, at the intersection of Pine and Front streets; they had a living room with fireplace on the second floor and, above it, two bedrooms, one of them soon to become Harry's nursery. For Louise, brought up privileged and protected, it was an education. Known as "the Bloody Fifth," this waterfront district was rough and poor; Tom's ministry did not include Harts or Lippincotts or Worrells. Instead there were drunks on the front steps, who shuffled away when the police rudely ousted them.

Occasionally there were irritations—called off hastily to the bedside of a dying man, Tom "returned home both indignant and hungry, having found the supposedly dying man sitting up and eating ham!"—but for Tom and Louise alike these were halcyon days. Once a week they held a shop in their house for the poor women of the parish, selling them muslin and gingham and other materials at cost. Across the street was a poultry market, where Louise got her Thanksgiving turkey for $1.50, "fully dressed!" On Sunday evenings William Henry Thorne regularly came in from Mount Airy; he and Tom liked and respected each other, and always inquired about their respective employments with genuine interest and curiosity.

The next year Harry was born. Before Louise was allowed to leave the maternal bed, Harry was carried across the street to the same church in which she had been married and given the rites of baptism, but not by his father; Tom baptized none of his three children, fearing that he might break down during what was, for him, an emotional service. As in years to come his brothers would also be, Harry was received in Christ's church with words that echo through the ages:

Hear the words of the Gospel, written by Saint Mark, in the tenth Chapter, at the thirteenth verse.

———

59

On the shore at Saunderstown: Tom, Louise and Harry

They brought young children to Christ, that he should touch them: and his disciples rebuked those that brought them. But when Jesus saw it, he was much displeased, and said unto them, Suffer the little children to come unto me, and forbid them not: for of such is the kingdom of God. Verily I say unto you, Whosoever shall not receive the kingdom of God as a little child, he shall not enter therein. And he took them up in his arms, put his hands upon them, and blessed them.

They stayed in Philadelphia and Mount Airy that summer, but the next year and for several to come they resumed their vacations at Saunderstown. Tom helped build a little cottage there for his mother, who by now was in a wheelchair with crippling arthritis. Jane Woolsey Yardley's bedroom was on the first floor, with an attendant's quarters adjacent and a ramp leading from the large porch to the ground. This spirited, indomitable woman presided cheerfully over the affairs of her family, never succumbing to self-pity or permitting the pain she suffered to diminish the pleasure of others.

Tom was blissful at Saunderstown. He "was always happiest in a boat—from a canoe to an ocean liner," but above all he loved to sail one of the many catboats his family owned over the years: lively little craft that raced over the water and gave the helmsman a good workout. On rainy days he and Louise and Harry might take the ferry to Newport, or go over to a lane called the Milky Way because so many small children spent their summers there.

At summer's end they returned not to Philadelphia but to Stockbridge, Massachusetts. Tom finally had his own church, and quite a church it was: St. Paul's, designed by Charles F. McKim and built, of south Berkshire granite, in 1884; its baptistry had been designed by Stanford White, its central tablet of sculptured angels by Augustus Saint-Gaudens, the windows flanking the angels by Louis Comfort Tiffany. Stockbridge was a resort for the wealthiest citizens of New York; the Yardleys quickly found it "a little difficult and rather expensive to get used to rural living at New York prices," and a few years later were shocked that it cost them $25 a month for the services of a maid who had just been rescued from the *Titanic*.

Another shock, the precise reverberations of which are impossible to calibrate, occurred when a vicar or deacon at St. Paul's, his name now unknown, fell in love with Louise. This strange episode, of which she is known to have spoken only once in the many years that followed, apparently caused great distress within the rectory and led, finally, to the gentleman's departure. We do not know whether Louise shared his feelings or gave him any encouragement, though the pensive manner in which she discussed the episode suggests that if nothing else she was flattered by his attentions. But an affair is quite out of the question; we all have our secrets, but Louise was too much the Victorian to permit herself behavior so far beyond the social pale. What does seem reasonable to assume is that the episode stirred a degree of tension within the marriage and did little to heighten Tom's or Louise's affection for Stockbridge.

For a time, though, they loved it there. Tom charmed his parishioners, who were touched by his self-effacing and good-humored manner. Asked if it was hard to replace his predecessor, who had been much beloved, Tom said, "On the contrary, it is a privilege to follow such a man." Once a woman spoke snidely about Louise's "lovely clothes." "Yes," Tom replied, "she is the only girl we have and we like her to look nice." Among those who fell for Tom, surely the most unlikely was Diamond Jim Brady, who ventured into town one time and found the young rector so to his liking that he proposed, most adamantly, to present him with a cow. This fancy Tom somehow persuaded him to abandon, being confident that the sight of a cow grazing on the lawn of St. Paul's rectory would give scant pleasure to his socialite parishioners, among them Austin Riggs, Miss Virginia Butler and the redoubtable Edith Wharton, whose pet monkey, Harry recalled, "peed indiscriminately on anyone and didn't even like his mistress."

The rectory was a large stucco house catercorner across the main street from the church. Not far away was an Indian burying ground where Louise often took Harry to play.

"Well, Harry," the archdeacon of the diocese asked him one day, "how do you feel playing over the bones of the Indians?"

"I feel very comfortable," Harry replied.

Tom also had a chapel a couple of miles away at Glendale, where he held a service on Sunday evenings. This, combined with his obligation to make visits in a parish that was widely scattered, led Tom to conclude that his two horses, Peter and Pilot, were insufficient to his needs, and prompted the purchase of the Yardleys' first automobile, a Pope-Hartford: "a monumental open two-seater, with oil lamps, a crank starter, running boards, all sorts of odd handles on the left to manipulate, no doors. It really was a beaut!"

Gradually, the pleasures and excitements of Stockbridge began to pall. Tom wanted "a more normal parish, with a more settled year-round congregation," and even a family that could afford a Pope-Hartford found it difficult to meet the expense of keeping the rectory's furnace and fireplaces burning during the long, cold winters. But escape was on the way. In August, 1913, not long before Bill's second birthday, Tom's step-cousin Elizabeth Gilman came for a visit. The heat was dreadful that summer; during a service at St. Paul's she and Louise were whispering sympathetic comments about Tom in his heavy vestments when Lizzie suddenly, to her amazement, spied two men in the congregation whom she knew in Baltimore. They turned out to be Blanchard Randall and Stanley Gary, vestrymen from St. Timothy's Church in Catonsville, a town just southwest of the Baltimore city limits. They dined at the rectory, were enchanted by the Yardleys, and offered Tom the rectorship of their church. After a muddy, rainy inspection of St. Timothy's, Tom accepted. Harry and Bill, and Paul soon to come, had found the town of their boyhood.

Catonsville, though it was on the fringe of a great city and had easy access to it by trolley, was in essence a small town. When the Yardleys moved there in the fall of 1913 the streets were mostly cobblestones and unpaved gravel, and horses, wagons and carriages were more common on them than automobiles; Tom's Pope-Hartford, if not exactly a rarity, was something of a novelty. Catonsville was a modest community of inexpensive clapboard dwellings and brick row houses, hardly a place that would qualify as fashionable, though its many spreading trees gave it considerable natural beauty.

St. Timothy's—St. Tim's, as it has always been called—was a

small stone church with a wooden steeple; a stone parish house was on its south side and the rectory on the north. This was a tall, ungainly Victorian building with clapboard siding and high French windows; the shutters outside were closed on chilly nights by Timothy Ebb, the yardman, when he brought in the firewood. Inside, the ceilings were high and the bannister on the front stairs was long, a perfect launching pad. In addition to Tim there were always live-in servants—during the war, when anti-German hysteria was rife, Tom hired a German cook and maid as an act of charity—but this was no token of Yardley wealth; domestic service was cheap and plentiful in those years, efficient kitchen appliances had yet to come onto the market, and servants were commonplace in middle-class households. For years the retainers were Annie and Bridget, whose story Harry must be allowed to tell:

> They weren't really quite lace-curtain Irish and still had traces of peat on their boots. However that may be, there is no denying that

St. Timothy's Church and Rectory in Catonsville

they were a pair of respectable drunks. Annie held her liquor much better than Bridget and usually had to push Bridget up the back stairs after their evening out. As I remember it, one of the Blands' chauffeurs was their nephew and they had apparently hospitable relations all over the village. One of the sights of my childhood was the picture of Annie and Bridget reeling home after an evening out, both of them barely able to walk but respectable to the end. They slept in the two little bedrooms over mine and I often remember the ceiling shaking when one of them hit the floor. Their hangovers must have been monumental and I'll never forget Annie's face when she served Monday morning breakfast. How they lasted as long as they did, I'll never know.

"Not at all a bad house to start growing up in," Harry wrote, "partly because it had so many exits, pigeons nesting in the third floor, rats and mice, and rabbits and goldfish." There were nine fireplaces, a double four-hole outhouse in the back—soon replaced by indoor plumbing—and plenty of pets, notably Louise's elderly pit bull, Prince, whom a "Bloody Fifth" saloon keeper had given her for protection, and after him a Boston bull terrier named Boy who had a particular attachment to Bill.

The Yardleys were hardly as familial or clannish as the Gregorys. The differences in the boys' ages had something to do with this, but the Yardleys simply were not people given to "togetherness," of which Bill spoke with bottomless scorn when the word acquired currency in the 1950s. The bad blood between Harry and Bill did nothing to improve matters, but it is unlikely that they would have been close even if they had liked each other; the Yardley boys, for all their marked similarities, were born to march to their own rhythms rather than those of any familial band.

Yet their childhoods were contented. They were together at table at least twice a day, eating the red meat and overcooked vegetables that were Louise's steady fare, and their dinner conversations were no more rancorous than any other family's. Everyone loved to sail; when one of the catboats was sold, it was the saddest day in Bill's young life. The Yardleys especially enjoyed Christmas, Tom's favorite day of the year. He insisted on postponing the family celebration until his church services were over so he could give the rites his full attention. They began with a massive dinner, the centerpiece being "a turkey as big as an ostrich," with background music provided by the firecrackers ritually set off all over Catonsville. At a designated moment Tom disappeared, and five minutes later Santa Claus burst in, wearing a black bearskin coat and a black fur hat and a pair of Wellington boots: the first time Bill saw this apparition he burst into tears, threw himself back in his high chair, and fell on the floor "in a Niagara of ice cream, plum pudding and champagne."

Then Santa threw open the doors to the front parlor and there it was: the tree, "glistening and shining with the ornaments that had accumulated since *his* boyhood just after the Civil War, lit with real candles." The presents were handed out and opened one by one; Tom couldn't stand to miss the fun of seeing each boy's joy as each package's contents were revealed: lead soldiers of the Coldstream Guards, French *poilus*, Irish Grenadiers, United States Marines, Napoleonic Hussars; "a tricycle, then at appropriate intervals a two-wheeler, followed by larger and larger ones as the boys grew"; then, as the boys became adolescents, "packages from Brooks and Abercrombie's supplanted the trains and bikes and rollerskates." It was a happy day, one Bill so loved that he later sought each year to re-create it within his own family.

The St. Tim's compound occupied about four acres, more than enough space for the Yardley boys and their friends to play; the size of the lot made it, in fact, a neighborhood gathering place. A further attraction was the presence immediately next door of St. Timothy's School for Girls, which had both day and boarding students. The church and school were connected by name only, but the girls attended Tom's services and he struck up a close friendship with the headmistress, Louisa Fowler; there is some reason to believe that his wife may have been jealous of this relationship with an attractive single woman, but she had no reason to be. Louisa Fowler was an old-fashioned woman of commanding presence who took on the Yardleys as her own adopted family— the boys, and in time their own children, called her Aunt Loulie—

and in later years became one of Bill's most trusted friends and
advisors. She was prosperous and lived accordingly, in a large
apartment overlooking Baltimore's Mount Vernon, surely one of
America's noblest urban spaces; she had the services of a chauffeur,
Isaac Bagwell, a black gentleman of impeccable dignity and self-
assurance who drove her about in a sedate, massive limousine.

Having a girls' school next door is not, as I can testify from
considerable experience, the best possible circumstance for a boy's
passage from youth to adolescence, but the Yardley brothers evidently handled it with aplomb. Louise was "pleased and proud" of
their good manners around the girls and their respect for the
school's regulations. She also knew that boys will be boys and was
hugely amused when Bill interrupted the bishop's Sunday confirmation ceremonies one sunlit, balmy spring day by dumping the
contents of the family's laundry basket on the girls as they paraded
past the rectory windows. "The procession from St. Timothy's
School came through the blitz convulsed," she recalled. "They
could scarcely sober down for church."

Such playfulness was not entirely characteristic of Bill, who was
a rather sedate and self-conscious boy, but he did have a mischie-
vous streak that occasionally slipped over into meanness. He
played all the usual boys' games, Kick the Can and Cowboys and
Indians and Capture the Flag, and he was good at sneaky business.
Once, when Louise was watching, he managed to slip undetected
behind trees and other objects, and avoid being caught in a game of
tag; "that's just the way he is," she said.

Still, people liked Bill, especially older people. Early in life he
discovered a knack—no, a genius—for ingratiating himself with
adults, women especially. He was deferential and charming, but he
also knew just how witty and irreverent and confiding he could be
so as to establish himself at their level. He was learning how to be
different things to different people, to assume and discard various
personae in order to accommodate the circumstances in which he
found himself; he never studied acting, but he was making himself
into a performer of immense skill and resourcefulness. He was a
secure boy at heart, but he had an abundance of tiny insecurities
that he sought to disguise by artifice; the older he grew, the more

adroit he became at drawing a line between artifice and reality that was so thin as to be invisible to all save those who knew him most intimately and who could see, as the world could not, when the curtain was rising on his next performance. Sometimes, though, the world caught on: his picture in his high school yearbook was accompanied by a line from Shakespeare, "My nature is subdued to what it works in."

Bill's formal education began in the Catonsville public schools; in later years he made a point of saying that "I always feel a little bit sorry for youngsters who go all the way up through twelve years of school without any taste of the public schools," but he was not happy there. The Yardley boys were not exactly typical red-blooded American boys; they were the preacher's kids, they lived next door to a girls' school, they hadn't much interest in baseball and football, they collected stamps and made model railroad cars—all of which is to say that in the relatively egalitarian atmosphere of a public school they were somewhat at sea. Bill further tended to be a sickly boy, with spinal difficulties and a general shortage of physical strength; he was not made for the rough-and-tumble.

So it came as a great relief to him when, in 1924, he transferred to the Boys Latin School in Baltimore. By this time Bill had developed the powerful sense of social stratification that would remain one of his strongest characteristics, so there can be no question that he would have preferred to attend the more socially prominent Gilman School, where for a time Harry had been enrolled, but Boys Latin was fine: it had enough social standing to suffice, it offered the daily pleasure of trolley rides to and from town, and it provided a first-class education, one demanding enough so that he had to repeat the seventh grade in order to obtain admission.

It was a proprietary school, owned and run for profit by its headmaster, a Johns Hopkins graduate named George Shipley, who had as fine an eye as Bill's for social nuance and standing. It was in a large brick building in a fashionable neighborhood called Bolton Hill, about a mile north of downtown Baltimore and near two of the city's major railroad stations. The curriculum was rigorously classical, which was just what Bill, with his strong taste for the past and its glories, thrived upon; he was a good student, at or near the top of his class each year, and was highly regarded by his teachers. But he was neither a grind nor a prig. Though his athletic activities were largely confined to serving, in his final year, as manager of Boys Latin's "fairly creditable" interscholastic basketball team, he was a big man on campus in extracurriculars. He was art editor of the yearbook for three years, class treasurer for two, a member of a social group called the Scoffer Club, and editor of the school newspaper, *The Ink Well*, in his senior year. "Combining his ability with his fine personality," his yearbook proclaimed, "Bill has been popular everywhere. At school, proof of his popularity is his being a member of the Scoffer Club. At dances and all other social functions, he is always welcome and popular because—er— well, look at him, girls! Yes, indeed, Friend Bill and his wavy hair plus his roomy Plymouth has really captivated the fair sex."

Yes, indeed: he *was* a handsome fellow. He had reached his adult height of just under five feet ten and had the full head of hair that in time he would lose. He was slender and graceful in manner, and he had learned how to dress himself to best effect. His sartorial education probably began in the households of the Blands and other wealthy Catonsville families, but it intensified at Boys Latin;

"Well, look at him, girls!"

how he managed the funds to make purchases at Hutzler's men's department or from the traveling Brooks Brothers representative is a mystery, but he always looked the glass of fashion and the mold of form. How disappointed he must have been that in his class ballot he finished second in "Best Dressed"; but he tied for first in "Handsomest"—and took first outright in "Thinks He Is."

He graduated from Boys Latin in June of 1930 and went off for a summer in England, Germany and France, a trip probably financed by one of his Woolsey aunts; his passport had on it the signature of the secretary of state, Henry L. Stimson, but unlike the signature on his grandfather's, it was a facsimile. On his return he matriculated not at Yale but at Johns Hopkins. He had badly wanted to go to New Haven, to what he thought of as "the family university," and had pleaded with his father to let him apply for a scholarship; but Tom Yardley declined to support him. Then, after he had been at Hopkins for two years, he asked his father if he could attempt to transfer to Yale. "No," Tom said, "you have made a four-year commitment to Johns Hopkins"—an uncharacteristically hypocritical comment from a man who had himself, as a youth, transferred in mid-career from Yale to M.I.T.

But these were hard times for Tom Yardley, and his peculiar behavior must be excused. The first decade of his life in Catonsville had been happy and productive: he had preached to an attentive and respectful flock, dined vinously with H. L. Mencken and Upton Sinclair, published a pious little book called *Was Christ Really Born of a Virgin?* (no, the answer was not in the negative), seen Sir Harry Lauder and the D'Oyly Carte in Baltimore with Louise, and watched his boys grow to the edge of manhood. But by 1925 there was trouble between him and his congregation; what its precise nature was we do not know, but it apparently was a conflict over forms of worship between Tom, who was passionately high church, and his low-church parishioners. Whatever the case, it clearly brought him to the edge of departure, for in the small collection of his remaining papers are a number of petitions, signed by dozens of people, urging him "to withdraw his resignation as our rector and to remain with us as long as his health or his wishes make it possible."

Tom Yardley in full ministerial regalia

He stayed, but in fact his health by now was poor. Diabetes had been diagnosed years before, a disease that even then subjected its victims to doses of insulin, administered by the patients themselves; Tom weighed his food at table, to the adolescent embarrassment of his sons and the pained concern of his wife. This ailment did nothing to ease his spirits, and his relationship with his congregation did not improve. He submitted a second resignation and this one was accepted. In June of 1930 he left St. Timothy's—if there were regrets on either side, no evidence of them remains—and took a two-month ministry in England. But that was only a brief reprieve from the pressures of self-inflicted unemployment, and by now the full weight of the Depression had begun to sink in.

Tom's response to these difficulties was to lose, for a time, his presence of mind. He was hospitalized at Sheppard-Pratt, a prominent psychiatric institution just north of Baltimore, while his family rented a house nearby in Towson. Upon his release in 1931 he took whatever ministerial work he could find, in New York and Connecticut briefly and then back in Philadelphia, where a part-time position, paying almost nothing, was available at the Church of St. James the Less. He and Louise found an apartment, and lived the rest of Tom's life there. In the spring of 1933 he was diagnosed as having throat cancer—he had smoked a pipe for years—and given no prospect of recovery. "My last memory of Dad," Harry has written, "was the look of love and compassion he gave me in the third-floor bedroom at 3216 West Penn Street a day or two before he died. I was so mowed down I could barely return it." Tom Yardley died on June 23, at the age of sixty-three; he was buried in the little graveyard at St. James the Less.

He did not live to see his middle son's graduation from college, but he had done much to make that education possible even if he had resisted Bill's longing for Yale. In May of 1930, while preparing to close out his career at St. Timothy's, he had taken time to write a personal letter to Joseph Sweetman Ames, the president of Johns Hopkins, asking if scholarship help would be available for Bill. "I have been under the necessity of resigning my parish," he wrote, "and as yet do not know where I shall be or how much I shall be earning. My cousin, Miss Gilman, has very generously offered to take Billy into her house . . . and this would of course solve a good deal of the problem of the expense. There is still, however, much else to be considered, and all I can say now is that if it is financially possible I shall hope to have Billy entered regularly in the class of 1934."

Tom's letter was followed by a scholarship application carefully filled out by Bill—"My father's salary is not sufficient to send me to college unassisted," he wrote in quiet understatement—and by two letters from George Shipley at Boys Latin endorsing Bill as "a chap who is certain to make good in any intellectual pursuit." Bill asked for, and was granted, $400 a year, which was sufficient to cover tuition and fees. Like many young men of Baltimore who might otherwise have sought admission to colleges of the Ivy League, Bill was forced by the realities of the Depression to look homeward; Johns Hopkins, with exceptional generosity, was finding scholarship funds for them.

The school was then little more than half a century old, a far smaller and less arrogant institution than the imperial university it has since become. Then as now it was a predominantly graduate institution; that had been the intention of its founders, who aimed to establish the first American university based on the German model. As its initial president they chose Bill's great-uncle, Daniel Coit Gilman, husband of Aunt Lily Woolsey, who in 1875 came to Baltimore from the University of California at Berkeley, of which he also had been the founding president; after leaving Hopkins in 1902 he became the first president of the Carnegie Institute, a record unparalleled in the history of American education. Of his years in Baltimore it is no exaggeration to say, as one historian has, that Johns Hopkins "was his lengthened shadow." He was a man of tact and determination and powerful intellectual integrity, with a gift for publicity and a single-minded devotion to the institution he served; he knew—it was perhaps from his example that Bill learned the lesson—that the institution is greater than the man and that it was the institution, not the man, he had been appointed to serve.

Gilman's retirement and death preceded Bill's enrollment by many years, but he was still a vigorous presence in the mythology of the campus and, through his daughter, Elizabeth, in its daily life as well. The diminutive Lizzie Gilman in her eccentric attire could regularly be seen walking along its pathways, stopping to talk with students, or promoting the socialist cause. Of this she was a tireless and, in the view of many, tiresome, advocate: she ran unsuccessfully for various offices from governor on down, participated in labor controversies, and served on innumerable boards. She was something of a common scold and thus was often dismissed as an eccentric; but it says something for her that at a dinner in 1941 at which she was honored for "outstanding service to her nation and to her community," the principal speaker was Norman Thomas, and the sponsors included Roger Baldwin, Robert M. La Follette, Jr., Harold J. Laski, Reinhold Niebuhr and Upton Sinclair.

Lizzie Gilman had no blood ties to the Yardleys—she was a child of Gilman's first marriage—but she was kin all the same in an era when family connections were more routinely honored than they are now. She was by no stretch of the imagination an attractive woman, which explains why Daniel Coit Gilman had offered his nephew Tom Yardley—this was before Louise Thorne had come along—a financial settlement if he would marry her. The offer was wisely if politely refused, but when coincidence brought the Yardleys to Baltimore, Lizzie welcomed them gladly. She lived in a large row house at 513 Park Avenue, a once-fashionable neighborhood beginning to go into decline, where she supported herself by taking Hopkins boys in as boarders. She had a decrepit old butler and a cook celebrated for incompetence; Thanksgiving dinner with Lizzie became a tradition for the Yardleys, one that none of them looked forward to.

In Lizzie's boardinghouse Bill was on scholarship, which he needed there every bit as much as he did at the university; no doubt she expected his occasional company as part payment for her generosity, for Bill's gratitude for her assistance was always tempered by exasperation at her personal deficiencies and political dogmatism. Her house was a couple of miles due south from the university, a distance Bill traveled by trolley in the morning and the evening; it takes no great leap of the imagination to surmise that he left as early, and returned as late, as he possibly could.

Much to his good fortune, he had somewhere else to go. In the fall of 1930 he pledged Alpha Delta Phi, a fraternity of high social prominence with a row house at 3004 North Calvert Street, two blocks from the university's eastern border on Charles Street. How Bill afforded the fraternity, impecunious as he was, nobody knows; but dues were low, lunch in the fraternity dining room was twenty-five cents, and in those days everyone was poor. There can be no question, though, of the fraternity's importance both to Bill's social life at the university and to his self-esteem. Only Delta Phi rivaled Alpha Delta Phi for standing on campus, and by admission to it—this at a campus of some eight hundred fifty students, nearly half of whom were fraternity members—Bill gained automatic entry to the upper echelon of the campus social structure.

Not merely that, but he found himself in a congenial place. Alpha Delta Phi was a "literary" fraternity, with monthly meetings at which members in formal dress read papers on topics of their own choosing and visiting critics commented on the proceedings. Bill was an active participant in this aspect of the fraternity's life and gained great respect for the literacy of his own contributions. He was thought of as intellectual, sophisticated, formal, aloof, discriminating; he liked a good time and enjoyed his drinks with the boys, but he wasn't a rowdy or a hail fellow well met. He participated fully and merrily in fraternity parties, but this was a quieter time; raucous boozing of the "animal house" tradition was most uncommon, girls were allowed in the fraternity house only on formal occasions, and buttons were kept decorously buttoned.

Bill's daily routine entailed classes in the morning, lunch at noon in the fraternity house, classes or other engagements in the afternoon. During his sophomore year these activities included membership in the Cane Club, a group of self-styled rakes who carried canes, wore top hats, and rode around in a tally-ho, making more of a spectacle of themselves than doubtless they realized. One of their initiation requirements was to pick a fight with a Jew, which Bill proudly if improbably claimed to have done. Alas, the prejudice if not the challenge would have been in character; Bill had absorbed his mother's virulent opinions about Jews and Negroes —the former were Shylocks, the latter fit only for servitude— and years passed before he began, however tentatively, to question them.

But his sentiments were certainly those of the age and the campus. Hopkins had a larger percentage of Jewish students than most universities then, and they mingled freely in the life of the school, but socially they lived quite apart. The atmosphere reflected not merely that of the period but that of the city as well. Baltimore was a conservative metropolis of an essentially southern character. Wardlaw Miles, an English professor of the utmost distinction who had lost a leg in World War I, was once asked at a dinner party if he hadn't paid too high a price in the war. "My only regret," he replied, "is that I did not lose it for the Confederacy"— and in so saying he spoke for many in old Baltimore, where venerated traditions, some of them discredited, still ran deep.

Yet the same city that harbored these retrograde prejudices and social taboos also tolerated a vocal and organized protest movement. Students at Hopkins, quite unlike those at Bennington, saw the Depression every day in the street-corner apple vendors, the men who knocked on doors pleading for money or food, the long lines of the unemployed. In response a Liberal Club was formed on the campus, and a Young Communist League; in the School of Business Economics a young professor named Broadus Mitchell was a passionate advocate for the dispossessed, organizing marches and protests, at one of which ROTC students turned fire hoses on the marchers and doused them into silence.

Where was Bill in all of this? Certainly not with the ROTC students, though membership in that organization was rewarded with a free suit of clothes and a bit of pocket change; the military never was Bill's cup of tea, unless it took the form of warships sailing serenely across a canvas or Civil War relics safely under glass. Nor could we expect to find him among the marchers, for he was entirely too fastidious for that. Yet we know that he did not go entirely untouched either by the turmoil of the times or by his association with Lizzie Gilman. In the fall of 1932 he cast his first presidential vote, and he gave it to Norman Thomas; he was ever after proud of that, and always said—quite accurately—that he had never cast one for a better man.

If a vote for the Socialist Party's candidate seems wildly out of character, it must be borne in mind that Bill's politics were hopelessly muddled. He had absorbed his father's Wilsonian big-D Democracy, but he also was sympathetic to his mother's prejudices and aristocratic longings. By 1932 he had seen enough poverty in Baltimore to have no patience with Hoover, but like many in the intelligentsia he found Roosevelt callow and opportunistic. Why not Thomas, whom he had met at Lizzie's house and whose own aristocratic bearing softened the radicalism of his message?

Politics was in any event not Bill's métier, as in later years his ill-informed and hilariously impassioned sentiments over and over confirmed. His world was the fraternity and, in his senior year, the Tudor and Stuart Club. This society, which had a handsomely paneled room in Gilman Hall, the university's principal academic building, brought professors, graduate students and a select group of undergraduates together under the common banner of literature. It had been endowed by the great physician Sir William Osler and his wife in memory of their son, Edward Revere Osler, a lover of old books who had been killed in World War I; in the ensuing decade and a half the club had assembled an impressive collection, specializing in the work of Edmund Spenser.

Election to the club was for an undergraduate a signal honor, though perhaps less so for members of Alpha Delta Phi, the membership of which substantially overlapped with Tudor and Stuart. But Bill doubtless was chosen on merit rather than social standing, for he had excelled in the study of literature, history and the classics. The club gave him a refuge from Lizzie; tea and coffee were available there, sometimes cheese and crackers, and always a comfortably overstuffed chair in which to read and relax. Surrounded by paneled walls and books in fine morocco, Bill saw in the Tudor and Stuart Club a vision of what was, for him, the good life: stimulating and congenial company in an atmosphere of civility and erudition. It was a vision to which he remained true and one he eventually realized in his own living room, in a small town in Virginia.

* * *

Given this strong interest in literature and a gift for prose that had won the attention of his professors, it may seem surprising that Bill did not pursue a career in writing, but it was not one that suited his particular talents. His mind did not have an imaginative turn, so fiction and poetry were out; he was not in the strict sense of the term a scholar, so academic or historical writing was out; and he looked down his nose at journalism, so that too was eliminated. Instead, after taking honors in the spring of 1934 in his comprehensive English literature examination and being presented with his Bachelor of Arts degree, he returned to Philadelphia and took a position as intern in the English Department of the William Penn Charter School. He had chosen for his life neither wealth nor power but the robes of a schoolmaster; Bill Yardley aimed to be a gentleman.

He lived for that year with his mother on West Penn Street; the school was within walking distance. After a summer during which Bill took a course at the University of Pennsylvania, Paul returned to the Kent School in Connecticut, which had granted him a scholarship. Harry, much to Bill's relief, had gone on his own. He had exercised all of his massive supply of charm on Elsie Dunning, an enchanting girl, and had married her; he was now trying to establish himself as an architect.

For Bill this first year of professional life must have been happy. He was learning to teach the only really effective way—by doing it—and he had his mother's undivided attention. She was still in mourning, and she had astonishingly little experience at supporting or even caring for herself, but she was a practical woman whose resources proved sufficient to the day. Doubtless she was grateful for Bill's regular presence; if it chafed him at all to be back under the parental roof, surely he knew that the benefits far outweighed the drawbacks.

He did well enough at Penn Charter to be offered a job for the academic year 1935–1936 at Bedford-Rippowam, a small private day school in Westchester County, and before the autumn term began he had an opportunity to become better acquainted with its headmaster, E. Trudeau Thomas, as both young men were enrolled in the Harvard School of Education's summer program, pursuing the degree of Master of Education. The two hit it off. Thomas, who was happily married, took it upon himself to encourage Bill's romantic life, as he made evident one day at class when they paused to chat.

"Say, Bill," Thomas said, "there's a girl I'd like you to meet. . . ."

*Bill Yardley and
Helen Gregory in 1936*

IT WAS about ten days later that Bill and Trudeau ran into each other again.

"Well!" Thomas said. "Did you have a chance to get together with Helen Gregory? How'd you like her?"

"Oh, I liked her very much," Bill replied. "In fact, we're engaged to be married."

"You're kidding! I knew you two would like each other, but isn't that just a little fast?"

That's what Louise Yardley thought; she also thought Trudeau Thomas was pushing her son into a premature match and resented him for this fancied intrusion. By now she had moved to the apartment at 212 West Highland Avenue in Chestnut Hill, on the inner portion of Philadelphia's Main Line, that would be her home for the next forty years, and she was establishing herself as an inescapable presence in her sons' lives. So Bill brought Helen down for the ritual introduction, and Louise's initial objections—among them was a peculiar fear that marrying "a college girl" somehow might be unwise—were overcome; the two women never were entirely comfortable with each other, but over the years they developed a mutual affection that was both genuine and deep.

The Gregorys were skeptical too, though for different reasons. Helen brought Bill out to the Cape that first summer, to the applause of her parents—Bill and Alfred Gregory hit it off at once, and thereafter treated each other as equals—but Al and Art were skeptical. These prototypically red-blooded American boys thought Bill too punctilious and intellectual and standoffish and "British": a sissy, in a word. He tried to ingratiate himself by eagerly joining them in their boat as they headed out for a sail; everyone labored to make the best of it, but it was an awkward afternoon. Then, that night, the Gregory boys and several of their friends were setting off skyrockets when one of the firecrackers accidentally ignited six or seven others, setting off a riot of noise and color. They thought it hilarious, but Bill rushed over from the porch, shouting, "Boys! Boys! Stop it! You can't do that!" They looked at him as if he were a creature from another planet.

Gradually, though, they came to accept and like him. At Christmas he visited the Gregorys in Maplewood. Art and Al were in their bedroom when first Helen and then Bill came in. They started horsing around, rather awkwardly, when suddenly Helen decided she'd had enough of Bill's teasing and elbowed him smack in the groin; it hurt, but it also got everyone laughing and broke the ice. In time Al and Art came to respect Bill's knowledge and seriousness of purpose; it meant a good deal to them as well that their parents admired him.

But before Bill could join the Gregory clan there was business to be done. He was intensely involved in the daily life of Bedford-Rippowam, which for an annual salary of $1,200 plus living quarters was placing stringent demands on his time: not merely did he have a heavy teaching load in the English Department, but as chairman of this tiny empire he had administrative work to dispatch; he also coached soccer and served as counselor to various extracurricular activities. The school, a couple of miles from the center of Bedford Village, had been established in 1917 to serve the children of families who had begun moving to the area from New York City; they were for the most part wealthy people, the fathers commuting to the city by train or automobile. The terrain was hilly, heavily wooded, spectacularly beautiful when the autumnal colors reached their peak intensity.

The school, which enrolled both boys and girls from kindergarten through ninth grade, at first occupied a wooden house and former barn; by the time of Bill's arrival two more wood-frame structures had been erected, giving the campus the cozy look and feel of New England. Bill fit in from the outset, quickly gaining a reputation among the students for his enthusiasm and patience, and among his colleagues for diligence and willingness to take on responsibility. He was going to make something of himself, by God, and he was willing to do whatever work was demanded of him.

Helen meanwhile was in the final year of college. She did not come rushing back to school breathless with the summer's happy news, but told Edie and other friends about her attachment to Bill quietly, almost shyly. Nor did she spend her premarital senior year pining away for the days to come. She awaited the mail eagerly, as all college students do, and was delighted when Bill could come up for a visit—Bedford was about a hundred miles to the south—but she had many other things on her mind beside trousseau and wedding cake. She was working on her senior thesis, "The Relation of the Aesthetic Structure of Henry James's Novels to His Conception of Morality"—a lucid, perceptive and meticulous piece of work—and she was closely involved, with the other members of her class, in plans for their graduation. In this as in so many other things they were making decisions that, if the results proved successful, would affect Bennington students for generations to come.

As it happens the Pioneers chose a ceremony that varied little from the traditional commencements held elsewhere. Apart from wearing beanies instead of mortarboards, they dressed as new graduates do in academic robes, they marched in procession to the ceremony, and they listened to the usual words of inspiration and admonition. This was on June 6, 1936, in the sunshine and crisp air of Vermont in springtime.

* * *

Two weeks later, at four o'clock on the afternoon of June 20, Helen walked down the aisle of St. George's Church in Maplewood on the arm of her father; she wore a white satin gown with a tulle veil, and carried a bouquet of roses and lilies of the valley. She and Alfred were preceded by Edie Noyes, Helen's maid of honor and her only attendant, who wore a pink marquisette dress and carried a bouquet of blue larkspur and pink daisies. At the altar they were met by Bill and his best man, Trudeau Thomas, both wearing tan gabardine slacks, blue blazers and regimental ties. The minister, the Reverend Mr. Francis H. Richey, then began to read, from *The Book of Common Prayer*, the words that would bind them to each other for half a century:

> O God, who hast so consecrated the state of Matrimony that in it is represented the spiritual marriage and unity betwixt Christ and his Church; Look mercifully upon these thy servants, that they may love, honor, and cherish each other, and so live together in faithfulness and patience, in wisdom and true godliness, that their home may be a haven of blessing and of peace; through the same Jesus Christ our Lord, who liveth and reigneth with Thee and the Holy Spirit ever, one God, world without end.

Then the Reverend Richey pronounced them Man and Wife, said a benediction over them, and sent them up the aisle with music in their ears and smiles on their faces. They and their several dozen guests went back up the hill to 42 Mountain Avenue, where in the back yard under the bright late-afternoon sky refreshments were served and champagne toasts drunk; the wedding cake was cut and several pieces of it were put in tiny boxes, which Bill and Helen saved for the rest of their lives. Louise was there with Paul and Harry and Elsie, a few of Helen's friends had come from Bennington, and there was a representative selection of Gregory friends from New Jersey and professional associates from New York; the party was gay but not raucous.

Inside the house and garage, packed and ready for shipment to Bedford Village, were the gifts with which the new husband and wife would begin to set up house. Many of them had been purchased, as would be expected of that time and place, at Reed & Barton, Samuel Kirk, Tiffany & Co., Bailey, Banks and Biddle, and Black, Starr, Frost & Gorham. They included the usual ice bucket and tongs, cigarette boxes, silver ladles and spoons, electric toasters and knickknacks. There was an antique drop-leaf table from Lizzie Gilman; a gold bedside clock from Alfred's friend and partner Dexter Hawkins; a forty-two-piece china set from Louisa Fowler; and, from Aunt Elizabeth Yardley at 91 Rhode Island Avenue, Great-grandmother Jane Andrews Woolsey's silver tea set. There were also checks to a total of $685, the most generous of these being for $500; this came from Helen's Bennington friends, Mr. and Mrs. James C. Colgate.

But the most princely gifts came, not surprisingly, from Alfred Gregory. Six months earlier he had presented Helen with thirty shares of stock in firms as blue-chip as Alfred himself: American Telephone & Telegraph, International Nickel, Sherwin-Williams, Union Carbide, United States Steel. These had been worth $2,819.38 at the time the gift was made, and had since risen to a total value of well over $3,000. To them he added his personal check for $5,000; Helen was marrying a schoolteacher, if not a churchmouse, but Alfred was determined that she be given enough of a nest egg to cushion the difficult times that surely lay ahead.

At the end of the afternoon Helen went to her room one last time and changed into traveling clothes. On the way down she stood at the landing where she had spent so many private and happy hours, and tossed her bouquet into a small sea of hands. Then she and Bill ran through a sprinkling of confetti and rice into the elderly Plymouth that had served Bill so well for so long. He started the engine and they were off: to Martha's Vineyard for a prolonged honeymoon—it was so happy that they agreed never to return to the island, lest their memories be sullied—and then to Bedford Village. Their half-century had begun.

PART TWO

Starting Out

IN AUGUST they came to Bedford Village, to a little house they had rented not far from the Bedford-Rippowam campus. In this small town they found two conditions that were to prevail, in their lives, for fifty years to come: they were in a physical setting of uncommon beauty both natural and manmade, and they were in the company of people who had the means to live in such surroundings. Certainly it is true that, thanks to Alfred Gregory, they had more financial resources with which to ease their way than are often afforded to an apprentice schoolmaster and his bride, but their income was laughably small and from the outset they had to train themselves to stretch it as far as they could.

Like most such communities in those days, Bedford Village was almost exclusively white, Anglo-Saxon and Episcopalian, and it certainly occurred to no one there—Bill and Helen included—to question this order of things. People of different colors, ancestries and denominations might enter Bedford from Mount Kisco and other neighboring communities to work in the shops along its lovely little main street or in the houses that perched on the hills beyond, but they were hired help. The stockbrokers and bankers and industrialists who daily traveled to the city, and the wives who stayed behind to tend their children and domiciles, belonged to the American ruling class and its quasi-official church.

The community's "Holy Trinity," they liked to say in Bedford, encompassed St. Matthew's Episcopal Church, the Bedford Golf and Tennis Club, and the Bedford-Rippowam School. By virtue of employment, both Bill and Helen were therefore immediately absorbed into what passed for the local establishment: Bill as chairman of the school's English Department and Helen as secretary to Trudeau Thomas, for which she was paid an annual salary of $600. Her job was to "answer the telephone, find out why children are absent, take the attendance and make out the list for lunch, not to mention writing letters and, worst of all, keeping the accounts, which means all sorts of bookkeeping"—"not at all what I thought I was preparing myself for when I started to write my paper on Henry James!" Indeed, Helen was quickly finding that life at Bennington and life in the world were anything except one and the same:

> I think marriage involves so many adjustments to another person and his habits and ideas that it is bound to influence the rest of your life. For that reason I found my job rather hard at first tho' now that I'm used to it and more used to married life the job is much easier.
>
> I also have found the adjustment to an entirely new community hard as I knew only four or five people in this locality. The hardest thing I've found is that people who are connected with a school are never allowed to forget it unless they get away from the school and everyone involved in its business. When we go out to dinner we have to talk about the school until I begin to think that in another year I won't be able to talk or think about anything else. It makes me furious that fairly intelligent people should think that other people as intelligent as they but connected with the local country day school, have no interests outside of the school.

Of course the obvious reality was that, for all their mutual interest in Bill's career, the two of them had strong, indeed passionate, interests elsewhere. To begin with they had each other. Whatever difficulties they may have encountered during their period of adjustment, these growing pains were eased and ameliorated by an ardent physical attraction to each other. Both had come as virgins to the marital bed, and both were eager to alter that condition. They had the good fortune to have come of age at a time when candor was replacing cant and misinformation about matters sexual. They had a book—*Sex Habits,* by Buschler and Jacobsohn—which they consulted regularly, the precepts of which they put into action; because they did not want a family until they were ready for one, Helen used a diaphragm. Their physical relations were ecstatic, frequent and imaginative; this—of which Bill once spoke to me in a moment of rare intimacy—seems to me quite enough for a product of those relations to say on the subject.

Their involvement with each other extended as well to a shared interest in each other's families, though the balance was decidedly in a Yardley direction. A born hobbyist—for years he had, among other such diversions, copied his father's practice of pasting pictures on thin sheets of wood and cutting them with a jigsaw into intricate puzzles—Bill elected to make an avocation of genealogy; Helen, who had not inherited her father's indifference to such matters, went along with him. Bill obtained a large sheet of heavy paper, some thirty-six by twenty inches, and on it drew a semicircle, which he then bisected directly up the middle. On each half he drew lines fanning out from the bottom in ever-increasing numbers; the left half of the semicircle was to be the Yardley family genealogy, the right half the Gregorys'. On that left side he fastidiously entered dozens of names, going back generation upon generation through an interminable, suffocating procession of Woolseys and Dwights and Worrells and Thornes. The Gregory side? Well, it comes as no surprise that Bill never got around to the Gregory side, and Helen was insufficiently interested to do the job herself.

What preoccupied both of them to the exclusion of almost everything else was furnishing and decorating their four-room house. This is of necessity a matter of paramount concern to all newlyweds, but Bill and Helen pursued it with exceptional zeal because furniture and decoration fascinated both of them: Helen because of her passion for design, Bill because of his passion for the past, both because of their shared passion for all that was beautiful and rare. Their wedding gifts supplied them more than adequately with silver and china, some of which was old and modestly valuable, and they had been given a few pieces of furniture, but they needed much more and they went about acquiring it with single-minded determination.

More than a half-century later it is quite impossible to realize how easily and cheaply good furniture could be obtained in those days; our age, in which Coca-Cola signs and Elvis Presley figurines are sold as "collectibles," can scarcely comprehend an earlier one in which Chippendale chairs and Sheffield candlesticks could be had for ludicrously small amounts. The Depression had demolished many households, and auctions were common; at one of these Helen and Bill purchased a massive round pedestal table of solid mahogany, with enough leaves to permit seating a dozen or more, for five dollars, and ended up paying more to transport it than for the table itself. They bought ladderback chairs with cane bottoms—country furniture now regarded as classic Americana—for a pittance, and nineteenth-century marine lithographs for pennies. They loved poking around in thrift shops, flea markets and used-book stores, but disdained antique shops; the prices were always too high there, they felt, and a canny, resourceful buyer could find better goods for less money elsewhere.

Though they had been reared in comfortable if not lavish circumstances, they adjusted to impecuniousness with astonishing ease and grace. Bill had become accustomed to that condition in the hard years after his father had left Catonsville, but Helen had been a privileged girl right up to the moment Bill slipped the ring on her finger. Yet for matter-of-fact Helen it was almost as if she had been presented a challenge, a puzzle to solve: on approximately $175 a month of combined income, how are we going to eat, pay the rent, furnish the house, afford ourselves some modest entertainment and save against the future?

The answer was that they pinched pennies, and in 1936 pennies went a long way. On November 19 Helen went to the grocery store and spent $8.39, for which she received: sardines, three grapefruits, sugar, rhubarb, lima beans, spinach, corn, coffee, eggs, Ritz crackers, bread, lemons, disinfectant, two lamb chops and a three-pound, two-ounce piece of roast beef. On March 21 of the next year she paid $3.67 for: cookies, butter, razor blades, spaghetti, mushroom soup, pea soup, chicken gumbo, four grapefruits, rhubarb, bread, a can of tomatoes, a can of corn, veal chops and a steak. The Depression may have been hard, but for those fortunate enough to have an income, even a small one went a very long way.

Not merely that, but Bill and Helen liked to do things for themselves. The lithographs that they bought Bill would carefully watercolor—he had the steadiest and most resourceful hands of anyone I have ever known, with long, nimble fingers—and mat with black paper trimmed by a gold-leaf border; in a frame they'd picked up at a yard sale, one of these—a view of New York Harbor, or Harvard Yard, or Washington at Valley Forge, or the battle between the *United States* and the *Macedonian*—made an elegant decoration, as did the little silhouettes Bill had taught himself to fashion. They also worked on their house, repainting all four of its rooms. The landlord saw the results and promptly raised the rent; when asked why, he replied, "The house has been improved."

This no doubt had much to do with their decision to move, after their first year, to the Kisco Gardens Apartments in Mount Kisco, five miles away; so too, surely, did Helen's sense that Bedford-Rippowam was taking up more than enough of their lives, and that a little physical distance between the Yardleys and the school could do them nothing except good. But in Mount Kisco as in Bedford, penny-watching was the order of the day. In 1937–1938 their pay was raised modestly, Bill's to $1,840 and Helen's to $620, for a total of $2,460, or $205 a month, every cent of which they needed. Not merely did they have regular expenses to meet, but each summer Harvard beckoned. In 1937, while Bill continued his slow, steady progress toward his Master's, Helen took two courses in secondary education but after that stopped: it "seemed rather pointless—I'm not interested in teaching and even if I had wanted a degree in Education it would have taken twenty years of summer work!"

If Helen had ever really wanted a career for herself—if she'd ever had any expectations beyond the conventional one of supporting herself in some kind of job until the right man came along—she had pretty well set them aside by now; beyond the house and school her activities were largely limited to studying wood en-

graving with a local sculptor. Otherwise she seems to have concluded by this point that her life, and whatever satisfactions it was
to give her, would be lived in the shadow and at the fortune of her
husband. Whether this gave her more than momentary pause we
do not know, though in her letters back to Bennington she indicated a strong curiosity about what lines of work her classmates
were pursuing. For herself, she had chosen the traditional help-
mate's role—"any position I could hold would have to be connected
with my husband's work"—and apparently without resentment.
The resentment came later.

As if she and Bill didn't have enough to do, in the summer of 1938,
before going off to summer school, they put a bit of Alfred's money
to good use by purchasing, for approximately $1,000, a farm in Fly
Creek Valley on the outskirts of Cooperstown, some one hundred
fifty miles to the northwest in Otsego County in upstate New
York. This consisted of eighty acres, mostly wooded, and a farm-

"Prospect Farm"

house and attendant structures all in a dilapidated, though habitable, condition; they gave it the name of "Prospect Farm," in tribute to William the Emigrant and his dwelling in the Delaware Valley. Their intention was to rehabilitate the farm themselves, and to that end they spent as much time there as they could in the summers and during school breaks.

They had long-term hopes for the farm, but these never came close to fruition because their lives simply became too busy to accommodate working on a farm in a location that then was even more difficult to reach than it is today. They sold the land in 1944 for $1,200, feeling that they had gotten something of a white elephant off their hands, but thereafter they always spoke of Cooperstown with affection. Because it was the first property they had jointly owned, they had an emotional purchase on it that had no book value and that they never entirely relinquished. They had loved the landscape of central New York State and the drive up to Cooperstown through the Catskills always thrilled them. They'd had happy relationships with their neighbors—Drakes, Shaws, Willseys, Lambs—and with an older couple who came to Cooperstown from Manhattan, Parker and Margaret Kuhn; a mutually affectionate attachment developed between the Yardleys and Kuhns, and over the years the couples kept in touch. They'd also had their first exposure to rural life, even to the extent of purchasing a share of stock in the Otsego Forest Products Cooperative Association, and they liked it enough to want more.

Decades later they were at dinner in Rhode Island with my wife, Sue, and me and my sons, Jim and Bill, when somehow the subject of toilets came up. Helen immediately brightened. "Oh, dear," she said, "in Cooperstown we had a terrible old toilet that was always in danger of breaking down, so we tried to use it as little as we could. We even had a little rhyme for it," and in unison, laughing, she and Bill, Sr., recited:

If it's yellow, let it mellow;
If it's brown, flush it down.

*   *   *

95

At about the same time as they were buying the Cooperstown farm, Bill and Helen determined that the moment had come to assemble an inventory of their effects. Ostensibly this was done for purposes of insurance, but the more likely reason is that it gave them an opportunity to compile a list—both of them loved list-making—and to create a document that authenticated the position they had assumed in life after two years of marriage; a further explanation is that in June of 1938 they acquired a modest amount of property from the estate of Bill's Aunt Lily—Elizabeth Woolsey Yardley—at 91 Rhode Island Avenue, and may have felt a need to catalogue it. Whatever the case, they bought a brown ledger with an alphabetical thumb index, pasted one of J. J. Lankes's green trees on the cover, and in Bill's precise hand, on the first page declared themselves:

INVENTORY

of

HOUSEHOLD GOODS & CHATTELS

of

HELEN GREGORY & WILLIAM WOOLSEY YARDLEY

June, 1938

Mt. Kisco, New York

They left almost nothing out. They noted that they owned four mahogany side chairs from Thomas Howe Yardley's house on Fourth Street in Philadelphia, with white leather seats that Bill and Helen had installed, in May of 1938, "at about $10 per seat"; a dozen cups and saucers, Aynsley English bone china, "one cup chipped as of June 1938"; a mahogany footstool covered in red-brown mohair (later, in pencil: "broke & in attic '46"); one white kitchen stool, purchased at R. H. Macy in September of 1936 for $3; a "miniature of W.W.Y., aged 3, by Emily Hayden, Catonsville, Md."; an "Oriental 'Akbar' India 9 x 12 rug gift of A. Gregory September, 1936 from W. & J. Sloane price $365 (reduced from $515)"; a maple sewing table Helen had bought while at Bennington (later, in pencil: "Broken in transit to Cooperstown, lost"); and one "black and gold Hitchcock-type side chair with silhouette of 'Prospect Farm.' Bought 1938 in junkyard Mt. Kisco, refinished and painted by W. W. Y."

It was on the whole an inventory such as any young middle-class couple of the day might have drawn up—if it is possible to imagine another couple so consumed by its household as to do so in such obsessive detail—with two notable exceptions. The first was that Bill and Helen had acquired, by gift or inheritance, an unusually large amount of antique furniture and tableware. Reading through the inventory I am startled at how much of what they owned in their mid-twenties was of such quality that they kept it for the rest of their lives, and at how much of it is now in my possession or that of my sisters and brother. In the front room of our house in Baltimore is a sofa, in a style that I would call Empire, the history of which was described in full a half-century ago in Bill's words:

> Early Victorian or "Regency" sofa, mahogany with lion's claw feet and curved ends. Came from Yardley house in Philadelphia, one of a pair the other of which is (1938) had by Aunt Isabel Marble. Reupholstered for us by Mr. Nielson in Pleasantville summer of 1938, in light green tapestry with bolster to match. Part of our share from 91 Rhode Island Avenue (cost to re-do and mend, $79.50). Probably made about 1820. (Appraised in estate at $50, before any refinishing or upholstering had been done.)

To those who say that earthly possessions are meaningless, I offer in rebuttal that sofa. It is for me as it sits in our house a direct, immediate connection to my past. That sofa was in Thomas Howe Yardley's house a century and a half ago, then in his son Henry's, then in Henry's sisters', then in Bill's, now in my own. That sofa connects me to my past as powerfully as the blood in my veins, just as does the silver-plated teapot in the shape of an early locomotive that sits on our mantel; it was given by Alfred Gregory to his clients at a railroad in Pennsylvania in 1938 and was returned by them to his daughter three decades later, in grateful recognition of his services. Every time I see that whimsical locomotive I think not of tea, or of silver, but of Alfred Gregory, and of those who went before me.

The second important difference between the Yardley inventory and those that other households of the time would have yielded was that it contained a disproportionately large number of books; Bill and Helen were readers of books then and collectors of books later, and to both of them books were as precious as anything else they owned—more precious, in fact, when years later Bill assembled a collection that, auctioned off in the early 1970s, gave them a small nest egg with which to begin their retirement. Imagine the patience it took for Helen and Bill—the handwriting of both is present in this section of the inventory—to record the title, author, publisher and date of acquisition of each of the nearly two hundred books they had acquired by the summer of 1938; more than anything else in the ledger, this clearly was a labor of love.

What the inventory tells us is what we know already: that Bill's taste was for the classics, while Helen was strongly sympathetic to modernism. To the joint collection Bill brought Thackeray and Trollope, Shakespeare and Smollett, Trevelyan and Boswell, while Helen contributed O'Neill and Dickinson, Joyce and Pound, Hemingway and Eliot. Yet there are surprises here as well: Bill's copies of Faulkner's *Sanctuary*, Lawrence's *Sons and Lovers*, Whitman's *Leaves of Grass*, and Helen's of Plato's *Five Dialogues on Poetic Inspiration*, Milton's *Poetical Works* and Pepys's *Diary*. Considering that they were children of the Anglo-Saxon middle-class, their reading tastes were refreshingly varied, undogmatic and imaginative; over the years they developed affections for certain authors and works they read over and over, but to the end they remained receptive to unknown writers and to books that explored worlds quite different from their own.

Whether they read aloud to each other in the evening I do not know, but chances are they did. Bill, with his highly developed sense of the dramatic, fancied himself a charismatic reader and reveled in a captive audience, which Helen gave him the rest of her life, though at times the captive was restive. So little is known of this period of their lives that there is not much to do except speculate about the Bedford years, but on the evidence of their later behavior I should imagine that after a day's work they had a cocktail or two—early in their marriage they drank Manhattans, but when they grew up they switched to martinis—and a boring meal of roast beef or broiled lamb chops or roast chicken, with boiled potato and steamed vegetable and most certainly dessert, without which Bill's existence would have been intolerable; afterward they probably settled into their separate armchairs and read their separate books, pausing from time to time to read aloud passages that were amusing or striking. Then, around eleven, they went to bed.

They had friends in these years, but virtually none of those friendships survived into their mature adulthood; they used to speak to each other in the presence of their children about certain people whose names became something of a litany, but we only rarely had the opportunity to attach faces to these names, and in my mind at least they are always associated with a dim and distant past that has little meaning for me except the obviously pleasurable nostalgia the names evoked for Helen and Bill. I think of them in those days as essentially apart: members of the Bedford-Rippowam community, of course, with the smothering intimacy this entailed, but alone in their living quarters, pursuing the interests and passions that were theirs alone.

By the beginning of the 1938–1939 school year Bill had been raised to $2,000 and Helen, under a new headmaster, to $800. Their gross earnings in 1938 were $2,859.67, which included $209.67 in dividends and interest; after earned income credit and personal exemption, they had taxable income of $51.92, on which they paid a federal tax of $2.08. The following spring they dipped into the Colgates' wedding gift—"the Colgate fund," they called it—to pay V. V. Nielson of Pleasantville $111 to make an upholstered barrel-shaped chair with matching ottoman; and on sale at Altman's in Manhattan, reduced from $450 to $195, they purchased a substantial mahogany breakfront with glass doors atop and drawers below, which became the storing place and showcase for the best of their silver and china.

They needed new furniture because they were moving; their Bedford period was over and soon they would have roomier quarters to outfit. At this point in his career Bill routinely had his name on file at the American and Foreign Teachers' Agency in New York, which kept its hand firmly on the pulse of the private-school job market. With his progress toward the Master's continuing apace, albeit a petty pace, Bill was acquiring the credentials for the administrative work he desired, and was looking for experience that would further his progress toward that goal. So when, in the spring of 1939, he learned of an opening at the Shady Side Academy in Pittsburgh, he seized it eagerly.

Shady Side offered Bill the same salary as he was making at Bedford-Rippowam, but other aspects of the job mattered more to him: the school was larger, which in private-school circles is almost always taken to mean better, it took boarding students, and it offered a free residence to Bill and Helen at Croft House, where in exchange for quarters he would serve as assistant housemaster. Besides, Shady Side provided yet another inducement; Bill and Helen knew the headmaster, E. Trudeau Thomas.

They needed the larger quarters, for in the summer of 1939 a new entry appeared in their accounts. It was called "Expenses for Baby," which by its completion had reached a total of $271.24, for doctors' fees and a nurse, a layette and a bassinet and baby clothes. As they drove to Pittsburgh in August of 1939 Helen was immensely pregnant, uncomfortable in the heavy heat and eager to get on with the business of motherhood. That she accomplished on October 27, 1939. Three decades later Bill recalled the day:

> Some twenty-nine years ago you made your appearance into the world. You changed my whole life from being a somewhat irresponsible young man to a somewhat irresponsible slightly older man who got less sleep every night.
>
> I wish you great joy upon your coming birthday. I can't tell you

how proud I am of being present at the laying of the keel, and of waiting outside the delivery room in the West Penn Hospital when you made your slightly traumatic entrance into Smokey City. Indeed you were a sorry-looking object; your head was bent to one side. Your face was bashed and bloody but unbowed.

The two Jonathans:
Edwards and Yardley

T HEY NAMED me Jonathan, in honor of Jonathan Edwards. As they would with each of their four children, they gave me no middle name. They told us when we were older that they had decided against middle names because both of them hated their own, but this is unconvincing. Helen certainly disliked hers, Marie, which struck her Scots nature as excessively Frenchified, and after her marriage she never used it. But Bill's pride in his Woolsey connections was intense, if not excessive, and he always signed his name either in full or with the middle initial; when he retired, he applied for and was granted the Rhode Island auto tag "WWY."

But that is neither here nor there, for the more immediate question is: *Jonathan Edwards?* How is it that this young couple of no more than passing attachment to theology or religiosity should have chosen to name its firstborn son after a darkly towering figure on the American religious landscape, a man whom one biographer has called "the father of American Puritanism" and whom a prominent historian has described as "one of a long succession of American Jeremiahs, brooding over the grievous faults of their strange Israel"? By what twist of contrivance or association did Bill and Helen elect to inflict upon this innocent babe the burden of attachment to a God-haunted preacher who began the line of succession that in time led, however circuitously, to Billy Sunday and Billy Graham and the television evangelists of the late twentieth century?

The answer borders on the bizarre, but it is the truth. Bill and Helen were bound to each other by more than the ties of love and marriage: each was a great-great-great-great-grandchild of Jonathan Edwards. One of the august divine's daughters married an Ingersoll, thereby establishing the connection on Helen's side of the family. Another married a Dwight, and a daughter of this union married William Walton Woolsey, Bill's namesake.

That Jonathan Edwards should be "family," as we say in this country, is a genealogical fact in which I have never taken inordinate pride. It seems to me a peculiarity best filed away in the category of "Believe It or Not," as well as a useful reminder that in the eighteenth century America was so thinly populated that every white Anglo-Saxon Protestant was kin to just about every other one. I find it interesting that Bill, whose glory in ancestry was immoderate, devoted little time to Edwards in his excursions into the familial past; it was a good name to have on the résumé, he seemed to feel, but scarcely of as much interest to any self-respecting Yardley as the noble procession of Woolseys and Badgers and Dwights.

There can be no question, though, that in the larger world Edwards occupies a formidably imposing place, one that has been examined and explicated by scholars beyond number. Sydney Ahlstrom, in his monumental *A Religious History of the American People*, describes Edwards as "a kind of perpetually misunderstood stranger" in the country's religious life, which seems to me entirely accurate. There are as many interpretations of Edwards as there are interpreters, and precious few of them agree about much of anything. During the Victorian era his harsh Calvinism was held in contempt, a judgment that prevailed well into the twentieth century; in time it was ameliorated by, most prominently, H. Richard Niebuhr and Perry Miller, and now toward the end of the century Edwards has become a growth industry in academia, where the number of doctoral dissertations devoted to him doubles every decade.

It is not my purpose to add further to this mountain of verbiage. I am neither a scholar nor a theologian, and my blood ties to the pious Edwards do not afford me, as best I can see, any particular perspective on his strange career. For what little it is worth, my own assessment of his role in American culture is far closer to that of the Victorians than of his current apologists. Though I share Edwards's doleful view of the human predicament, and respect his standing as a theologian, his overwrought descriptions of hellfire and damnation strike me as cheap rhetorical tricks designed to terrify his congregation into abject capitulation to his morbid theology. Edwards loved his God and his theological exercises, but he did not love his fellow man. A biographer who admired him was to the point when he wrote, "The great wrong which Edwards did, which haunts us as an evil dream throughout his writings, was to assert God at the expense of humanity."

Yet for all of that his presence in the family's history cannot be lightly dismissed, for it is a forcible reminder of the prominent role religion has played in that history. This to be sure is not true of Helen's side of the family. There is no evidence of strong religious sentiment among the Gregorys, and the Ingersolls drifted from denomination to denomination, taking whatever was offered wherever they happened to have settled; my sense is that they were so intimately connected to God's natural world, they had no particular need of God himself.

But on the Yardley side it is another matter altogether. From the devout Quakers who brought the family to America to the equally devout Episcopalians who assumed the pulpit two centuries later, Yardleys have until quite recent memory been people of the church. When Bill Yardley decided, well into his career as an educator, to study for the Episcopal ministry, he did so less for spiritual than for professional reasons, but he was also answering a powerful familial call; in the most literal sense, he was choosing to follow the faith of his fathers.

The first of these was William the Emigrant, the gentleman who came to Pennsylvania in 1682 with his wife and children and whose nephew, Thomas, subsequently gave the family permanent establishment in the New World. This William was born in Stafford-shire in 1632 and trained to be a farmer, but "the operation of the Holy Spirit within him whilst yet a youth, stained the beauty and the glory of earthly things in his view, and he was concerned diligently to seek for a saving knowledge of the Truth as it is in Jesus." He became a "Seeker," and in time found his truth in the words of two "faithful ministers, called in scorn Quakers, out of the north of England."

It was his moment of awakening, for which he paid dearly. "Called and constrained to lift up his voice for the Truth," William boldly attempted to convert "the nominal Christians around him," who responded violently. He was arrested and sent to prison for nineteen weeks, "during seventeen of which he was obliged to sleep and rest on the bare floor, the keeper with cruel malignity not even allowing straw to be brought in for him to lie on." That was in 1655. Five years later he was imprisoned at Shrewsbury, "for his testimony for the Truth in Shropshire," and in 1661 he was placed in the stocks at Derbyshire and then committed to the house of correction. According to *The Friend*, an eighteenth-century Quaker publication in which William's biographical sketch can be found,

> Ralph Sharpley and William Yardley were inhumanly used by the keeper of the prison, who confined them in a close hole, too low to allow them to stand up in, and which they were not permitted on any account to leave. Their books and letters were taken from them and never restored; and when sometimes in their place of strait confinement, their voices were raised in prayer to the Lord, the helper of his people, the keeper would strike them brutally in the face, and endeavor to stop their mouths. During the time of their confinement, their Friends were neither permitted to visit nor relieve them.

So what a relief it must have been for this stout-hearted man to set sail aboard *Friends' Adventure*, two decades later, for Penn's young colony. The land was unknown and his prospects there anything but certain, but there would be no more persecution—or prosecution—for his unpopular religious convictions. As we know, he lived for eleven years in America; before his family was decimated by smallpox he rose to a position of prominence and respect within the Society of Friends. "He dearly loved the society of his brethren," his memorial stated, "and much prized unity as one who knew the comfort and benefit thereof."

A similar tradition, though in a different denomination, took hold elsewhere in the family. The Reverend Benjamin Woolsey, who in 1709 was graduated from the "collegiate school" at New Haven that nine years later became Yale College, entered the ministry and became noted in various parishes on Long Island as a "dissenting Protestant Congregationalist." He preached to Presbyterian congregations but was of an ecumenical turn of mind and mounted whatever pulpit was available, even that of an Episcopal church in Hopewell, New Jersey: he was "willing to preach in any edifice devoted to the worship of God." Such benign tolerance was rare then, even in a new land dedicated to religious freedom: "Living as he did in an age of prejudice and bigotry his life and teachings were such as to make him a conspicuous figure." Like William the Emigrant he was much loved and admired for "his steady attachment to the religious principles he professed, ever attempered with the most amiable character and condescension towards those of a contrary mind."

After the deaths of these two gentlemen religion moves slightly away from the center of family records, but not far and not for long. As we have seen, both Henry Yardley and his son, Tom, were drawn to the ministry by irresistible calls, and both took leave of other endeavors in order to answer them: Henry abandoning the law, Tom architecture. Within the frail bodies of these two men burned bright fires of faith and commitment, and as best I can determine they were ministers in the deepest sense of the word: acolytes before God, and shepherds of his flock.

That their example helped inspire Bill when he chose to study for the ministry is beyond question, but in his case the secular world intrudes in a fashion that most certainly would have given both his father and his grandfather pause. The full story will be told presently, but for now it must be noted that in 1948, when Bill was first approached about the rectorship of Chatham Hall School, he was informed that preference would be given to a candidate who was an Episcopal minister as well as an educator and administrator. At that time Bill was thirty-six years old, well past the age at which most enter the seminary, yet he promptly let it be known that he was prepared to assume the cloth. "The more I think about it," he told Edmund J. Lee, the incumbent rector, "the more I like the idea of reading for orders. There comes a point in the life of a school-man when the discipline and authority of the Church as well as its spiritual guidance and security stand like a rock in a chaotic world. You can go only so far in the training of young people without it."

Those are the words not of a man who had heard his call, but of one who wanted a job so badly that he was ready to change his life in order to obtain it. Within Bill's family there has always been unanimous agreement that, whatever the quality of his ministry once he had attained it, his motives in entering it were considerably less than pure. A church-affiliated school had a headmastership to offer him, and there was little doubt that he was the preferred choice of the person whom the board of trustees had empowered to make that choice; but Chatham Hall had been Dr. Lee's life for nearly two decades, and he was deeply committed to the religious aspects of the education it offered. The best way Bill could overcome Dr. Lee's qualms was to offer himself up for the church. This he did, and the results were as desired.

As it happens he went on to become a minister of impressive dignity and compassion; in part this was merely one of the personae in and out of which he slipped with such ease, but he also came naturally by the therapeutic gifts that made him a trusted counselor, first for students and faculty at Chatham, then for the aged and infirm at several small parishes in Rhode Island. Yet almost always one sensed that he was more attracted to the forms of his ministry— *The Book of Common Prayer* and the King James Bible, the chasubles and altar linens, the stained glass and silver patens—than to the spirituality of it. His was the secular world, not the ecclesiastical one, as a delegation from the Virginia Department of Highways learned one day when it visited the rector to solicit his views on a bypass that, if constructed, would cut through Chatham Hall property; the head of the delegation rolled his eyes upon leaving Bill's office, and said, "That's the cussingest preacher I ever saw."

*   *   *

Nobody knew this better than Bill's wife and children. Helen never criticized any member of the family within the hearing of any other, so her feelings about Bill's ministry died with her, but its effect on his children was pronounced. The positive side of being the offspring of this unholy minister was that one was exposed daily to a liturgy that is, in my biased view, the most majestic man has yet devised. Unlike his father, Bill was determinedly low church, despising incense and bells and elaborate ritual, believing instead that the words themselves were sufficient unto the day; the result was that those words became as much a part of our daily lives as what we ate and drank, and connected us to our familial past more than anything recorded in any of Bill's treasured genealogies.

But for none of the children was this what could be called a religious experience. It was cultural, rooted in our family and even literary, and its effects on all of us were immeasurable, but it drew none of us into the church. I say this with no pride, for I envy my forebears the satisfaction and strength that the church gave them, but it remains that spiritual faith is notable in the lives of Bill's children largely for its absence. Only Jane regularly attends church, and for her a chief attraction is the pleasure she derives from singing in the choir. I alone among the four regularly say grace at the evening meal, which I do in deference not to religion but to tradition. We are children of the age of science and secularity, mindful and respectful of our religious past but unable—so far, at least—to find its appropriate place in our own lives.

For this Bill, as well as the age, must be held accountable. If he taught us the beauties of the liturgy, he also taught us that the cleric's vestments do not always garb a holy man. His characteristic gesture was the wink: he winked at the world and, his children knew, he winked at God. This left us with a suspicion about the church and those who toil for it, a suspicion that it harbored the pretender as well as the pious and that its protestations of holiness should be taken with an ample dose of salt. It is hard enough for any preacher's child to be true to the faith; it was doubly hard for the children of Bill Yardley.

But he made certain that we had full exposure to it. He required us to be in faithful attendance at Sunday school, which in my experience is a potent antidote to religious inclinations. When Jane and I were young he gave each of us two nickels, one for the collection plate and one for Mr. Jones's soda fountain, and sent us walking down the hill from the school to the Episcopal church on Main Street in Chatham. I was ten years old and Jane eight when, as we crossed the little wooden bridge over the creek at the bottom of the hill, we heard a *plink!* and then a *plop!* I looked in my fist and saw only one coin.

"Uh-oh," I said. "There goes the Sunday-school nickel."

I was, by all accounts, an agreeable and pliable baby; my intractable side, which later caused Bill and Helen so much vexation, was not scheduled to appear until early adolescence. I was fed, according to what was then received middle-class wisdom, by bottle, and I slept in a heavy metal crib, painted white, that earlier had been used by all three Yardley brothers; a generation later, both of my own sons slept in it. I developed tolerable nocturnal habits within a reasonable period, acquired no infantile illnesses of note, and received my first haircut on May 1, 1941, the thin blond remainders of which Bill lovingly stored in a small envelope. I had my own nursery in the sunny apartment at Croft House on the Shady Side Academy grounds, and was often visited by students who found it amusing to encounter so tiny a male creature in their boisterous midst.

My arrival brought with it enormous changes in the lives of Bill and Helen Yardley: especially Helen, for whom the duties of motherhood were to linger far longer than for most women of her time and background. As is to be expected of two people who had been reared as they were, they discharged their parental obligations in fundamentally conservative ways. Though Bill made token gestures toward feeding and diaper-removal, these were seen as

Helen's tasks by virtue of maternity and she discharged them without recorded complaint.

Had she been inclined to protest, she surely would have resisted the temptation out of deference to Bill, who was trying to absorb the double impact of new child and new job. By contrast with hermetic, bucolic and intimate Bedford-Rippowam, Shady Side was a school of several hundred boys located in an industrial metropolis that was already beginning to gear up for the huge wartime manufacturing effort that soon would be expected of it. Pittsburgh in those years, for all its rough virtues and honest labor, deserved many of the unkind epithets its critics heaped upon it; it was filthy with soot and grime and noise, and not even Shady Side, with its green campus on a hill above the hurly-burly, could quite escape the choking smoke. Their four years there were important to Helen and Bill for personal and professional reasons, but they fled the city whenever they could and cited "dislike of Pittsburgh environment" as a principal reason for wanting to leave it.

Still, they had little time to sit around and formulate grievances. Helen was busy with her baby, and Shady Side kept Bill hopping every bit as much as had Bedford-Rippowam. His primary obligations were in the classroom, where he taught English to grades seven through twelve and history to seven through nine, but that was only the beginning; he was also director of the student-operated library, faculty advisor to the biweekly *Shady Side News* (to a reporter for which he said, "I consider *Vanity Fair* by William Makepeace Thackeray the greatest novel ever written"), coach of intramural soccer and other sports, and assistant housemaster at Croft House. The apartment was attached to the dormitory, which meant that students were a ceaseless presence in his life; such privacy as a dormitory master and his wife enjoy is hard-earned, squeezed out late at night after the students are in bed and the campus has gone silent. Small wonder that Bill and Helen looked with great anticipation to their summers at Cooperstown and, when war broke out, saved their gasoline ration stamps so as to have enough fuel for the four-hundred-mile journey.

After 1942 they were able to spend the full summer there, for Bill's Cambridge years finally were over. That year Harvard awarded him the Master's in education, in an experimental program that had been established in the early thirties to prepare graduate students for the administration of private secondary schools; by the end of the forties Bill and all his classmates had risen to headmasterships, but it irritated these young men that shortly after they completed the demanding Harvard curriculum the requirements for the degree were reduced by half.

To have this diploma was not perhaps so grand a distinction for Bill as one from Yale would have been, but he prized it and ever after referred to himself as "a graduate of Harvard and Johns Hopkins," from time to time neglecting to mention the latter.

Bill went to Cambridge and Cooperstown during these years, but he did not go to war. He was a father and an educator, a combination that persuaded the Selective Service System, which had been established in 1940, that his wartime years would be most productively spent on the homefront. There is no evidence that he resisted this classification, and there is in the Tuxedo years a fair amount of evidence that he openly encouraged it. When Jane and I grew old enough to understand this we were quietly embarrassed by it, especially as Bill's wartime service contrasted unfavorably with those of his contemporaries within the family: Harry, though he was thirty-five by the time of Pearl Harbor and had a child (my cousin Louise, called Lolly, born six months after me), tried repeatedly to enlist, only to be rejected apparently because of questionable political associations during the Depression. Paul enlisted in the Navy at the earliest moment, rose to the rank of lieutenant, and served with great distinction as a member of the intelligence team that broke the Japanese code; he was personally responsible for monitoring the movements of the Japanese destroyer fleet. Art and Al, Helen's brothers, both were trained as pilots, Art in the Air Corps and Al in the Navy, and both saw duty overseas.

Everyone in the family is proud of the wartime records these three young men compiled, but there no longer seems to me any point in condemning Bill for staying home. The government had decided as a matter of national policy that schoolteachers were in their own way important to the defense effort, as were policemen and doctors and others in occupations necessary to the maintenance of the civilian fabric, and it declared thousands of them exempt from service; most found, as Bill later did, other ways to contribute to the national defense. I do think it likely, though I cannot recall his ever raising the subject, that Bill probably missed something of real value in the male camaraderie and shared sense of danger that wartime service provided. He had too little of this in his life, but who am I to lecture him? Neither I nor my brother served in the military, for which we do not apologize but which leaves us, as I suspect it left Bill, with a sense that something is missing.

It may, perhaps, have been as compensation for this deficiency that Bill made a point of instructing his children in what he saw as the family's honorable record of service. He was interested in the Harts, who "seem to have been enterprising and warlike." The Badgers, we were told, were "fighting Quakers," and seven Badger brothers fought in the Revolution. One of the original Thomas Yardley's sons is believed to have rented—*rented*, let it be noted, not donated—to George Washington one or more of the Durham boats he used to cross the Delaware on December 11, 1776, not far from Yardley's Ferry. But after the Revolution the family is scarcely to be found in the chronicles of war; a cousin, Theodore Winthrop, was the first Union officer killed in the Civil War, at Fort Sumter, but the family must stretch a point—as Bill was rarely loath to do—in order to claim a share in his heroics.

On Helen's side the record is more or less the same. We have already encountered the doughty Deacon David Ingersoll, who flitted in and out of combat in the Berkshires, but there is no evidence that the Ingersolls further served the Revolution. Their principal military action was seen in Canada during the rebellions against the queen in the 1830s. Helen's grandmother, Nancy Agnes Wright, was a small girl near Toronto when British troops came searching for her father, Joshua, who had been active among the rebels. While he hid in a haystack, Nancy's mother refused to answer the soldiers' questions. They repeatedly poked their bayonets into the hay but somehow missed Joshua. In their frustration

they slashed his wife's arms and then vanished; when she told this
story to her granddaughter Helen Ingersoll, she always concluded
by rolling up her sleeves and proudly displaying her scars.

But that, so far as the family's military history is concerned, is
that. The Hales may have been warlike, but the Yardleys and
Gregorys are not. They have willingly done what their country has
asked of them, but only rarely have they gone the extra mile. In
this I suspect that they have more in common with most Americans than most Americans would care to admit.

War in any event did not come until Bill and Helen had been at
Shady Side for almost a year and a half, and it was some time
thereafter before its full effects began to be felt. In the months
before Pearl Harbor they, like countless other Americans of the
middle class, were preoccupied by the knowledge that war quite
surely was in the offing and by the determination to outfit themselves before the time of shortages began. The sudden burst of
prewar defense spending had, after a decade of Depression,
brought the country close enough to prosperity to permit people to
make substantial purchases, and its manufacturers were rolling out
exciting new products that offered conveniences guaranteed to ease
the path through domestic life.

Helen and Bill joined the march into the new age. In May of
1941 they went to Sears, Roebuck and purchased, for $40, a
vacuum cleaner. In December, surely made aware by Pearl Harbor
that if they did not act at once there would be nothing left on which
to act, they made two substantial purchases. They obtained a new
Apex washing machine for $63. Then they went to the Danforth
Company, which offered a discount to the school, and traded in the
little old Frigidaire that Harry and Elsie had passed on to them;
they replaced it with a "new 6-foot Westinghouse electric refrigerator," for which they paid $87.50.

These were, for a young couple with a two-year-old son and a
second child soon to be born, substantial acquisitions; they were
made, moreover, only a year after Bill and Helen had bought the
new 1940 Ford—they had a prejudice against used cars—that

would take them through the war and well beyond. These purchases were made with cash; as children of the Depression and of self-sufficient parents, Bill and Helen shared a prejudice against credit even stronger than that against "pre-owned" automobiles, though it is a bias they were unsuccessful in passing along to their children. Since they declined to borrow, presumably they used up what remained of the Colgate fund in making these acquisitions, as well as part of a $500 gift that Alfred Gregory bestowed upon his daughter in October of 1941.

It is the last such benefaction of which I can find a record. Not long after sending that check Alfred resigned from Hawkins, Delafield & Longfellow. He was by now in his early sixties, and he remembered the beginning of his own career when he had felt held back by "older men cornering the market." He was determined not to follow their example. "It's totally unfair that the old men are in charge," he said. "They keep the younger men from developing." So he stepped down from his prominent partnership and retired to his living room, where he read murder mysteries, listened to the

Alfred and Helen Gregory, in their maturity

war news on the radio, and smoked an endless succession of Fatima cigarettes. He had some $150,000 in stocks and bonds and, for a time, an annual pension of about $5,000 from the railroad in Pennsylvania that he had helped through the Depression.

On this he and Helen were able to live comfortable if monotonous lives, nibbling gradually into capital but leaving enough untouched to preserve a small inheritance for each of their children. What is puzzling about their retirement is that Alfred, who had been so vigorous as a younger man, made virtually nothing of it. He was content to sit in his chair, whether in Maplewood or Brewster, and idle the hours away; after the war a neighbor said, "Mr. Gregory looks as though he's just waiting to die." But he and Helen were always delighted to see their daughter and her children, who loved both of their grandparents and the morning routine they followed. Alfred made breakfast each day and called his wife—"One more minute!"—as the eggs neared readiness. After the meal he removed his false teeth, washed them in a glass, and put them back in. Then he ignited a wooden match by flicking it against the bottom of his shoe, lit up a Fatima, and contentedly blew smoke rings.

Which is why, when I was three or four, I said, "I want to be just like Grandpa Gregory."

"Why's that?" Helen asked.

"So I can take my teeth out and pull fire out of my shoes."

It is of Gregorys and Shady Side that my first memory is made. I am sitting in my high chair, with Helen and Grandma Gregory somewhere in the room, talking cheerfully to me. Outside it is bright and boys are playing on the grass. I remember red brick and sunshine and happiness, and nothing else.

That is because we left Pittsburgh long before it had a chance to make any strong imprint on my mind; when, at the age of nineteen, I spent some time with a girlfriend who lived there, I might as well have been in a foreign country. Bill and Helen left because, though Bill was reasonably happy in his job, his income scarcely increased at all—in four years he inched up from $2,000 a year to

$2,100—and he became convinced that there was no future for him there. Helen, too, was restless, though for different reasons, as she wrote in her annual letter to Bennington. She had been swapping notes with other graduates of women's colleges:

> In talking over our college experiences we have wondered whether college gives women a tendency to dissatisfaction with housekeeping, family life and its routine, etc. You have so much excitement and fun for several years that the adjustment to being a plain housewife is hard. Much of the difficulty in my present adjustment is due to the fact that a boys' school seems to offer no life for the faculty wives. There is no easy way for us to contribute to the school as a whole. Everyone knows this (at this school) but no one does anything. Also life in a boarding school is different from community life. So much is done for us in the way of housekeeping and meals that we are placed in a leisure class far beyond our incomes. Perhaps it is not a very serious matter but I feel that I am not a useful or contributing member of my community and that is something which I hoped Bennington would help me be.

So they decided to look for another community and another school. Bill was on file not merely at the American and Foreign Teachers' Agency, but also at Clark-Brewer and Associated Teachers', all of which were busily distributing his résumé. On it he was able to add a line that could only help his cause. Since 1941 he had traveled to Princeton for a couple of weeks each summer to serve as "reader in English" of essays written for the College Entrance Examination Board. He was paid for this at a rate of $1.50 an hour, which the family exchequer welcomed, but more to the point he spent this brief period in the company of his fellow readers, people who were known and respected in secondary education and in higher education as well. These acquaintanceships were, in the usual manner of such things, both cordial and useful; they moved Bill a step or two closer to the inner circle of the tiny world in which he had chosen to live his life, and they gave him reputable references should such be needed.

By late 1942 he was fully committed to the decision to move. Letters flew this way and that, but desirable opportunities were hard to come by. A letter to Andover elicited a discouraging response from its headmaster: "The trouble with your situation lies in the fact that you are married, with two small children. Here at Andover we have some teaching vacancies, but no living quarters for married men. A bachelor, ineligible for military service, is at this time worth almost his weight in gold." So he turned then to St. Paul's, where his friend Bill Oates offered no immediate prospects but sound advice: "1. investigate as widely and as vigorously as possible *everything*. 2. do not take hope that anything possible will materialize from generalities. 3. Never lose hope that something will come, unexpectedly."

Bill followed that counsel faithfully. From time to time a nibble came his way, but the few that actually turned into firm offers he rejected as inadequate for one reason or another. Then, through Nellie R. Talbot at the American and Foreign Teachers' Agency, he learned of an opening at a small country day school in Tuxedo Park, New York. It was interviewing numerous candidates for the headmastership that Anthony V. Barber was leaving. "I do hope that the trustees will engage you," Nellie Talbot told Bill. "As I have written you, and still believe, I have no one who is better qualified to step into Mr. Barber's shoes." But, as she added, "It always takes some time for trustees to make up their minds," and those of the Tuxedo Park School were no exception. They wanted to learn more about the training Bill had received at Harvard, and there were other candidates whose merits had to be weighed. But in truth they did not dally long. They notified Bill by telephone on March 7 that the position was his, and soon a letter followed:

> In accordance with a resolution of the Board of Trustees of the Tuxedo Park Country Day School held March 7th, 1943, we wish to confirm that the Board has offered you and you have accepted the position as Headmaster of the Tuxedo Park Country Day School for the coming years at a Salary of $4,000.00 payable in ten equal monthly installments beginning September 1, 1943 and ending June 1, 1944.
>
> We wish to confirm further that by resolution of the Board you will be given full authority with respect to tuition rates to be charged and the curriculum of the School during your first year.

It was, at that stage of his career, all that Bill could have hoped for, and he accepted the job with delight: "Everything about the school seems completely as it should be," he told the trustees. He sent the good news to Nellie Talbot, together with one-half of her $200 placement fee (he paid the balance in November), and in turn received her enthusiastic congratulations. "My only regret is that the other candidates are disappointed," she wrote. "You may be amused to know that each time I sent the credentials of other candidates (out of fairness I cannot limit myself to only one or two) I would write Mr. Barber that 'Mr. Yardley is still my first choice.'"

So in June of 1943, off Bill and Helen went, with the regrets and good wishes of their friends at Shady Side. The movers came for the mahogany dining table and the books—the number of which had steadily grown—and Lizzie Gilman's antique table and that amazing new Westinghouse electric refrigerator. Now the Yardleys' real life as adults was about to begin, so they filled the Ford with a precious tank of gas and pointed it to the east.

There I was in the back seat, an excited little boy only a few months short of his fourth birthday, just tall enough to peer out at the blur of passing scenery and to be induced by that blur, as for a decade again and again I would be, to carsickness. Beside me, too young to view the passing scene with any sense of what she was leaving or where she was going, slept the new kid in town: my sister, who had been born on January 25, 1942, and was now nearly a year and a half in age.

THEY NAMED her Jane, in honor of Jane Andrews Woolsey. This singular woman, who was born in 1804 and lived a full eighty years, was the granddaughter of a gentleman who plays no role in this story but cannot be allowed to pass without mention. His name was Aaron Andrews; he was a physician in Wallingford, Connecticut, where he became a local legend for his absentmindedness and his Scots crustiness. One day he was descending the cellar stairs to fetch a drink of cider, his wife Sarah's finest china pitcher in his hand, when suddenly he slipped and fell. Sarah ran to the top of the stairs and called, "Oh, Doctor, have you broken the pitcher?"

"No," he called back, "but I will now!"—and smashed it against the wall.

Many years later, in his seventieth year and suffering his last illness, the good doctor was visited by a fellow physician of earnest intentions and infuriatingly circumlocutory manner. The attending doctor huffed and puffed and hemmed and hawed before at last saying, "I think, perhaps, Doctor, that I ought to make you aware, that your time upon earth, is likely to be short."

"Well!" snorted Aaron Andrews, who knew perfectly well what awaited him. "I know it, but a man can't die all in a minute!" With

The two Janes:
Woolsey and Yardley

that he pulled the sheet over his head, turned his face to the wall, and prepared to die in his own good time.

He was succeeded as head of the family by his son John, Jane's father, himself also both a physician and a man of vigorous opinion. As a young man he left Wallingford for Guilford, where an opportunity for practice had presented itself, but he did not remain there long because he learned that back in his hometown another suitor was "paying attention to Miss Mabby Atwater." John hastened back to Wallingford, elbowed aside the gentleman who had been so presumptuous as to court the seventeen-year-old Abigail, and married her forthwith. They lived thereafter in Wallingford, where Dr. Andrews divided his time between his practice and the local Episcopal church, his passion for which bordered on the obsessive.

Jane and her brother, Sherlock, were reared in a pious but lively household; everything we know about her indicates that she had a tart, irreverent sense of humor and a deep well of quiet self-assurance. This was tested when as a young woman she became betrothed to a Dr. Holmes, whose attentions proved unworthy and deceitful. However much it may have hurt her to break off this engagement, it did not prevent her from leading an active social life. This included a trip with her mother in the fall of 1831 to Cleveland, where Sherlock was in business. In the course of their excursions through Cleveland society her brother introduced her to John Mumford Woolsey, a bachelor eight years her senior who was managing his family's extensive land investment in that young city; to say that the two liked each other is an understatement.

Jane's charms must have been irresistible, at least to John Woolsey. Evidently she professed herself unworthy of him, for in the ardent letter he addressed to her immediately upon her departure he was at pains to say, "I have seen too many ladies who would force our admiration by their accomplishments—too many who had learn'd to think that they were made for display and that more unobtrusive charms were valueless. I value more that plain, useful common-sense which you possess—the affectionate heart—the domestic habits—the straight-going integrity—the ready usefulness and unfading cheerfulness which characterize you, more than all the embellishments that art or education can give." Her flirtatious reply arrived several days later:

> I passed Sunday very quietly in my own room, having a severe cold, and on Monday morning I was cheered with the arrival of a little messenger from Cleveland who said so many kind and flattering things to me that I was in the highest enjoyment of self-complacency some hours afterward, and if ever poetically inspired I should from pure gratitude for such a comfortable state of mind have penned Ode to Vanity. Serious—the fear that your imagination might have invested me with qualities I did not possess, induced me to make some of the remarks to which you refer, but now having had leisure to take a comprehensive view of the subject I give you permission, nay, even *command* you henceforth to be as *blind* as you *can*.

Thus this nineteenth-century courtship began, conducted largely through the mails, which were not then notably more reliable than they are now: "I never was more decidedly anti-Jacksonite," John wrote on November 19, "than after reflecting that under the management of his officers your letter was two whole weeks reaching me." But even by mail, the courtship moved swiftly. Barely ten days later John sent to Dr. Andrews "a request which you may perhaps think unreasonable and improper," this being "for your permission to address your daughter Miss Jane Andrews," who "has created in my heart a strong affection and esteem for her and a confidence that I may safely commit to her keeping (if she will accept the task) my future happiness." John then introduced himself and offered several references, among them "Professor Silliman, and Mrs. Sereno, and Timothy Dwight of New Haven," but that was quite unnecessary; Dr. Andrews replied forthwith, "I have no doubt, sir, that your character is good, and that the honor you intend my family is what any Parent might well be satisfied with."

In the spring of 1832 they were married, Jane being twenty-eight and John thirty-six. They made the rocky journey westward from Connecticut—it took a week, exposing them to the dangers and discomforts of stagecoach roads and shaky bridges—and established themselves in Cleveland, eventually constructing the pleasant house on Euclid Street where all of their children were born: Sarah Chauncey, Jane Andrews, Elizabeth Dwight, Theodora Walton and William Walton. Many happy households have been mentioned in this chronicle, but none, surely, was happier than this one. Jane and John Woolsey were loving, confident parents who created an atmosphere in which flourished childhoods so idyllic that years later an immensely popular series of children's books was inspired by them. "Freedom, play and out-of-doors made our happiness," their daughter Jane recalled. "We were never 'dressed up' as children call it, to walk in the street. . . . Nobody took much notice of us, excepting to see that we were obedient and not quarrelsome, and had dry feet. We had bread and milk for tea and went to bed *very* early. Nobody theorized about us, or studied our dispositions closely, or talked of the sacredness of the body! If we were naughty we had a quick slap from mother or nurse, and that was the end of it; if we were pert and talked too much, we were told to hold our tongues, children should be seen and not heard."

When the children were in adolescence their parents decided to move back to Connecticut, where they acquired a large brick house on Wooster Street in New Haven. John became a respected member of the local intelligentsia—his brother, Theodore Dwight Woolsey of Yale, was fond of saying, "John is so full of information that if you prick him it runs out!"—and the girls were so enthusiastically courted that "if there were not at least six hats on the hat rack every evening we were getting to be old maids!" But New Haven proved to be less happy for the family than had been hoped. John's investments took a turn for the worse, as did his health, and in 1870 he died, at the age of seventy-four.

With John's death Jane promptly quit New Haven—given her devotion to her husband, the likelihood is that she could not bear to remain in the city where he had suffered and died—and removed herself to Newport with her daughters Susan (Sadie), Elizabeth (Lily) and Theodora (Dora), who had not yet married and remained with her. At first they occupied quarters on Washington

Street, near the waterfront, but before the year was out they had bought the property at 93 Rhode Island Avenue—on higher ground, and therefore less damp—that for so long would be Woolsey, and then Yardley, headquarters. It was here that the women of the family gathered, in an extraordinary gynecocracy.

As mother of them all Jane Andrews Woolsey presided over "The Jungle" from 1870 until her death fourteen years later. She was by then a woman of looks that can most charitably be described as forbidding, but she was loved and deferred to. Her decorative tastes ran to clutter: fine pieces from the turn of the nineteenth century or earlier wildly mixed in with the most appalling Victorian atrocities; a pair of small Fra Angelicos intermingled with family landscapes of dubious artistic merit; statuettes (mostly hideous) and silverware (much of it exquisite) and gimcracks (largely defying description). But home, be it ever so strange, is home: after Lily's marriage to Daniel Coit Gilman in 1877, Jane and Sadie and Dora remained in this roomy, eccentric building for the rest of their lives.

Dora is a shadowy figure, recalled mainly as "a little old lady with a sense of fun and pleasure in very young people," but Sadie is more formidable even than her mother. She was, as before long will be seen, by profession a writer, but she was also the dominant figure in an animated household. In the Civil War she served as a nurse; the war, Lily recalled, "aroused in Sadie a passion of enthusiasm and devotion, and she threw herself with all her heart and soul into work for the soldiers at home and afield." She was a prodigious traveler, sometimes with Dora as companion, who visited Alaska before the Gold Rush and all the great countries of Europe; she did sketches, in pencil or pen-and-ink, of the notable landscapes she saw. She also, among her many activities, found time to manage 93 Rhode Island down to the most mundane domestic detail, including supervision of the several cooks, maids and yardmen who were employed there. One of the latter was a "highly prized" fellow named John, who handled all the heavy-duty chores and who lived precisely as he wished, with a woman not his wife. This outraged a pious visitor, who complained directly to Sadie: she "gave a whoop and said she did not employ him for his moral character, but for his faithfulness!"

Two houses away, at Number 89, lived yet another grande dame of the clan, this being cousin Eliza Woolsey Howland, the widow of Colonel Joseph Howland of the New York Seventh Regiment; she had met him while serving as a nurse with the Sanitary Corps in the Civil War. She was "round and pink and dimpled and purple plush with an obnoxious and asthmatic Pekinese with a penetrating, falsetto yap." She rode about in a carriage with purple upholstery drawn by a large black horse, and beside her fireplace hung a leather cat-o'-nine-tails. God knows why.

Then, upon Henry Yardley's death in 1882, the ladies of Numbers 89 and 93 were joined by those of Number 91. We are by now well acquainted with the head of that household, Jane Woolsey Yardley, and with her son, Tom, as well, but there were also his sisters, Isabel, Elizabeth (Lily) and Laura (Lolly). The first of these was a woman of regal bearing who in time took as her husband Frank Marble, a commander in the United States Navy whom she regarded as the greatest sailor since Lord Nelson. She was at once his servant—if he left his shoes outside his bedroom at night, she surreptitiously shined them "for the honor of the house"—and his apologist. For a time they lived in Tokyo, where Frank served as naval attaché to the American embassy, but more often they lived at the Newport War College. It was there that he blew his brains out. Isabel noisily contended that he had been murdered by an intruder; the Navy said that, no, it was suicide pure and simple, but settled a pension on her—which she promptly, if crazily, refused "on principle." Later this peculiar woman ran the Belgian hospital in London during the First World War—she was the only immediate family member to participate in that conflict—and after the armistice was decorated by the Belgian government.

The other of the Yardley sisters to marry was Lolly, whose husband, Graham Sumner, was an immensely successful New York lawyer. After their marriage they bought a hundred-acre estate on Round Hill Road in Greenwich, Connecticut, from which Grae, as he was known, commuted daily to the city. Apart from an office there he also had a mistress, whose existence Lolly discovered in the classic manner: she picked up the phone at the wrong time. Grae gave up his paramour and settled into an uneasy existence with Lolly, who eventually died of cancer; before that she had the unhappy luck to witness the death of her adult son, Graham Jr., who choked one Christmas on his roast beef. She was a charming, effervescent, temperamental woman who was deeply attached to the Yardleys and, thanks to her husband's prosperity, was able to give Tom's widow financial assistance at a time when it was sorely needed, in the hard months following Tom's death.

Then there is Lily. She stayed her entire adult life at "Brown Beeches," nursing her invalid mother and Aunt Dora Woolsey as well: she was a quiet, kind soul, one of those people—women, mostly—who give up their lives to the service of others. She drove about in a 1917 or 1918 Model T, in which she taught Harry to drive, and managed a tidy social life for herself on a decidedly limited income. The family money had run out by now, such of it as there had been, so she supported herself by moving to Florida in the winter and renting out the house to Navy people. She was devoted to her three Yardley nephews, who thought of the house at 91 Rhode Island as their own. No doubt it was after one of her winters in Florida that Bill, breakfasting alone, was served a pink grapefruit; never having seen or heard of such an oddity, he assumed that the cook had bled on it and rushed outside to hide the hideous thing under a tree.

These were the ladies of Rhode Island Avenue. There is also one other who never made it there, but for whom I have developed a great affection: Ella Yardley, the second daughter born to Jane and Henry Yardley. On August 18, 1879, this girl sat down at her desk. "I am going to keep a journal," she wrote. "I shall be sixteen in a month, and I think it is high time I began to do something." She was on Nantucket then, with "the Yardley family in full force." Her diary contains nothing of consequence, and before long she tired of writing it, but even the briefest of samples presents us with a lively, sympathetic, irreverent and wholly appealing girl:

> August 20th. Morning. Perhaps we are going to Sacacha Pond today to go fishing; that is if Papa feels well enough. Tom is just backing out and saying he won't go. I should like to have the management of him for a few months. I think he is altogether too

Elly Yardley

much "Lord of Creation." Evening. Went to Sacacha Pond and caught sixty three perch and three eels. Had a lovely time. Played whist in the evening. Mr. B my partner. Papa beat both games. Always had the luck on his side. Am too sleepy to write more tonight.

"In 1880," her mother wrote many years later, "our dear and beautiful Elly—the oldest living child, aged seventeen—went to Saint Agnes School in Albany, and after six weeks of happy school life was taken with typhoid fever and I went to nurse her—only to bring her back in her white coffin after one week's illness." It was a loss Jane Woolsey Yardley never quite got over. "I wish you could remember her better," she told her surviving children, "for she was most lovely in her face and with a great musical gift—far beyond most girls. She was a great companion to her father, whose intellectual training had been the greatest boon to her and a close tie between them."

OF THE four Yardleys who pulled into Tuxedo Park one June day in 1943, it was Jane who came to love the place most and to retain the fondest memories of it: walking down the hundred steps from the school to our house at day's end, her hand in Bill's, feeling so privileged that he was head of the very school she attended; learning to skate, on the pond called Little Wee-Wah, by pushing big wooden chairs with steel runners; having hot chocolate with Helen in the warming hut, where a bonfire had been built right out on the ice. She grew into a cheerful, pretty, self-effacing girl of whom Bill used to say, "It doesn't take much to make Jane happy," and who eventually became categorized in family mythology as the child who might not be all that smart but who worked hard and thus did well.

It was, like all such mythologies, off the mark, just as were the ones that grew up around me in my grammar-school days: that I was, as Aunt Loulie once put it, "eager of mind and nature." Because Jane was perky and sociable and blonde, attention was diverted from her intelligence, which was considerable, and from her capacity to see life's dark side as well as its bright. This mythology further ignored her eccentricities, which over the years have taken various forms, perhaps most notable among them a blithe independence that quite belies her parents' conviction that she was fated for a life of contented conformity. They should have seen the early warning signs in Tuxedo, where she liked to retreat into the heart of the dining-room table—the pedestal expanded when leaves were added—and sit there for hours with a box of dog biscuits, happily munching away.

Tuxedo Park was a private town of several hundred people that had been founded in 1885 by Pierre Lorillard, whose fortune came from tobacco. New York City had entirely too many people then, too many of whom insisted on rubbing their soiled shoulders against Lorillard's, so in time he came upon the idea of establishing a town to which admission could be gained only by those possessing sufficient wealth and—this being desirable but not mandatory—social standing. For the site of this exquisitely undemocratic settlement he chose a location of such natural beauty as to border on the majestic: a thousand acres in the Ramapo Mountains, thirty-two miles west-northwest of Manhattan, with a long, narrow lake as focal point and two smaller bodies of water immediately above it. The hills were thickly wooded with evergreens and deciduous trees that annually satisfied every cliché of autumnal splendor; the water in the lakes was of a blue so deep and rich that the sky, even on the sunniest day, offered only pale competition.

For the convenience of his prospective neighbors Lorillard located both the Main Gate and the North Gate across the road from the Erie Railroad, which constructed Tuxedo Station to serve these privileged commuters. Inside the Main Gate, hard to the right, he erected St. Mary's Church: Episcopalian, of course. Like the Main Gate and many of the mansions that were rising in the hills overlooking the lake, the church was made of stone and wood; it had the same permanent, prosperous, plutocratic look with which the previous generation of Yardleys had been acquainted at St. Paul's in Stockbridge. Finally, because the residents of Tuxedo Park would require a place to meet in collective splendor, Lorillard built for them the Tuxedo Club, on the northern shore of Tuxedo Lake, and adjacent to it he erected the Tennis Club; the unwritten but strenuously enforced rule was that before a person purchased a house or a lot in the park, he obtained admission to the club, thereby certifying his acceptability.

One cannot have a private town without servants and tradesmen, so outside the gates the Village of Tuxedo was established. It had a row of shops, an assortment of modest houses and cottages, and the Church of Our Lady of Mount Carmel. This last was provided to meet the spiritual needs of the Italian stonecutters, East European laborers and Irish domestics who had been imported to construct the private town and attend its tables. In the settlement's early years the residents of the village were docile and respectful, but gradually it dawned on them that they, too, were now Americans and they began to look to the hills not with awe but with loathing.

By the time the Yardleys reached Tuxedo, relations between the private and public towns had severely deteriorated; a Tuxedo Park child whose parents were foolish and/or impecunious enough to send him to public school in the village could be confident that each day would deliver its appointed thrashing. This is not to say that the proletariat had achieved its millennium but that the bloom was off Lorillard's rose. Even behind the walls of Tuxedo Park, the Depression had taken its toll. Fortunes made of paper were fortunes no more, and houses in the Ramapo hills suddenly had gone vacant; others had mysteriously gone up in smoke, much to the distress of the insurance companies, and their ruined hulks now stood above the lakes as instructive testimony to human vanity.

No, Tuxedo Park had not been impoverished, but it had been taken down a peg or two. Real estate that now sells for many millions could be had for $10,000 or less, if you could come up with $10,000. The Autumn Ball was still held, if with a shade less magnificence, but the Dog Show was a thing of the past. Some of the older residents had managed to hang on to their money, but the younger ones were regular working stiffs who went into the city each day, bringing home paychecks from the brokerages and the banks and the advertising agencies. Years later Bill said Tuxedo had been a sobering experience for him "because I couldn't afford to return the hospitality I had been given," but he must have been

Bill and Helen, circa 1943

referring to the old folks on the hill; the men and women of his own generation, though certainly they were more prosperous than he and Helen, received them as equals and became their lifelong friends.

No residence was then provided for the headmaster of the Tuxedo Park Country Day School, but he was automatically and at no cost—save his own bar and dining room charges—made a member of the Tuxedo Club, and each year he received a similar notice from the club's secretary: "I have the honour to inform you that at a meeting of the Governing Committee held on Thursday evening, June 24, 1943, you were extended the privileges of the Club, without charge, for the fiscal year ending April 30, 1944." Yet for Bill and Helen, even this became a burden, once their son and daughter figured out that all it took to get a "free" Coca-Cola was a childish signature on a piece of paper.

Financial struggle was a daily reality for Bill and Helen in Tuxedo, but it always had been and evermore would be; Helen's comment at Shady Side about being "placed in a leisure class far beyond our incomes" was a fact of life with which they never ceased to contend, but to which eventually they became so accustomed that they no longer gave it much thought. They had chosen to work and live among people who as a matter of course sent their children to private schools; they knew that in going to Tuxedo Park

133

they were in a community whose name rang all the right bells in such people's minds. "Tuxedo was a distinguished place for me to have been," Bill used to say: "the proper kind of place."

It was also, at that point in his career, the proper place for him professionally, because the Tuxedo Park Country Day School gave him ample opportunity to show what he was made of. Like the park in which it was situated, the school had seen better days. Founded in 1900 by residents "who wished to provide their children with the best possible elementary education," it had existed for four decades as an unaccredited institution; not until 1942 did the school obtain a charter from the New York Board of Regents and membership in the Secondary Education Board—and by then, in the view of some trustees and parents, these steps toward institutional legitimacy may have come too late.

The school of which Bill became headmaster in June of 1943 had in its kindergarten and nine grades only a few dozen students, none of them boarders, and five teachers; faculty turnover, sometimes as much as one hundred percent, was an annual headache because the school had insufficient funds to pay competitive salaries. It was in an old, run-down stucco building across the street from the house Bill and Helen had rented. Classrooms were in disrepair; students quite literally were endangered by plaster falling from the crumbling ceilings. Even for a school so small as this there was not enough space, and there was no room in which to expand; growth, Bill and his board well knew, was absolutely necessary if the school was to survive. So Bill took a look at what he had been given and said: "This is it. I'm not going to put up with this any longer." The school needed a new building; Bill made it his first and largest task, the central mission of his headmastership, to obtain one.

Of Bill's six years in the Tuxedo headmastership, the first three were consumed by the search for a new building; bricks, as much as brains, are the stuff of a schoolmaster's life. Bill had to persuade the trustees that the old building was inadequate; he had to locate either an existing structure or an undeveloped site that would be suitable for the school's needs; he had to obtain the building and/or land, either by gift or purchase, and if the latter he had to find enough contributors to make the purchase possible; he had to persuade the school community, alumni and parents primarily, to make a long-term commitment of support for it; and he had to preside over the remodeling of an older building or the construction of a new one.

It is remarkable, inasmuch as the country was at war and the economic state of Tuxedo Park had declined, that Bill succeeded. It took two years, but on September 21, 1945, the Finance Committee of the Tuxedo Park Country Day School's Board of Trustees announced that "due to the generosity of certain friends" the estate of the late Mr. and Mrs. Henry Tilford on Tower Hill had been donated for conversion into a new schoolhouse and grounds, and that they hoped to enlarge it "to a day and boarding school of upwards of 100 pupils." They reported that before the decision to move had been made, "sufficient funds were on hand to cover estimated deficits for the first three years of operation, after which time the school should be entirely self-supporting." They asked for contributions of $25,000 to cover "the additional cost of making necessary repairs and equipping and adapting the Tilford property for use as a school."

The trustees' letter to parents and alumni was accompanied by one from Bill in which he outlined the educational advantages to be gained from moving into new quarters. The letter provided a precise description of the school's present condition and future hopes:

> There are today many children in the school whose parents and even grandparents attended the same school. This is in itself a good thing, making for continuity and tradition; but the point is that it is the same building without a single major improvement. We have an inadequate kitchen, an inefficient heating plant, virtually no library, less than an acre of hillside playground, and no means whatever of developing our educational program through the use of modern stage equipment, workshops, radio, or moving pictures. Our teachers live under substandard conditions and our children are taught in classrooms only one of which will hold more than ten desks and chairs.
>
> Further, through the small size of the school, our children miss a great deal. They miss that kind of experience which comes only

with being a part of a large group—varied friendships, competition, fuller classes, team games. When the boarding department of our school becomes established, the Tuxedo children will be the gainers rather than the losers. We can provide a larger faculty, for another thing; classes will not have to be doubled-up and teachers can be real specialists in one field or age-level. Classes of sufficient size can be maintained to make it desirable and practicable to keep Tuxedo children at home through the eighth or ninth grade instead of having them go away to senior boarding school for five or six years.

Here for the first time we have Bill, at the age of thirty-four, speaking in his headmasterly voice, one that over the next quarter-century he refined and perfected as few before or since have done. His tone was candid, avuncular, practical, slightly inspirational; he spoke of community and tradition as qualities as much to be valued in a school as in life; he revealed, without flaunting it, an intimately detailed knowledge of the minutiae out of which a school is fashioned; he addressed himself to the pride parents take in their children and the upbringing they want to give them. When Bill spoke of these matters, it was without artifice or sham; he shaped his language to the ears of his audience, of course, but the convictions he expressed about schools and their educational mission were passionately held, in the heart of his heart. Whatever else he may have been, he was a schoolman.

He was also husband and father, and at this period of his life he was in top form as both. The cynicism that crept upon him in early middle age was only dimly visible now; he was in love with his wife, he delighted in his children, he was surrounded by friends whom he liked and respected and who returned the compliment. In photographs from that time his hair is beginning to recede, but he is still trim and youthfully handsome; his smile is confident and kind; his demeanor is that of a young man who is going somewhere, a fellow who in due time will make a name for himself.

I was old enough by now to be a student in his school, first in kindergarten and then in the elementary grades; through the

Greetings from Tuxedo Park: silhouettes by Bill Yardley

fourth grade he was my headmaster as well as my father. Given that he and I had our full share of hard times in years to come, I find it remarkable that from this period I harbor not a single unpleasant memory of him; not even being spanked or having my mouth washed out with soap—punishments for which Bill had a sadistic enthusiasm—clouds my recollections of a time that was just what childhood should be. Instead I remember the four of us driving north on Route 17 for day trips to the huge stone inn at Bear Mountain or the stirring campus at West Point; having stories read to me at night and receiving instruction in the rudiments of model making; standing by in worshipful admiration as Bill mended a faucet or sawed out a jigsaw puzzle; being taught to catch and throw in the spacious back yard of the house on Stable Road.

This house, which Bill and Helen rented for $100 a month from an elderly woman named Lucia H. Hull in the spring of 1943, was a two-and-a-half-story wooden building with white clapboard siding. It was situated in Tuxedo Park's least moneyed and pretentious quarters, an area of smaller houses originally inhabited by people building and servicing the large estates. It had an odd little front hall that ran parallel rather than perpendicular to the front wall of the house; the living room was behind it to the right, and the pantry, kitchen and dining room to the left. Both upstairs floors were finished, with five bedrooms and as many bathrooms, all with spacious ball-and-claw tubs.

It was a comfortable building into which the family fitted easily, so when Mrs. Hull died later in the year Bill and Helen decided to see if they could purchase it. This in time they did, but only after protracted negotiations with the widow's son, an amusing fellow who was quite convinced that no lawyer need be party to this transaction; this was reason enough to acquire the services of an attorney in Goshen, who steered matters past the younger (though not much) Hull with diplomacy and patience. By March of 1944 the deal had been made: for $11,000 Bill and Helen acquired, on approximately an acre of land, the house in which they lived, a second dwelling of slightly smaller dimensions but similar appearance, and a three-car garage with an apartment upstairs. They also obtained from the estate of Lucia H. Hull, "in consideration of the sum of One Dollar to it paid," all of the furniture in the two houses, a bargain if ever there was one: these chattels included a large, uncommonly comfortable overstuffed sofa, which sat in their living rooms for the rest of their shared lives, the small fall-front desk that Helen used, and a number of other pieces that now have found their way into the houses of their children.

The purchase proved a good investment, but in 1944 it was more than they could handle on their own. Later in the year they received a modest return on the sale of the Cooperstown property, but they found it necessary to obtain from the National Bank of Tuxedo a five-year mortgage in the amount of $5,000; in subsequent years they made an elaborate point of claiming to their children that they had never taken out a loan, so the discovery of this document gave me no small amount of wry pleasure. But mortgage or no, they had little cause for doubting the wisdom of their purchase. In the first two years of ownership they took in more than $2,000 in rent on the second house; in 1946 they sold the garage for $1,350, and in 1947 the second house went for $8,000; in the summers of 1947 and 1948, while vacationing in New Hampshire, they rented their own house for a total of $1,250; and in 1949 they sold that house for $16,000. Although we can only guess at what they spent on utilities and maintenance for the rental property, it seems reasonable to assume that they nearly doubled their initial investment.

Their profit would have been higher except that in 1946 the joys of home ownership descended upon them in full force. From April through October the plumbers from J. Ezra Conklin's and the carpenters and painters from Mead & Taft Company were Helen's daily companions. Conklin's men ripped out much of Lucia Hull's plumbing; they also put in a new boiler, oil burner and electric hot-water heater, for which they charged a total of $887.34. Mead & Taft's crew worked inside and out, upstairs and down, putting in new windows and screens, installing asphalt strip shingles on the roof, tearing down the coal bin in the basement, and putting two coats of paint on the exterior; for this they billed the Yardleys

The house on Stable Road

$1,048.24, which when added to Conklin's charges produced a grand total of $1,935.58. So much for the $1,350 (less $67.50 commission) on the sale of the garage.

But it was money well spent. Not merely was the house thoroughly improved, both as a residence and as an investment, but the elimination of the coal-burning furnace made the basement a wholly different and infinitely less dreadful place. Going into its black depths to stoke the furnace had been an assignment despised by all: not because the coal was dirty and heavy, not because the furnace was hot and dangerous, but because in the years before the oil burner the basement was host to a colony of rats. None of these creatures was pleasant, but one of them was worse than all combined. He was a large, malign fiend who prowled the pipes in hopes that one of us would be so foolish as to venture into his realm; if one did, that person was likely to find King Rat on a pipe inches from his face, teeth bared, ready to pounce. The rat lived in my nightmares for years, long after Conklin's men had sent him to his reward.

But rats were simply something you lived with in those days, an inescapable fact of life visited with more or less equal regularity upon the rich people in the stone houses overlooking Tuxedo Lake and the struggling ones on Stable Road. Helen was oblivious to the rodents below as she prepared the evening meal, listening to *Make Believe Ballroom* as it broadcast the latest hits by Glenn Miller and Tommy Dorsey and—her particular favorite—Benny Goodman. Bill had little use for music and even less for swing, though he had vehement opinions about both; but Helen loved music and dancing, and those afternoons in the kitchen, alone or with the children, gave her the chance to listen with no carping interruptions.

By now Helen was virtually a full-time housewife, and I think a happy one. She had a bit of an outlet for her artistic interests in a part-time job with a ceramicist and potter, a friend named Nan Benziger, but her real life was in the house. She devoted herself to it wholeheartedly, taking on without complaint duties that her mother had been able to pass along to others. She had no servants, hence the vacuum cleaner they'd bought in Pittsburgh; housecleaning was not her favorite chore, nor was she an absolute stickler for it, but she kept things orderly and tidy. As a girl she had been given full instruction in domestic crafts—she spent hours making bound buttonholes, for example—and now she practiced them with genuine pleasure. She loved to sew dresses for herself and Jane, to knit sweaters for all of us—I did not have a store-bought sweater until I was a married adult—and to do other needlework. She was not merely enthusiastic about these crafts, she was also exceptionally good at them; years later, in Rhode Island, she planned, organized, and presided over a collective needlepoint project the result of which was nothing less than a work of art.

In all of these activities she was invariably calm, poised, serene; she was punctual (but not ostentatiously so) in all appointments and fastidious (but not fussy) in all habits. With her children she was matter-of-fact but loving, though in an undemonstrative fashion; she did not equate *mother* with *smother*, so she meted out her affections reservedly, but they most surely were there for the taking. Of the many lessons she taught me, I value none more than this: the love of another must be accepted as it is offered, not as one might wish it to be, because we must always take others on their own terms. In the picture that remains in my mind she is sitting in her dark-red wing chair reading a book, a quiet smile on her face, and when she hears someone enter the room she looks up expectantly: What interesting thing, she wonders, will this person bring into my life?

She was now in her early thirties, she had gained some experience in her small world, and she was beginning to develop more self-confidence than as a girl she had possessed. Perhaps because she had been modestly privileged on Mountain Avenue, she suffered no sense of inferiority or self-doubt at being impecunious on Stable Road; she knew who she was. If she and her husband had little money, they were obviously people of some culture and refinement, and of broader educational background than some of the parvenus up the hill; the schoolmaster is hired for his intellect, after all, just as the minister is for his faith, and these qualities have their own coin even in circles where money is valued above all.

Indeed the social life that she and Bill had in Tuxedo was livelier and more congenial than any in their marriage save the one they enjoyed in Rhode Island many years later. Their friends were also their customers, but business rarely intruded on pleasure; indeed business *was* pleasure, for the future of the Tuxedo Park Country Day School was a matter of the most intense communal interest and, as that future began to take shape, pride. A prominent fact of Tuxedo social life was a "cocktail circuit," in which women of leisure paused at the end of the day for liquid refreshment, often to excess, in each other's houses, but this was not the world in which Helen and Bill moved; instead they had their own circle of friends, whom to their everlasting pleasure they discovered to be people entirely like themselves.

It was not until the end of the war, though, that their social life came into full flower. Tuxedo Park may have been an enclave of privilege and isolation, but it scarcely went untouched by the war. A number of local men were overseas in the service; those men and women who had stayed at home found various ways to assist the war effort. Bill retained his 2-A classification throughout, though in 1944 he received a brief scare when suddenly he was reclassified 1-A; a letter from the president of the school's trustees to the local draft board advised that "it would be an irreparable loss to this country community were Mr. Yardley to be drafted into the Army," and the mistake, if mistake it was, was soon corrected. Helen worked for the Tuxedo chapter of the American Red Cross, of which by war's end she had become secretary. Bill was a member of the Orange County War Price and Rationing Board, playing a small role in the local allocation of stamps for gasoline, food and other necessities; he did his part for relations between the park and the village by serving as a member of the board of education of Tuxedo Union School. Bill also served in the Army Air Forces Aircraft Warning Service, for which he had been trained before leaving Pittsburgh. His duties in that regard consisted primarily of going out at night with binoculars to scan the skies against the unlikely prospect of enemy fighters zeroing in on the Ramapos. It was as close to combat as he ever got, but he took his duties seriously and so, too, did I; standing in the back yard with him when the night was dark and ominous, I felt the war with all its terrors and uncertainties draw near, and was both proud and relieved to have the protection of this brave man whom President Roosevelt, in his wisdom, had selected for a position in the line of defense.

Not that President Roosevelt was especially popular in the Yardley household. Both Bill and Helen thought he had been in office too long; Bill in particular disliked F.D.R.'s aristocratic theatricality, perhaps finding it too close in style to his own, though in later years his disdain turned to admiration. I in any event thought I was the bearer of good tidings when, on the afternoon of April 12, 1945, I raced into the pantry to report the news I had heard outside. "Mummy! Mummy!" I shouted. "President Roosevelt is dead! The president is dead!" Much to my surprise, she burst into tears.

Then all of a sudden the war was over and the men began to come home. None of them elicited greater admiration in Tuxedo than Crawford Blagden, universally known as Sonny. An exceptional athlete in prep school and college, he lost an arm in the service but declined to let this disability slow him down; he commuted daily to New York and taught himself to play one-armed golf and tennis with startling expertise, in the process setting a vivid example for grown men and small boys alike. Bill admired Sonny Blagden immensely, and liked him as well; along with the Brighams and the Fields and the Crofuts and the Woolstons and others, the Blagdens were part of the tight social circle in which the Yardleys moved and in which they felt wholly at home. Though from time to time there were gatherings at the club, these people saw each other primarily at each other's houses, for cocktails and dinner; these were relaxed, informal evenings where people pitched in to help with the cooking and the dishes, where the talk was of children and school and jobs and the longing for new cars and appliances that bound all Americans together in those days.

War's end also brought the climax of Bill's headmastership: on April 8, 1946, the newly renamed Tuxedo Park School moved into the Tilford mansion. Among the Yardleys the excitement was positively electric, since the school was the focus of our lives outside the immediate household, but I can only guess at the elation Bill must have felt upon that certifiably red-letter day. It had taken no small amount of courage for him to come to Tuxedo three years before, considering that the school's situation was then as dim as its prospects, but he had a clear vision: he saw that there was a real possibility of building a good school in a community so richly endowed in so many ways, and he devoted himself to the fulfill-ment of that possibility. To say that the day when the new school became reality was his moment of personal triumph is no mere expression of filial pride; it is the truth.

Now that Bill had his building, he could get about the business of making it into a school. But what a building it was! In a commu-nity of mansions, it stood apart. Styled vaguely in the manner of English country houses, of ivied redbrick walls and leaded-glass windows, it was three stories high and a city block in length. It occupied a hilly piece of ground with spectacular views of the lakes and the Tuxedo Valley, through which in 1777 Washington's men had marched en route to West Point and New England; its many terraces were more valuable for their scenic views than as athletic fields, since footballs and field-hockey balls kept disappearing into the wooded banks below. Inside were numerous rooms of widely varying dimensions, from the capacious public spaces on the first floor to the tiny servants' quarters on the third; some of the first-floor rooms had huge fireplaces with carved stone mantels, before which on winter evenings students gathered for songs and stories.

These were boarding students; Bill believed that because the school had only a limited clientele within driving distance, a boarding department was absolutely necessary if the school was to grow and become competitive with other institutions. So he turned the third floor into a dormitory, hired a housemother, and found teachers who could work weekends; soon enough the boarders began to come; some were the children of local parents who disappeared into Palm Beach and Sarasota and other winter refuges of the rich, and who therefore welcomed the opportunity to leave their children in familiar surroundings while they improved their tans and their golf games. The boarders' numbers were relatively small—twenty-five students in a total enrollment three times as large—but they played a disproportionately large

The new Tuxedo Park School; Bill is in the doorway

part in Bill's life for the simple reason that he was responsible for them twenty-four hours a day, seven days a week. Nothing worried him more than the prospect of harm coming to one of them, so when several girls decided one evening to run away, his consternation must have been terrible; soon all returned but one, and finally—at about eleven-thirty that night—this last lost sheep knocked timidly at the Blagdens' door. Bill rushed over to rescue her, but not to castigate her; as he always was with students, he was gentle and kind, reassuring the girl rather than excoriating her.

On another occasion Bill found himself confronted with a small group of frightened, tearful six-year-olds. It was rest hour, during which an impish boy in the class had done precisely what every impish child in his right mind longs to do: he had ripped from his mattress the tag that read, "DO NOT REMOVE THIS TAG UNDER PENALTY OF LAW." The other children were terrified—as was the culprit, once the enormity of his action had sunk in—and rushed to the headmaster's office.

"Oh, Mr. Yardley," one of them cried. "Look what Tommy has done! Tommy has broken the law! Will he have to go to jail?"

Bill took the tag from the boy and looked at it solemnly. "Well," he said at last, "Tommy has done something very serious. But it is not a criminal offense and I do not think it will be necessary to call the police. You see, the manufacturer puts that tag on the mattress so customers will know it is clean and safe, but once someone buys the mattress he can take the tag off if he wants to. Tommy shouldn't have removed it because the mattress belongs to the school, but I am the headmaster of the school and I am not going to punish him. Now why don't you be good children and finish your naps?"

Of such ordinary crises are the life of a headmaster usually made, but from time to time there are exceptions. Briefly, Bill had as a student a boy whose grandfather had been a flamboyant figure widely known as the Boy Wizard of Wall Street. One day his grandson was seen brandishing a revolver, which Bill promptly confiscated. Then he telephoned the boy's father.

"I'm sorry to tell you that your son came to school with a pistol," Bill said.

"What does it look like?"

"It's a silver-plated revolver, with a pearl handle."

"Heavens!" the gentleman said. "That's the pistol my mother tried to shoot my father with! You keep it—and never let me hear about it again!"

Bill did just that; the pistol remained "among my treasured artifacts," its story one he ever after delighted in telling.

His style as headmaster was formal and conservative. His manners were exquisite, and he expected the same of students and staff alike. He may at times have overdone the Mr. Chips routine—this being a notable inconsistency, inasmuch as he loathed the sentimentality of *Goodbye, Mr. Chips*—but it was part of his deliberate effort to set an example, a standard to which his students could aspire. To his family it often had the appearance of yet another act, and at times indeed it became one, but it was an act born of conviction rather than mere artifice.

"Since the School occupies a large estate," Bill wrote, "with all the natural beauty of Tuxedo Park at its door, life here closely approximates that of a large family living contentedly together in their country home." The metaphor was by no means fanciful. Bill had a gift for creating and presiding over orderly, peaceful enclaves that somehow closed out the troubles of the real world, and Tuxedo Park School was such a place. It was small enough to be intimate, large enough not to be suffocating; the atmosphere was one of friendliness and mutual support; the children were given "constant but unobtrusive" supervision by teachers who seemed genuinely to like them and each other; the headmaster's door was open to all, and none feared to pass through it.

Bill made certain that Tuxedo Park School was "a conservative one in its academic program, avoiding the extremes of repression and unrestricted freedom." From kindergarten through ninth grade, his students were required to steep themselves in the fundamentals of the humanities and sciences at the same time as they were encouraged to develop their artistic and creative urges. By the third grade they were introduced to history and geography; in the sixth grade they studied the Middle Ages, and in the seventh they began the mandatory study of Latin. They also, from first grade to last, studied woodworking in Toimi Paarsinen's shop, taking home to their parents ashtrays and wastebaskets and letter openers, some of which were fashioned with more than passing care; they studied music and art, went on field trips and nature walks, staged plays and had dances. For this their parents paid tuition ranging from $200 (kindergarten) to $1,400 (boarding), as well as modest fees for books and stationery.

If their parents needed to reach the headmaster outside school hours, they could call Bill at Tuxedo 439, the number at the house on Stable Road; the Yardleys may not have been on campus, as they had been at Shady Side, but Bill was very much on full-time duty at Tuxedo Park School. He responded quickly and sympathetically to calls, even those from parents whose concerns or complaints were largely imaginary, but he did not let them interfere with his busy and happy private life. By 1947 his children were old enough to have developed an interest in the world, one that he and Helen were quick to encourage. They loaded Jane and me into the Ford and took us to museums, to battlegrounds, to historic houses and sites: to whatever they could find, and in that part of the country there was much, that would help us understand and revere our American heritage.

By no means was this all edification and no play. Every winter we took the train to Manhattan for a matinee performance by the Ringling Bros. and Barnum & Bailey Circus, all three rings of it in the old Madison Square Garden at Eighth Avenue and Forty-ninth Street; one year it presented a fellow named Unus, who raised himself on a single finger atop a brightly shining orb, and who in my memory has stood there ever since. Bill was no lover of films—on the general subject of popular culture he had a large, stubborn, willfully blind spot—but we did drive over to Suffern one day for my first trip to a movie theater, to see Laurence Olivier's production of *Henry V*, the majesty of which still reduces me to wonder four decades later.

The most amazing of these excursions, though, involved only Bill and me. Through the good offices of my next-door neighbor and best friend, Walter Crofut, I had become an ardent fan of baseball generally and the New York Yankees specifically. Bill had no use for sports except as part of school life, and even less for professional sports, but one fine day he loaded me into the car and drove to Yankee Stadium. There, in seats along the left-field line, we watched not one baseball game but two: a doubleheader between the Yankees and the St. Louis Browns. Even though to my inexpressible disappointment Joe DiMaggio did not play—he had a minor injury, but he did me the courtesy of standing briefly on the top dugout step and thus permitting me a glimpse of immortality—the Yankees won both games and I went home in bliss. It was not until many years later, when I became a father myself, that I fully realized what Bill had done for me that day; there could have been, for him, no greater expression of love than to suffer through two baseball games in a single afternoon.

But then that morning he had had his own treat. We had gone downtown to Bannerman's, a retail establishment that for a time rivaled Brooks Brothers in Bill's affections, and in mine as well. For a boy, and for the boy in Bill, Bannerman's was heaven. It specialized in the sale of military artifacts both antique and modern, and its inventory—regularly catalogued in a fat volume with black-and-white illustrations—was so vast as to defy comprehension. From Bannerman's one could purchase, at modest prices, a medieval suit of armor, Civil War buttons and buckles in astonishing profusion, swords and long rifles, hats and helmets of every description; some of this was on view in the Manhattan store, but the real treasure house was at Bannerman's Castle, a great structure on an island in the Hudson just south of Newburgh. For Bill, who loved all things military so long as they did not require his enlistment, Bannerman's was a never-ending delight; from it he purchased swords, buttons and buckles, parade helmets—a small collection that provided handsome, if somewhat peculiar, ornaments for the walls and shelves of the house on Stable Road.

In that house matters proceeded quietly and serenely during the postwar years. The perennial financial difficulties had been somewhat alleviated by 1948, when Bill's salary was raised to $5,300. This, combined with the income they received from renting their own house during the summer, permitted Bill and Helen to spend July and August of 1947 and 1948 at a bungalow in Little Boar's Head, New Hampshire, that was owned by Cord Meyer, then a figure of some renown both for his own pioneering accomplishments as an aviator in World War I and for those of his son and namesake, a leader of the World Federalism movement. The bungalow was an intimate green-shingled affair nestled amid pines, in which each cool evening a whippoorwill sang; not far away was the tiny New Hampshire coastline, where we went daily for swimming and the construction of various elaborate sand structures, in which both Bill and Helen participated enthusiastically.

From their friendship with the Meyers, Bill and Helen received not merely access to the bungalow but also the mixed blessing of a cocker spaniel puppy, the runt of a Meyer litter, of whom they took possession in the late summer of 1948. He was the first of a long succession of Yardley dogs—cats, so far as Bill and Helen were concerned, were anathema—but the first and last cocker. They called him Boy, in honor of the dog of Bill's childhood, but he never really lived up to Bill's idea of what a dog should be; that came later, in the person of a gentlemanly dachshund named John Sebastian.

Boy was not the only addition to the family that summer. It had been Bill and Helen's careful plan to have two children, but some evening late in 1947 their passions got the better of their plan. In August of the next year they ended their vacation prematurely, so as to be back in Tuxedo for the birth of their third child. This unexpected but welcome girl appeared, in Suffern, on August 22, 1948.

THEY NAMED her Sarah, in honor of Sarah Chauncey Woolsey. So far as Bill was concerned, though, they really named her after Susan Coolidge: this being the pen name that Sarah Chauncey Woolsey took in her other life, that of an established if no longer remembered author, primarily of books for children.

She did not become a writer until 1870, when at the age of thirty-five she began to set down on paper the little stories that the next year were published as *The New Year's Bargain*, the first of her many books; for this volume she received the congratulations of Christina Rossetti, who commended "the originality and beauty of the story," which consisted of a dozen tales, each told to a little boy by a month of the year. She also at this time began to try her hand at verse, though poesy might be a more suitable word for it. Over the ensuing years she wrote countless poems, most of them cheerful and few of them memorable, yet if there is any of her writing that survives, it is not one of her books but this couplet, one that readers are likely to assume was written by James Whitcomb Riley or Edgar A. Guest:

> *Every day is a fresh beginning,*
> *Every morn is the world made new.*

———

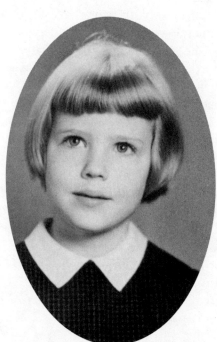

The two Sarahs:
Woolsey and Yardley

She wrote rosy poetry because her outlook on life was optimistic and, for all her travel and wide acquaintance, rather innocent. It had been shaped in the Woolsey children's idyllic childhood in Cleveland, and it was when she came to write about this childhood that her fiction blossomed. She wrote many books—among them *Mischief's Thanksgiving*, *Nine Little Goslings*, *A Guernsey Lily* and *A Little Country Girl*—but it is for those thinly veiled depictions of her own childhood that she was best known in her lifetime. Unlike the prissily moralistic books for children that were in vogue in the late Victorian age, Susan Coolidge's were merry and irreverent; a British critic wrote that "the girls of England loved them and they introduced into this country a class of schoolgirl heroine whose popularity has never waned." In all there were five of these books—*What Katy Did*, *What Katy Did at School*, *What Katy Did Next*, *Clover* and *In the High Valley*—and all of them sold well; they did not elevate Sarah to the popularity enjoyed by her contemporary and acquaintance Louisa May Alcott, but they brought her a substantial, loyal readership.

The first of them, *What Katy Did*, set the tone for the series. The Carr family lives in the town of Burnet, "which wasn't a very big town, but was growing as fast as it knew how." The father is Dr. Carr, "a dear, kind, busy man, who was away from home all day, and sometimes all night, too, taking care of sick people"; he is a widower, his beloved wife having died four years before in childbirth, so his five children are cared for by his spinster sister, Aunt Izzie, "sharp-faced and thin, rather old-looking, and very neat and particular about everything." The eldest of the children is Katy, who is twelve as the series begins and is Sarah Chauncey Woolsey to the core; the others are Clover, Elsie, Joanna and Phil, and they are joined by their orphaned cousin, Dorry, a six-year-old boy.

Katy is their ringleader and heroine, a spirited girl who makes her obligatory bows to the piety of the age but is determined to go her own way. When she grows up, she says, "I mean to *do* something grand," and then she speculates about what glories this future may hold for her:

> Perhaps it will be rowing out in boats, and saving people's lives, like that girl in the book. Or perhaps I shall go and nurse in the

hospital, like Miss Nightingale. Or else I'll head a crusade and ride on a white horse, with armor and a helmet on my head, and carry a sacred flag. Or if I don't do that, I'll paint figures, or sing, or scalp—sculp,—what is it? you know—make figures in marble. Anyhow it shall be *something*. And when Aunt Izzie sees it, and reads about me in the newspapers, she will say, "The dear child! I always knew she would turn out an ornament to the family."

But then a terrible accident happens: Katy falls from a swing and is severely injured. For months she lies in her bed, cheered only by the love of her family and the occasional presence of her cousin, Helen, who tells Katy that "God is going to let you go to *His* school—where He teaches all sorts of beautiful things to people." That, she says, is "The School of Pain," and the lessons it teaches are those of Patience, Cheerfulness, Making the Best of Things, Neatness and Hopefulness: an entirely respectable Victorian agenda. After many months Katy's recovery slowly begins, and in time she is actually able to go downstairs. There Cousin Helen tells her, "You have been learning by yourself all this time. You have won the place, which, you recollect, I once told you an invalid should try to gain, of being to everybody 'The Heart of the House.'

"Oh, Cousin Helen, don't!" said Katy, her eyes filling with sudden tears. "I haven't been brave. You can't think how badly I sometimes have behaved—how cross and ungrateful I am, and how stupid and slow. Every day I see things which ought to be done, and I don't do them. It's too delightful to have you praise me—but you mustn't. I don't deserve it."
But although she said she didn't deserve it, I think that Katy did!

It's a lovely little book, really, very much of its time but hardly irrelevant to our own, especially with its clear insistence that girls as well as boys can lead interesting, productive lives; the Katy books, three of which remain in print, are of interest both as Americana and as children's literature. Certainly they were the capstone of Sarah Chauncey Woolsey's writing career, though by no means did that career end when the last of them was published in 1884. In 1892, under her own name, she edited an edition of Jane

Austen's letters, to which she appended a brief, gracious introduction. During the 1890s she served her publisher, Roberts Brothers of Boston, as a reader and advisor. She loved Boston and made regular visits there, staying at 77 Mount Vernon Street with her friend Sarah Wyman Whitman, at whose literary salon the likes of Sarah Orne Jewett and William James were in frequent attendance. James much admired Sarah Chauncey Woolsey, but could not resist commenting on her manner. She had grown quite elderly and fat but was as lively as a child; she was, James declared, "a cross between an elephant and a butterfly."

With her death in 1905 the family lost its only regularly published writer since Jonathan Edwards, whose sermons, treatises and theological speculations were widely issued during and after his lifetime. Though some of his admirers have made claims for Edwards as a literary stylist, few readers of our day are likely to find his prose either delightful or digestible; whatever its importance in the country's religious life, his work seems to me to have little merit as literature and I propose to make no such claims for it. Neither shall I say more for Sarah Chauncey Woolsey than that, apart from being an unusually energetic and amiable and interesting person, she wrote slender books that gave pleasure to many people, most of whom by now surely are dead.

But she was a figure to whom Bill attached particular importance, and with good reason: he saw her as emblematic of the family's abiding love for books and reading, its commitment to those traditions and customs that the word *literature* embraces. For the same reason he had the most ardent admiration for Sarah's nephew, John Munro Woolsey, who served on the United States District Court for the Southern District of New York from 1929 until 1943. He was an authority on admiralty law, but in the course of his judicial career was obliged to settle several cases of a literary nature. In one he rejected charges of plagiarism against Eugene O'Neill, noting that "inasmuch as the plaintiff cannot claim a copyright on words in the dictionary, or on usual English idioms, or on ideas, the alleged paraphrasing comes to naught"; later he

ruled that *Contraception*, a study of birth control by Marie C.
Stopes, was neither obscene nor immoral and thus could not be
banned under the customs laws of the United States.

But it was in 1933 that Judge Woolsey took his place in history.
The previous year James Joyce had been approached by Bennett A.
Cerf, of a young publishing firm called Random House, about the
possibility of bringing out an American edition of his monumental
novel *Ulysses*. Random House promised to defend the book against
censorship or suppression, in return for which Joyce approved its
edition as "the only authentic one in the United States." As
expected, the book was seized by the Customs Service, on the
grounds that it might provoke "impure and lustful thoughts"
among American readers. The case eventually found its way to
Judge Woolsey's courtroom, where he gave it the most careful and
studious attention. He spent a month reading and rereading the
novel, and on December 6, 1933, one day after the repeal of
Prohibition, handed down a verdict that was as salubrious for
American literature as repeal was for American society. In all
respects he found in favor of the plaintiffs, thereby opening the
way for full American publication of what is, in the minds of many,
the transcendent work of twentieth-century literature in English or
any other language. Not merely did Judge Woolsey find for Random House and Joyce, but he explained that finding in no uncertain terms. "In *Ulysses*," he wrote, "in spite of its unusual frankness,
I do not detect anywhere the leer of the sensualist. I hold, therefore, that it is not pornographic." He continued:

The words which are criticized as dirty are old Saxon words
known to almost all men and, I venture, to many women, and are
such words as would be naturally and habitually used, I believe, by
the types of folk whose life, physical and mental, Joyce is seeking to
describe. In respect of the recurrent emergence of the theme of sex
in the minds of his characters, it must always be remembered that
his locale was Celtic and his season Spring. . . .

I am quite aware that owing to some of its scenes *Ulysses* is a rather
strong draught to ask some sensitive, though normal, persons to
take. But my considered opinion, after long reflection, is that whilst

in many places the effect of *Ulysses* on the reader undoubtedly is somewhat emetic, nowhere does it tend to be an aphrodisiac.

Ulysses may, therefore, be admitted into the United States.

It was in every sense of the term a landmark ruling, one that not merely opened the ports of America to *Ulysses* but tore away the last significant vestige of Victorianism in the country's literary life. To the authors and publishers of America, Judge Woolsey's decision said that literature was no closed room into which certain subjects were not admitted. In his eloquent and witty opinion he opened the door to that room and let in the real world of men and women.

The literary community rejoiced at the decision, as did Bill; not merely was he proud of his cousin's forthright ruling, but he had a pronounced taste for ribaldry. Over the years, as censorship steadily weakened and subsequent court decisions broadened the rights of writers and publishers, he accumulated a tidy little shelf of paperback erotica: Frank Harris's *My Life and Loves* and the anonymous memoirs of a Victorian Gentleman, *My Secret Life*, not to mention *Fanny Hill*, *The Story of O* and—one he especially treasured—*Candy*. He found these books immensely amusing, and passed them along to friends with laudatory reviews. "You'll find some chuckles in this one," he'd say with a wink and a leer, or, "Here's a nice piece of gen-u-wine dirt." All hail John Woolsey!

But dirt, however pleasurable, was the exception rather than the rule on the many shelves that over the years Bill and Helen filled with books. Although their tastes were unpredictable and catholic, they preferred, as most passionate readers do, books that connected in one way or another with the lives that they led and the world they inhabited. Though they were sympathetic to experimentation and the avant-garde, Helen especially, they had no patience with or interest in books that addressed themselves to narrow, self-infatuated readerships; their world may have been small, but they knew that in the hands of a skillful and perceptive writer, the small can yield the universal.

Above all else they loved novels of middle-class manners. They had been brought up on the great fiction of Victorian England, which they read and reread with undiminished pleasure. In time Bill transferred his attention from Thackeray to Trollope, whom he collected in stupendous volume, but his admiration for *Vanity Fair* never wavered. Helen in particular loved the work of Jane Austen, a five-volume set of which she obtained in the 1950s and kept by her bedside thereafter; like Mr. Bennet in *Pride and Prejudice*, Helen with a book was "regardless of time." Their Anglophilia, which in Bill's case was a lifelong passion, extended to nonfiction as well; in their Rhode Island years they spent countless hours with Mark Girouard's *The Victorian Country House* and other volumes of that ilk; on the shelves of Bill's study could be found *Happy England*, by Helen Allingham and Marcuse Huish; *Cromwell: The Lord Protector* and *Royal Charles*, both by Antonia Fraser; and *The Oxford Book of Oxford*.

Yet on those same shelves were *Sophie's Choice*, by William Styron, *A Good Man in Africa*, by William Boyd, *Tigers Are Better Looking*, by Jean Rhys, and *Go Down, Moses*, by William Faulkner. Unlikely as this last may seem, in their late sixties Bill and Helen embarked jointly on an all-stops excursion through Faulkner's Yoknapatawpha County, reading all the books and absorbing the full genealogy of Compsons, Sutpens and McCaslins. They were especially attached to the Snopes trilogy, which they found uproarious; Bill was so amused by the machinations of this nefarious clan that he once sent me as a birthday present a "grandfather's necktie" on which the names of more than a dozen Snopeses had been carefully inked: Flem, Mink, Eck, Bilbo, Lump, Vardaman, Wallstreet Panic, Clarence, Ab, Byron, Colonel Sartoris, Admiral Dewey and Montgomery Ward. It made for quite a conversation piece.

But of all the writers whose work they read and loved, two stand out. Neither was a major figure in American literature, nor did Bill and Helen make insupportable claims for the merits of either. But the truth is that among people who read regularly for pleasure, relatively few books that pass through their hands are of any lasting literary distinction. Reading is scarcely pleasurable if one must constantly be deciphering an author's arcane codes or untangling a mess of unfamiliar names; the books to which we turn for relaxation make relatively small demands on us, and either transport us into worlds we do not know or engulf us in familiar places and sensations.

This is why each week Bill and Helen eagerly awaited the delivery of the latest issue of *The New Yorker*. They enjoyed its fiction and cartoons and reviews, but above all they loved the satirical poems of Ogden Nash. Now those poems are beginning to fade from our consciousness, but in the 1940s and 1950s they were celebrated among the educated middle class; it was in those days said that among American poets only Nash and Robert Frost could support themselves solely on the royalties from their work. The explanation for Nash's popularity lay both in his cleverness—puns, outrageous rhymes, ingenious coinages—and in his indignation at what he saw in the new American world. Like Russell Baker a couple of decades later, Nash used humor to cloak his anger and sorrow at what was being done to America. The cheap ruses of advertising, the blare of broadcasting, the encroaching tide of asphalt—all of this troubled him deeply, but he hid his rancor behind a laugh:

> *I think that I shall never see*
> *A billboard lovely as a tree.*
> *Indeed, unless the billboards fall*
> *I'll never see a tree at all.*

Helen and Bill loved Nash, but Bill especially; he and the poet shared the same anger and the same wit, though Bill's was more bitter and thus less palatable than Nash's. When he learned that Nash and his family summered at Little Boar's Head, Bill finagled an introduction and subsequently made it a point to be on the beach when the great man arrived for his daily swim. The two had in common, besides a mutual *Weltanschauung*, roots in Baltimore, and Bill milked these for all they were worth. For years afterward he said, "As Ogden Nash told me one day . . ." but the name-dropping was excusable because his pleasure in the slight acquaintanceship was so obvious and heartfelt.

* * *

But the writer whom they loved above all others was John Phillips Marquand, who became, with the publication in 1937 of *The Late George Apley*, the family's unofficial novelist laureate. Like Ogden Nash—like Bill and Helen Yardley and the world they knew—Marquand is fading away now, but in his day his novels were every bit as popular as Nash's poems, and Yardleys everywhere read and collected them avidly. In the spring of 1987, when I visited my Uncle Paul and Aunt Maili on the Hawaiian island of Kauai, I felt upon the moment of arrival as though I were back home in Middletown, six thousand miles to the east: there were dachshunds nipping at my heels, and volumes of Marquand on the bookshelves.

He was a novelist loved by readers and dismissed by critics, who could not tolerate his shady past: as a young man he had written hack fiction for *The Saturday Evening Post* and other mass-circulation magazines. He left the "smooths," as he called these publications, with the writing of *Apley*, his affectionate satire of Brahmin Boston, but the critics never acknowledged his departure and always, with only the rarest of exceptions, dismissed him as a lightweight; he did not improve himself in their eyes when he became a regular in the book clubs and best-seller lists, inasmuch as popularity is routinely regarded in American literary circles as prima facie evidence of deficiency.

This bothered Marquand immensely—he regarded himself as a "consistent craftsman of fiction," and believed himself to be more closely in touch with American reality than most more honored writers—but his readers cared not a whit. Bill and Helen knew he was no Thackeray or Austen, Wharton or Dreiser, but they correctly appreciated his clear eye for social and cultural nuance, and his sharp critical intelligence. They also, Bill in particular, were sympathetic to his relationship to privileged Americans; he stood as they did, one foot in and the other out, giving him an outsider's perspective with which they were all too familiar.

His novels came forth in prolific succession, eventually in uniform editions of light brown cloth with blue and dark-brown decorations on their spines. Bill and Helen bought them all, saved them all, and read them all over and again. As well they knew, the early ones were best: *Apley, Wickford Point, H. M. Pulham, Esq., So*

Little Time, but they delighted in the others even as they recognized their shortcomings. Bill understood, for example, that *Sincerely, Willis Wayde* was a hamhanded satire of the new American Babbit-try, but Marquand's prejudices were his own and he was overjoyed, not to mention richly amused, at finding them so pungently expressed.

Of all these novels, the one they most loved and most often returned to was *Wickford Point*. It is a book about which I cannot hope to write objectively, because Bill and Helen loved it so and because I identify so strongly with its narrator, a free-lance writer named Jim Calder, a.k.a. John Marquand, whose inside-outside position precisely reflects Marquand's, and my own. But it is easy to see why Bill and Helen were so drawn to it, for *Wickford Point* is among many other things a book about the American past and the families who lived it. For all its tart satire—Bill positively thrilled at Marquand's depiction of Allen Southby, an artificially tweedy Harvard professor whose "ideas were as unconnected with reality as the furnishings of his study"—*Wickford Point* is at heart a lamen-tation for a lost America:

> I could remember when there had been security at Wickford Point, when the house had a clean, soapy smell, when there were plenty of people in the kitchen to do the work, and two outside men to tend the garden and the grounds. That was when my grandfather was alive and before my great-aunt Sarah's mind was failing. The subsequent change was gradual, like the decline of the Roman Empire, and children do not often notice such essentials, although they observe most of the things that grown-ups forget or take for granted.

Satirists are usually moralists at heart, and Marquand was no exception; like Nash, like Bill and Helen, he lamented what he saw happening around him and yearned for a past that he believed, whether legitimately or not is scarcely the point, to have been better. Though Bill and Helen did not often talk about this aspect of his novels, I believe it to have been the strong undercurrent that drew them to Marquand, from the triumph of *The Late George Apley* to the final disappointment of *Women and Thomas Harrow*.

Marquand's world was their own, as was his view of it, and they treasured his every word.

But not without reservation. This was brought home to me when, at the age of fourteen, I returned to school from the Christmas recess. In English class we had been assigned a theme on what we had done over the holidays, which I seized as an opportunity to flex my own Marquandian muscles. "Thoughts at the Beginning of a New Year" I called the story, which was a depiction of Chatham, Virginia, with the names changed. "It was an insignificant town in Southern Virginia," I began, "not any larger than the average, not any smaller," and from there I slid steadily downhill. I described a "bi-annual egg-nog party—that was a puissant drink for this small, sedate town"; the "radically Baptist teacher of the sixth grade in the very low-class public school and her husband, a teacher at the local military academy"; the "laconic old men grouped around the drugstore, hungrily eyeing the girls in the ads for Kodak cameras and Maidenform bras"—and then concluded with exquisitely sophomoric condescension:

> The coming year might mean anything to these people—success, happiness, pain, sadness. No matter what the year would come to, though, these people would go on living their ordinary lives, not changing, but plodding on, never bothering to "leave a footprint on the sands of time."

For this I got a mark of 88—my satiric barbs were blunted by numerous misspellings and grammatical infelicities—and a swollen head. Knowing full well that the prejudices enumerated in the paper faithfully reflected those expressed daily at the breakfast hour in the privacy of the Yardley dining room, I sent the paper home in full expectation of parental approval. This I received, but with a surprising twist. Bill used the occasion to deliver a gentle lecture, one that—precisely because of its gentleness—took some years to sink in but that remains perhaps the most valuable he ever gave me. The letter, on Chatham Hall stationery, is dated January 22, 1954:

Many thanks for your grand letter and for letting us see the theme which received the deservedly high mark. Your mother and I chuckled over it a good deal and would certainly agree that you show a flair for writing unusual at your age. It would be wonderful to develop this talent and make something of it. There have been quite a number of writers in the family in the past though since your great-aunt Sarah's day none of us seem to have achieved too much success.

The list of books you have been reading is mighty interesting. I have read most of them myself and enjoyed all that I read. Incidentally, it has always seemed to me that the really great writers are great because they have a depth of passion and sympathy for their characters. They can laugh at their foibles and put them into funny or pathetic situations, but they still *feel* very deeply the human emotions of the people about whom they are writing. I had some glimmer of that in your series of sketches of home town folks. Don't ever be cynical about people even though they may be trapped in a narrow environment.

The reason that, of our southern writers, William Faulkner is head and shoulders above Erskine Caldwell is that Faulkner has deep human compassion. Melville had it, as did Dostoyevski. Marquand has it but to a limited extent. He is much more concerned with surface manners and the contact between obvious types that you and I know. The reader knows Marquand characters intimately yet superficially. He knows the way they look and act without really knowing the inner person.

However unplanned Sarah may have been, she hastened her way into the center of Bill's heart. Like Jane she was a lively child, but there was a seriousness about her that neither her sister nor her brother then possessed. Before long the tag attached to her read, "Sarah is the smartest of all the children," and virtually everything she did confirmed it. She displayed a lively interest in the world around her, she talked precociously, and later she excelled in school. Bill began to sense that in naming her after Sarah Chauncey Woolsey he had chosen well; this, he thought, was the child whose future was brightest.

In time she became his favorite child, though the early partiality that he had shown to Jane never quite faded. His expectations for Sarah were at once conventional and not; he thought she could make a name for herself, which was unusual in a man who expected women to marry after being properly educated and thenceforth to subordinate themselves to their husbands, but he assumed this success would come in one or another of the paths that Yardleys traditionally had followed. What he did not know was that he had on his hands an unconventional child, and that in the future unconventional times awaited her.

* * *

But for now all was quiet in Tuxedo Park. At home the only crisis was a sudden attack of acute abdominal pain that led to the removal of Helen's appendix. She weathered the operation routinely and even derived a substantial side benefit from it: she followed doctor's orders and quit smoking, a habit with which she had been afflicted since college. Bill declined to follow her example. His Chester-fields, later to be followed by a succession of progressively blander and blander filtered cigarettes, were the core of his daily diet. As a boy he had been bribed not to smoke by one of his great-aunts, but as soon as he turned twenty-one and the bribes stopped, he started. For a time in the early thirties he smoked a pipe, in a self-admitted "effort to look academic," but the cigarette was his true instru-ment. From time to time he quit—by the early seventies he claimed to have stopped nine times—but these brief withdrawals served primarily to offer the pleasure of starting all over again. He was a born smoker: in later years, when the rest of his plumbing began to spring leaks, his lungs roared mightily along, unencum-bered by any of the dire circumstances about which innumerable surgeons general had warned him.

His life at school was as serene as that at home. Tuxedo Park School had become, thanks almost entirely to Bill's expert direc-tion, a self-steering ship that moved calmly and predictably through each year's academic waters. If there was anything about it that disappointed Bill, this was the failure of its boarding depart-ment to grow beyond a couple of dozen students. Even among the idle and peripatetic rich, there evidently were not many parents who had much enthusiasm for sending eight-year-olds away to school, so it must have become apparent to Bill by now that Tuxedo Park School would grow largely to the extent that Tuxedo Park itself grew. Yet if after five years in the job he was getting restless, he gave no visible sign of it; he was an established figure in a community of no small prestige, he was respected near-univer-sally in that community, and his family was happy there. In all likelihood he could have stayed forever, to the gratitude and satis-faction of all.

Then, quite unexpectedly, came word of a bright opportunity, far away in what was for Bill and Helen an unknown land. The

The Yardleys in 1948: Jonathan, Jane, Bill, Sarah and Helen

word was delivered by Alice Murray, a friend to whom the Yardleys were devoted; her several daughters had attended first Tuxedo Park School and then Chatham Hall, a four-year secondary school in a region of south-central Virginia known as Southside. Edmund Jennings Lee, the rector of Chatham Hall, was to retire at the end of the 1948–1949 academic year, and the trustees were about to authorize a search for his successor. Alice Murray suggested that they have a look at the young man who had worked such wonders with the little school in Tuxedo Park.

The trustees had empowered Dr. Lee to conduct the search himself, reserving final approval of his choice for themselves. On February 24, 1948, he wrote to Bill. "Mrs. Francis Murray talked to us about you and Mrs. Yardley when she was here a few days ago," he said, "and we should very much like to make your acquaintance." He would be in New York four days hence: "Would it be possible for you and Mrs. Yardley to take lunch with me in the

Coffee Room at the Biltmore Hotel on that day, say at one o'clock?"
As an afterthought he added: "The idea of your coming to a girls'
school may seem fantastic, but that is exactly what I thought about
it when the position was offered me."

Thus began a process—*minuet* is more the word for it—that did
not reach its conclusion for nearly a year. Bill wrote Dr. Lee that of
course he and Helen would be honored to meet him at the Biltmore, and the engagement was duly made. No record of it exists
beyond an exchange of notes between the two principals expressing mutual satisfaction about the meeting, but matters progressed
with sufficient dispatch for Dr. Lee to extend an invitation to the
Yardleys for a visit to Chatham. It is also clear that Dr. Lee raised
the troubling question of Bill's lack of clerical standing and that
Bill—perhaps cued in advance by Alice Murray?—indicated he
was prepared to consider entering the ministry.

Though one must read between the lines to do so, it is difficult
not to conclude that Bill was eager for the Chatham job from the
outset. Probably he thought that if he did not soon move along, he
would find himself in Tuxedo for far longer than would be good for
him or the school, and doubtless he knew that at the age of thirty-
six he may well have been too old to enter the rarefied circle of boys'
preparatory schools at a level appropriate to his experience. He was
ready to do whatever it took to get the Chatham job, because what
he saw there looked for all the world like his future.

In pursuing the position at Chatham he behaved precisely contrary to the counsel of Louisa Fowler at St. Timothy's in Baltimore.
He had telephoned her shortly after being apprised by Mrs. Murray of the situation in Chatham, and Aunt Loulie had not been
encouraging. With "a heartful of love and understanding," she
advised him in a subsequent letter that "it seems to me wiser for
you to stand by the smaller school of younger children in your own
part of the country where you are known and liked than to make
such a radical change in so many ways at the present uncertain
times." Her words were kind and understanding, but forthright:

If you and Helen were ten or twelve years older and had at least
some experience in dealing with girls between fourteen and eigh-

teen, creating their life as well as planning their work, my feeling
would be different. A boarding school of over a hundred, and a girls'
school at that, would be a tremendous task even with age and
experience added, but without either it might be too great a challenge. Then, too, both you and Helen in Virginia would be very far
from your homes and close ties.

All things considered I cannot encourage you to consider Chatham. I know so well the demands of a girls' boarding school that I
cannot encourage you to give up the known for the entirely
unknown.

Everything Aunt Loulie said was right and necessary, and Bill
and Helen certainly gave it the most serious consideration; they
loved and respected her too much not to weigh her words as
deliberately as they had been offered. But Aunt Loulie failed to
reckon with two vital considerations: Bill's deep belief, an out-
growth of his success at Tuxedo Park School, that he could do any
job in private secondary education; and his great desire, one that
intensified every day, to win this particular job—girls' school or
no, Virginia or no, he wanted it.

So at 9:50 P.M. on Friday, April 9, 1948, he and Helen boarded
the train at Pennsylvania Station in Manhattan. Eleven hours later
they were met by Pete Taylor, foreman of Chatham Hall and its
chief greeter, at the tiny station in Chatham. They stayed the
weekend at the Rectory, where Edmund and Lucy Lee had the
opportunity to examine the young couple at leisure, and vice versa.

What the Yardleys found was an odd but entirely engaging
couple. The Lees were in their early seventies and presented a stark
contrast: Edmund Lee was small, gentle, absentminded, while
Lucy Lee was aristocratic, vigorous, commanding. They had met
years before in China, where Edmund was a missionary, and had
devoted their subsequent lives to the church and its works. They
ran an abstemious household. Once at the end of the day Dr. Lee
asked a visitor from the North, "How would you like a Rectory
Cocktail?" "Sounds wonderful!" the gentleman said, rubbing his
hands in anticipation—whereupon the maid emerged from the
kitchen with two glasses of milk on the rocks, generously laced
with ginger ale.

Now the Lees were to retire, rather reluctantly, and they were determined that the school they so loved should be passed on to a couple capable of giving it as much devotion as they had.

The weekend was a happy one, but its conclusion was not. Dr. Lee met with his trustees shortly after the Yardleys' departure and expressed his high opinion of them. But the trustees were concerned that if the new headmaster was not a minister they would have to hire a chaplain as well, and as a result they directed Dr. Lee to pursue all leads that might produce a rector who could wear both the ministerial and the headmasterly hats. Bill feared that his chance had been lost. "What a grand place it is!" he told Dr. Lee. "Although I feel sure that you will find the right clergyman to be rector, it cannot help but be a disappointment to the Yardleys."

For two months there was no further word from Dr. Lee; the Southern adventure appeared to be over. Then in late June the Lees came to New York on personal business and motored out to Tuxedo to see the Yardleys in situ. I wish I could report from memory about this visit, but at eight years of age I was more interested in Walter Crofut and Joe DiMaggio than two old people from Virginia; evidently the engagement went well, because to his thank-you note of July 2 Dr. Lee attached a postscript that read, "We are increasingly impressed with the qualifications of the headmaster of the Tuxedo Park School."

That can only have been cold comfort for Bill and Helen, who heard nothing more for two more months. Then, early in September, came word that the tide might be shifting in their favor. "Our strenuous efforts to find the clergyman for the Chatham Hall succession have so far been unsuccessful," Dr. Lee wrote on September 4. "We must make one or two efforts, but about that I am discouraged. We would feel very badly about this if we did not think so highly of Mr. and Mrs. Yardley. In your letter please let me know that you have not made commitments that make you unavailable, and that you are still interested."

Most certainly they were, but at this point there is a strange and frustrating lacuna in the correspondence. Suddenly their negotiations must have shifted from the mails to the long-distance telephone—which even as recently as 1948 was still regarded as an extravagance—because the next letter is dated December 8. It is from Bill to Dr. Lee, expressing satisfaction with a "whirlwind trip through Tidewater Virginia" on which his newly revived candidacy had just taken him; he met with influential friends of Chatham Hall, and found this "a delightful experience which will never be forgotten." Then, though denying that "I am trying to put on pressure in this respect," he turned the screws a trifle:

> I have deep obligations to the Tuxedo Park School and a strong moral equity in its future success and am deeply anxious to be quite certain that, should I leave Tuxedo, my successor be the finest available person. For that reason I hope it will not be too many weeks or months before I know definitely one way or the other about Chatham. You know how unsettling it is to a school faculty to have its leadership uncertain.

Dr. Lee counseled patience. There was by now only one other candidate, a minister for whom Dr. Lee displayed little enthusiasm; surely Bill knew that he and he alone was Edmund Lee's favored candidate, as perhaps he had been from the outset. On December 17 Dr. Lee sent his Christmas greetings to Bill and Helen along with the news that "Yardley stock seems to be very definitely on the rise and it was already well above par." Then, on the first day of the new year, he wrote: "There will probably be a meeting of the Board of Trustees next Saturday after which I am hoping to send you a telegram." Now Bill and Helen were on pins and needles: "Your news is more exciting than any I have received for a long time and I am afraid that this next week will be a long one for Helen and me."

But even the longest of weeks eventually end. Theirs did when Edmund Lee telephoned Bill with the good news: the job, so long just beyond his grasp, at last was his. Two days later the appointment was confirmed by the Right Reverend William A. Brown, bishop of the Diocese of Southern Virginia. "I am very happy to inform you," he wrote, "as you probably already know, that the Board of Trustees of Chatham Hall at its meeting Saturday, January 8th, unanimously elected you as the successor to Dr. Lee as Rector of Chatham Hall to take effect, if satisfactory to you, July 1st, 1949." The job paid $6,500 a year and included "many perquisites."

Again, alas, memory does me no good service. I have no recollection of what it was like that day in the house on Stable Road, but
I can make a reasonably intelligent guess. Bill, warm-blooded as he
was, must have raised a mighty whoop of jubilation; Helen, cooler
and more self-contained, would have been every bit as thrilled but
more reserved in expressing her pleasure. To Jane and me they
must have said, "How would you like to live down in Virginia?" or
words to that effect, but neither of us recalls their words. What, in
any event, does memory matter? What matters is that we were on
our way.

"I feel myself resisting an irresistible urge to call you Uncle
Edmund," Bill wrote in his first formal communication with the
man whom he could now think of as his predecessor-to-be, "but
shall save that for your personal permission when we meet in
Chatham next month." With his unerring instinct for flattering
older people Bill had struck Dr. Lee at just the right moment, and
Uncle Edmund he happily became. In a letter accepting that
affectionate honorific he also outlined to Bill the perquisites of the
job, which were generous indeed: free occupancy of the Rectory;
"the general expenses of your household, including heat, light and
repairs," as well as "the wages of one servant and the supplies for
the kitchen"; free washing and ironing at the school laundry; "the
care of the school physician, but not hospital expenses or medi-
cine"; and "the up-keep of your car, which means while in
Chatham and does not include expenses of personal trips away
from Chatham."

What this meant, in sum, was that Bill's salary was effectively
doubled; $6,500 a year was not much for a man assuming the large
responsibilities of the rectorship—and it made no provision for
Helen, whose duties would prove numerous and inescapable—but
the perquisites meant that the Yardleys could breathe a bit more
easily and could save at least a little for the education of their own
children.

In February the Yardleys made their return to Chatham and
were affectionately welcomed. Dr. Lee had already paved their way
with an exceptionally gracious letter to the school community in

which he wrote words that Bill unconsciously echoed upon his own retirement twenty-three years later. "I want to ask one thing of you with all the earnestness that I can command," Dr. Lee said. "It is that there be no loss of your loyalty and devotion to Chatham Hall because we are not here." Later he told Bill that he wanted a photograph to be taken of the Lees and Yardleys together on the Rectory porch: "This will symbolize the relationship and help us to transfer all the loyalty felt to the school through us to you."

Dr. Lee meant those words with all his heart, but despite his good desires he was having trouble breaking away. He told Bill that he planned to continue his custom of sending birthday cards to all of his own alumnae—a task Bill was more than happy to let him continue—and, more disturbingly, he proposed to be named president of the board of trustees. Bill wrote supportively about this, but he can only have been alarmed at the prospect of having his near-legendary predecessor hovering over him; since nothing ever came of the idea, it seems safe to assume either that the trustees themselves gently dissuaded Dr. Lee or that Bill himself surreptitiously intervened to head it off.

Dr. Lee also did not seem to understand that Bill still had a school to run in Tuxedo Park, for he constantly badgered him to represent Chatham Hall at one conference or another. Somehow Bill managed to work all of this in, but he felt constrained to note, a trifle abruptly, that "I am very anxious to avoid any local criticism in Tuxedo that I have lost interest in the Tuxedo Park School and am being away more than I should be." The words fell on deaf ears. Dr. Lee now consulted Bill about virtually every detail of Chatham Hall business, from teachers' salaries to building plans to redecoration of the Rectory, and Bill dutifully responded to each inquiry. But surely he must have gnashed his teeth when, in mid-April, this one came in:

> Now prepare yourself for a shock! Dr. Andrews, the Commencement speaker, has had to withdraw his acceptance and we must secure someone else. Miss Holt, Lucy and I think the proper man to do it is Mr. William W. Yardley and I hope you will approve. It would, I think, be a wonderful way to make your entree to the Chatham Hall constituency.

The Yardleys and the Lees, on the steps of the Rectory

Rolling their eyes, no doubt, Bill and Helen agreed; they thought "that it would be a fine thing to do and further that it would be most unenterprising and most ungracious to decline." Then, before this blow had fully sunk in, dear Edmund Lee delivered another. The Chatham Hall Fund was driving for its last $5,000, he wrote in May, "which we expect to come in $100 gifts from fifty people." Then: "The letters of appeal state that the first two $100 gifts are from you and me. You may send me that check whenever you have a mind to do so!" Wearily, Bill replied that "the contribution of $100 from Helen and me will be with you before very long."

What Dr. Lee either failed or refused to understand was that quite apart from the incessant missives he was receiving from Virginia, Bill was up to his ears at Tuxedo Park. Principally, he owed one final duty to the school: presentation of his annual report to the board of trustees, a report he offered "with somewhat mixed emotions: pride in our solid growth and increasing maturity as a school, and sorrow at leaving what for me has been a happy and stimulating responsibility." He noted that the enrollment was now seventy-seven, thirty-one boys and forty-six girls; that the school's academic life was healthy and "for the third consecutive year the faculty situation has been quite stable"; and that "the biggest physical need has been recognized already as being a house for the headmaster and his family." He closed with "a benediction of thanks to the Board for your friendship, wisdom and support during six exciting years."

He was saying farewell to people about whom he indeed cared deeply, as he made clear to one of them:

> Leaving Tuxedo is going to be a terrible wrench for Helen and me with all the nice friends we have had the privilege of making since we came six years ago. This was certainly not a case where we were restless or dissatisfied. Chatham Hall seems a much greater responsibility, and an opportunity for wider service, as well as being a professional advance. I cannot pretend that I am not excited by the prospect, but I would be ungrateful if I pretended to leave Tuxedo without great reluctance.

The reluctance was genuine. Whatever discomfort they may have felt at being churchmice in the cathedral of privilege, Bill and Helen had been happy at Tuxedo in every way. They were leaving a school Bill almost singlehandedly had built, a house they loved dearly, and friends whom they treasured. Ahead lay a region of the country about which neither of them knew anything, a region that spoke a peculiar tongue and observed customs they barely comprehended. In that strange new world they knew no one except the people who soon would be their employees, and they could not hope to imagine what their life in this place might be like. But it was the life they had chosen; they went off to meet it with high hearts, certain that here at last was a challenge for a lifetime.

PART THREE

Chatham Hall

BILL KNEW scarcely a thing about Virginia but he knew his genealogy, and he quickly made a connection between the two. To a distant cousin who congratulated him upon the appointment at Chatham, Bill replied: "I fully expect that our many times great-uncle, George, will be the most useful relation that we have once we live in Virginia. I have found already that the name of Yardley carries much the same eclat in Virginia that Cabot would in Boston, or Biddle in Philadelphia, even though Sir George passed away something over three hundred years ago."

This was one snob corresponding with another; the truth is that the name Yardley meant approximately as much in Virginia as in South Dakota, which is to say almost nothing at all. In fact, the George to whom Bill referred did not even spell the name as Bill did: he put in the extra *e*—Yeardley—that most of the family had abandoned by the early eighteenth century. But in deference to Bill it must be acknowledged that George was a figure of some consequence in the history of the nation; even if his name meant nothing to all but a few of the fine old Virginians upon whom Bill dropped it, still it was a name to be reckoned with.

He was a native Englishman, born at Southwark in 1588, who took up the profession of arms not long after the ascension to the

179

throne of James I in 1603. He rose to the rank of captain, serving under Sir Thomas Gates in various adventures, and sailed with him to the new colony in Virginia, aboard the *Sea-Adventure*, in 1610; they were marooned at Bermuda and presided over the construction of two new vessels, *Patience* and *Deliverance*, aboard which they reached Virginia on May 24. There, at Jamestown, George was witness to a dramatic moment when Lord Delaware, governor and captain general of Virginia, came ashore and, in the words of another witness, "fell upon his knees and before us all, made a long and silent Prayer."

George stayed in Virginia for seven years, during which he was acquainted with John Rolfe and Pocahontas, and became the owner of extensive properties. Then in 1616 Sir Thomas Dale, the deputy governor, returned to England and chose George to serve in his place, as acting deputy. It was a popular appointment; George "applied himself for the most part in planting Tobacco, as the most present commoditie they could devise," and thus deserves much of the credit, if credit it is, for establishing the tobacco plantations of Virginia. In 1617 he was succeeded by the permanent appointee, Samuel Argall, and subsequently returned to England.

He stayed with his older brother, Ralph, from whom our line of the family is descended, and presented to Ralph the bride whom he had recently taken in Virginia. She is notable as a woman of great character, but her noblest distinction is her name: Temperance Flowerdew. What a comedown, from Flowerdew to Yeardley! But she took it, and over the years presented George with three children, Elizabeth, Francis and Argall. The namesake of this last was discharged by Lord Delaware while George and Temperance were still in England, Samuel Argall having proved himself "arrogant, self-willed, and greedy of gain"; to replace him James I chose George—in November, 1618, when George was a mere thirty years of age—and several days later conferred a knighthood upon him. George spoke to the king at this ceremony of matters Virginian, as one witness reported:

> This morning the King knighted the New Governor of Virginia,
> Sir George Yeardley, who upon a long discourse with the Kinge,

doth prove very understandinge. Amongst many other things, he told the King that the people of that country doe believe the resurrection of the body, and that when the bodye dies, the soul goes into certain faire pleasant fields, there to solace itself until the end of the world, and then the soule is to retourne to the body againe and they shall live both together happily and perpetually. Hereupon the Kinge inferred that the Gosple must have been heretofore known in that countrie, though it be lost, and this fragment only remaynes.

On January 29, 1619, Sir George and Lady Temperance sailed for Virginia aboard the *George,* which encountered rough weather all the way across but landed safely on April 19 at Jamestown. Among the new governor's first responsibilities was the arrest and deportation of Argall, a task that cannot have pleased Sir George; the possibility that he named his son after his old friend by way of atonement cannot be discounted. In any event it is from his arrival that the civilized life of Virginia is dated. He had charters from the London Council empowering him to end the feudal rule of the planters and establish government by law; this he did, convening at Jamestown on July 30, 1619, the first American parliament.

Sir George's three-year appointment ended in 1621; he was replaced by Sir Francis Wyatt. Now he established himself as a private citizen, becoming the largest landowner in Virginia, having several plantations as well as a manor on seven acres in Jamestown, with frontage on the James River. But in 1625 Sir Francis resigned his governorship and Charles I, newly risen to the throne, turned as his father had to Sir George. He served until his death in November, 1627, leaving an estate of more than ten thousand pounds. His fellow colonists mourned him as "a main pillar of this our building." Two centuries later George Bancroft, in his pathfinding *History of the United States,* wrote: "Posterity retains a grateful recollection of the man who first convened a representative Assembly in the Western Hemisphere: the colonists in a letter to the Privy Council, pronounced an eulogy on his virtues."

So, too, did Bill: over and over—and over and over—again. He saw Sir George as his ticket to the great mansions of the Tidewater—which soon enough he began pronouncing "*Tahd*-woe-tuh"—and as authentication of his own standing among the First Families of Virginia. Before the first red clay had hardened on his shoes he was at work on his Virginian accent: "There's a mouse in the house and there's no doubt about it" became, in his new locution, "There's a moose in the hoose and there's no doot aboot it." In the mansions of Richmond and Lynchburg, Alexandria and Roanoke, to which from time to time his headmasterly duties took him, Bill played the act for all it was worth. What the *real* Virginians thought of this—the Carters and Walkers and Randolphs and Dardens—is not recorded; at worst, I hope, they were amused.

His arrival was anything but auspicious. In the middle of June he packed Boy into the back seat of the Ford—a new car, one of the hundreds of thousands of redesigned 1949 Fords that had so excited American consumers—and set off, alone, for his first motor trip into terra incognita. Along the way he stopped to have lunch with friends and let Boy out for a trip to the fire hydrant. The spaniel, a creature of considerable stupidity, took this as license to vanish into the woods.

Bill furiously chased after him: "Boy! God damn it, where are you! Boy! You imbecile! God damn it, come here!" Around and around he raced, in his bare feet, for he was unaccustomed to the heat of Virginia in June: raced through woods and fields and patches of leafy green. He never found Boy—someone else did, and shipped him to his new home a couple of weeks later—but for his pains was rewarded with a glorious dose of poison ivy, between his toes and all over his feet. I have no recollection that he kicked Boy upon that sorry fellow's return, but certainly he felt like it.

A few days later he squeezed his swollen feet into loafers and drove to the airport in Danville. That morning his wife and three children had departed Idlewild Airport, flying first to Washington and then taking a puddle-jumper through the Virginia Piedmont. Poor Helen: on her lap she had the not-inconsiderable weight of Sarah, and beside her she had Johnny and Jane, each retching furiously into a paper bag, whining for attention, and inquiring endlessly about the duration of the journey. She was exhausted by the time the plane landed, but somehow she found the energy to perk up for her husband and Virginia Holt, the dean who had been Edmund Lee's strong right hand and now was to be Bill's.

The eighteen-mile drive from Danville—a drive we made so many times in years to come that all of us, even now, can take every curve of it in our sleep—was for Jane and me our introduction to the South. If ever before we had seen black people, I do not recall it: now here they were, walking along the roadside in shabby clothes, working in fields over rows of peculiar plants, some of them chained together in gangs and herded along by sullen white men holding shotguns. The air was hot and heavy with moisture, hanging over dilapidated shacks and battered gasoline stations. In some of the fields were cows, in others horses; plows and wagons were pulled by bizarre animals that we later learned were called mules. And the people spoke a language we had never before heard. "How y'all doin'?" "Mighty glad to welcome you to Chatham!" "Reckon that's a storm buildin' over yonder?"

Dixie: how strange and quaint and distant it now seems, a mere forty years ago, yet lost forever. How difficult it is to cast our minds back to those vanished days, when to move from suburban New York to Southside Virginia was to enter another country. The age of mass communications was in its early phases then, the Interstate highways had not been constructed and air travel was relatively novel, and the regions of the nation were separate and distinct, none more so than the South. The legacy of slavery and defeat permeated its air, the resentment against the conquering North still seethed just below hatred. Its economy was primitive by Northern standards, depending on cash crops and cheap labor. Many good people lived there but it was a backward land, awaiting the liberation that began in the 1960s when at last all Southerners gained their freedom.

But of its beauty there could be no doubt. When for the first time we drove up the hill to Chatham Hall, Jane and I were dumbfounded by what we saw: rich fields of the deepest green rolling away toward the Blue Ridge Mountains, great thick trees that stood on the land like monuments, tiny hummingbirds—hummingbirds!—darting through the air. Upon this majestic site man had erected a row of three large redbrick buildings—Pruden,

183

Dabney and Willis halls—and at the end of the line, perpendicular to these three, St. Mary's Chapel with its bright stained-glass windows that called forth the glory of God. And there, only a few yards from the chapel, it was: the Rectory. Home.

But it was not to be that until the fall. Over the summer it was the preserve of carpenters and painters, freshening it up for the new rector and his family. Meantime we stayed in a far smaller building, Brush House, a faculty residence named for a former business manager of the school. Its close rooms held on to each breath of the summer heat, and all we had to condition the air were fans, none of them sufficient. We boiled, and Helen fretted. Not far to the west was a terrible epidemic of poliomyelitis; Wytheville, a mere one hundred miles away, had been devastated by the disease. Sunstroke, Helen had heard, could provoke polio's onslaught; she bought large straw hats and made us wear them whenever we went outdoors.

The polio epidemic scared us, but it didn't keep us from exploring the campus—"Paradise!"—that we thought was ours alone. Together and apart—Jane with her newfound friend, Brenda Taylor, the foreman's daughter; I with Henry Hammer, the doctor's son—we roamed through Chatham Hall's three hundred sixty-five acres: Mr. Henry Gatewood's poultry farm and dairy, Mr. Charlie Taylor's stables, the tennis courts and playing fields, the empty classrooms, the peculiar little indoor swimming pool. It was heaven, and heaven had its headquarters: the Powerhouse. There Pete Taylor held sway, and there he supplemented his income by operating a Coca-Cola machine. From it one could receive, for a nickel, a frosty Coke in a green glass bottle, but who needed nickels and who needed cold drinks? Right there on the floor were cases of warm Cokes awaiting their turns in the machine: cases from which bottles began to disappear at an alarming and mysterious rate.

Finally Pete put two and two together. Most reluctantly he went to the rector's office in Pruden Hall and, straw hat in hand, said, "Mr. Yardley, somebody has been taking Cokes from the Powerhouse, and I'm afraid it is little Johnny and Jane."

Bill looked at him with astonishment and embarrassment.

"Are you quite sure of this, Pete?"

"Yessir, I am."

So he called us in and put the question to us. We could steal, but we couldn't lie: "Yes, Daddy," we said tearfully and fearfully.

Those Coca-Colas cost us a session with the hairbrush, which Bill wielded fiercely, and an evening in our rooms without dinner. What it cost Bill he never told us, but his shame must have been excruciating. Here he was new on the job, determined to gain the respect of his staff, and what do his children do but prove themselves common thieves?

Chatham Hall: a lovely name, and to Yardleys one with deep resonance, but not its original one. The school had been established late in the nineteenth century by the Episcopal Church of Virginia, which was attempting to reconstruct an educational system that had been devastated by civil war. The Reverend Clevius Orlando Pruden came to Pittsylvania County in the early 1890s with a lay reader, Chiswell Dabney, and reported that the county was in dire need of educational institutions. Accordingly it was resolved to found a school for "girls of gentle breeding and daughters of clergy," one that would educate "according to the best modern methods along church lines and at actual cost." It opened, as Chatham Episcopal Institute, in September of 1894, with Pruden as headmaster, Dabney as treasurer, and Bishop A. M. Randolph as chairman of the board of trustees; the school was "purely a venture in faith."

Its original building was an elderly mansion overlooking the town of Chatham. That sufficed until 1907, when the first of the brick school buildings was erected, followed four years later by the second; these in time were named, respectively, for Pruden and Dabney. Sometime in these early years the school's most famous alumnae were enrolled: a girl with artistic ambitions named Georgia O'Keeffe, and a promising actress named Margaret Sullavan. In 1925, under a new principal, Mabel Stone, the school became Chatham Hall and the swimming pool was built near the Powerhouse, but the school's prospects were poor. By 1929 only a dozen girls were enrolled and the debt was $30,000. In desperation Bishop Beverley Tucker reached all the way to China, whence he hired his old friend Edmund Lee as the school's rector and, the bishop hoped, its savior.

For a time it seemed that Dr. Lee had been retained merely to preside over the school's demise. He called in the head waiter, William Morrison, to warn him that the hired help had better start looking for work elsewhere. "This school was founded on faith and prayer," Morrison responded, "and it will never have to close. And when you get where you don't know what to do or where to turn, then the good Lord will fix things up for you." Which is just what happened. That very day Dr. Lee persuaded a philanthropist in Lynchburg to give the school $15,000, and later to add an extra $18,000; combined with a $25,000 donation from another source, this gave Dr. Lee enough money to erase much of the school's debt and put it back in business.

"Mrs. Lee and I left no stone unturned if there was a chance of finding a girl beneath it," Edmund Lee said. The Lees were able recruiters who soon discovered that they were working with an unexpected advantage: parents who had been hurt by the Depression learned that the little school in Virginia offered a tuition far lower than those charged by more prestigious institutions, and all of a sudden girls from the North began pouring in. Now the school was reborn. Dr. Lee had to undergo a period of adjustment: "I knew a great deal about Chinese boys," he said, "but little about American girls. When I made the discovery that American girls were a good deal like Chinese boys, my problems became easier"—but it did not take long for him to establish himself as a headmaster of presence and dignity. He hired Virginia Holt as dean, he expanded the faculty, and within four years of his arrival he had a student body of more than a hundred girls—and was accepting only one applicant in ten.

Though it suffered, as all girls' boarding schools of the day did, under the opprobrium of "finishing school," Edmund Lee's Chatham Hall was anything but. He stressed the social graces and was well aware that most of his graduates would go on to become housewives and mothers, but Dr. Lee was deeply committed to education and social service. Virginia Holt was a diminutive, soft-spoken woman who felt as ardently as he did about liberal education and formulated an academic program that, in the minds of many college admissions directors, was the best among all the country's girls' schools. As for public service, Edmund and Lucy Lee made this their particular province by establishing the Service League, to which each girl in the school belonged; the several departments of the league involved themselves in numerous projects, the most successful and enduring of which was a community center constructed for the black residents of Chatham.

The town was the county seat of Pittsylvania, having a population of less than two thousand, a high number of whom were lawyers and courthouse politicians. Much has changed for the better there, but in the 1930s Chatham was a bad place to be black. Racial tensions ran high, discrimination was merciless, and blacks were relegated to the bottom of an economic heap that wasn't very high to begin with. Those who worked at Chatham Hall—as waiters, maids, laborers, farmhands—were thought to be exceptionally fortunate, and were respected in the black community as a local aristocracy; three decades later the black workers of Chatham Hall repaid that respect by playing leading roles in the Pittsylvania County civil-rights movement: and Bill Yardley, who had come a long way by then, gave them a helping hand.

By the time Bill and Helen arrived there in 1949, Chatham Hall was an established school. Unlike Tuxedo Park Country Day School in 1943, it had no serious financial worries and no gloomy prospects. It had one hundred sixty students, a faculty of twenty, sixteen administrators and staff, and a work force of several dozen. It produced its own eggs at its poultry farm, its own milk and butter at its dairy—the milk came in thick glass bottles, the heavy cream rising just below the paper caps—and its own horses occupied the stable a few hundred yards beyond the main campus.

If it sounds a bit like a plantation, well, in a way that's just what it was; Bill, to his joy and astonishment, was Massa. Atop his hill in Chatham he was lord of all he surveyed, and he reveled in it.

Any school, especially any private school, is a self-contained, hermetic institution, but it is all the more intensely so when, like Chatham, it is so isolated. The students and faculty and staff, when they looked above them, saw only Bill between them and God; he was, on that tiny postage stamp of earthly soil, the final authority on all matters temporal and, in time, spiritual as well.

Under Bill, as it had been under Dr. Lee, it was a benign despotism; above all else, Chatham Hall in the 1950s was a happy place. With the exception of Bill, a succession of business managers and an occasional teacher, its white-collar population was entirely female—and, as a pleasant ramble through the yearbooks of the day reminds me, most agreeably so. The faculty lived in little cottages scattered about the campus; Miss Holt had built her own house behind Dabney, at her own expense, some years before. With the most infrequent exceptions these women liked each other and worked together in harmony. Though younger women were forever coming and going through their ranks, it was the older ones who kept the school going and contributed so much to its character: Pansy Andrus, the music teacher, a tiny, birdlike woman who lived in a suitably tiny house behind the Rectory with her tiny dogs and trinkets and whose sudden death a few years later devastated the community; Catherine Curtis, the senior mathematics teacher, a handsome woman of great dignity and good humor; Maria Gagarine, who taught Russian—yes, Russian—and French, an aristocrat who had known the Tolstoys and whose erudition was bottomless; Ann Elizabeth Taliaferro—Tollie—a housemother and occasional Rectory baby-sitter, fat and jolly and patient with children of all ages; Lillian Hensleigh, who taught science for a quarter-century, a quiet, forceful person whose students were intensely loyal.

Ah yes, the students: I can no more be objective about the girls of Chatham Hall than I can leap tall buildings with a single bound. I had crushes on more of them than I can count or remember, they figured in my dreams in roles of which they would not care to know, they in great measure defined my idea of what a girl, and then a woman, should be. In my memory they are all shapely and pert and blonde, though in truth they came in all shapes and dispositions and shades of hair. Though the school was in the South, most came from the Middle Atlantic and New England: Park Avenue, Chestnut Hill, Tuxedo Park, Long Island, Scarsdale, Newport, Princeton, Rumson, Wethersfield, Ardmore, Greenwich. Those who were Southern also came from the right places: Charlotte, Richmond, Charleston, Roanoke. A few were on scholarship—the school awarded about $15,000 a year in grants—but most had been born into prosperous families whose names were well known in their own communities if not in the world at large; to these parents, the tuition of $1,800 was a small price to pay for the value their daughters received.

Chatham Hall was very much in loco parentis for these girls and highly conscious of its disciplinary obligations. Rules were strict and inflexible: no student could leave campus without permission; smoking was "absolutely forbidden"; the words "WHITE FLAG" on a door meant that it could not be entered, and on an object that it could not be touched or moved; at the snack bar in the Tea Room, students could spend only twenty-five cents a day, "including ten cents worth of candy or crackers to be taken outside"; contraband articles, apart from cigarettes, included matches, chewing gum, radios and phonographs, "an unnecessary amount of cosmetics," flashlights and "movie and other trashy magazines"; students wishing to make telephone calls had to have the dean's permission, calls could be taken only at certain hours—and only from parents. Offenses that resulted in automatic expulsion were cheating, stealing and drinking; each year a couple of girls usually were sent packing, often after unpleasant confrontations between the rector and distraught, infuriated parents.

Rules governing dress were no less stringent; they were designed not only to impose a degree of uniformity, but also to discourage the conspicuous display of wealth: "We are deeply anxious to preserve a certain simplicity in the life of our students, and to keep them from being extravagant and from competing with each other with elaborate wardrobes." Each girl could have a total of fifteen dresses, with "a sweater, jacket or skirt to count as one-half of a dress." One heavy coat was recommended, but fur coats were forbidden, and "all jewelry except that of an inexpensive kind will be sent home." All clothing was required to be distinctly and conspicuously marked, to facilitate sorting in the laundry. Students could bring "one *small* pillow and one *small* stuffed animal" to put on their beds, could hang no more than two framed pictures on the walls of their double rooms, and could have no more than four pictures, framed or unframed, on their dressers.

Spartan though it may sound, it was a life that produced remarkably little complaint. The girls were kept so busy that they had hardly any time in which to formulate anything more than passing gripes about the conditions of their existence. They rose at seven, breakfasted at eight, attended a brief assembly, then spent the morning in class, with a ten-minute break for milk and cookies. Lunch was at noon. If a guest was there for a meal, he or she was subjected to a welcoming ditty, which over the years I heard more times than I care to remember:

> *Johnny, we're glad to see you,*
> *Johnny, we're glad to hear you,*
> *Johnny, we're glad to have you*
> *Back at Chatham Hall.*
>
> *Since you went away,*
> *We've waited here to say,*
> *Johnny, we're glad to have you—*
> *Stand up and bow to all!*

After lunch came a period during which students rested in their rooms or consulted with teachers; athletics began in mid-afternoon and lasted for a couple of hours; the daily chapel service was held in early evening, followed immediately by dinner; the night was given over to a brief free period and then study hall; all girls had to be in their rooms at ten before ten, and at ten sharp lights went out.

In the classroom and in extracurricular life, stringent demands were placed on them. The curriculum, both the general course and the college preparatory, placed a heavy emphasis on traditional studies: English, modern languages, religious education, history, mathematics, science; Latin was required for at least three years, and there were no courses in the domestic sciences. Outside of class, opportunities were everywhere. There were, as there always are in schools, clubs galore: the Astronomy Club and the Bird Club and the Camera Club and the Junior and Senior French Clubs and the Music Club. The most admired and responsible students rose to the Student Council, the chief instrument of student government, or to leadership of one of the Service League's seven departments: School Life, Devotional, World Outlook, Altar Guild, Social Outlook, Race Relations and Northfield League—this last being an interscholastic organization devoted to worship and service, which met each summer in New England. For horsy girls there was the Bit and Spur Club, for singers the Choir and Glee Club, for thespians the Sherwood Dramatic Club, for those of a literary bent the *Anonymous* and the *Chathamite*—not to mention the Bootery Committee and the Junior Proctors and the Citizenship League and the Mail Marshals and the Color Squad.

Speaking of which: the school's colors were purple and gold, because its first literary magazine, the *Iris*, had been bound with purple and gold ribbons. The intramural teams were the Purples and the Golds; once an incoming student was placed on her team, she was there for life. Among the annual events of that life were the Christmas Pageant, at which the great moment was the unveiling of the Madonna—a girl secretly chosen by the rector because of her kindness, generosity and character—and the Lantern Ceremony at commencement, when under the moonlight the graduating seniors passed along their lanterns to the girls whose class would succeed them. In "The Well," at the center of Pruden Hall, was a staircase that could be used only by seniors; to sit there after dinner, singing songs and chatting, basking in the envy of the underclassmen (as in those days they were called), was the height of glory. And of course there was an Alma Mater:

> *School days bright, that fly so swiftly*
> *Down life's stream beyond recall,*
> *Leave within our hearts abiding*
> *Loyalty to Chatham Hall.*

Chorus

Chatham Hall, our Alma Mater,
  Love for thee, a pledge for all,
And forever and forever,
  We'll be true to Chatham Hall.

When the golden sun is sinking
And the shadows o'er us fall,
Memories will take us backward
  To our days at Chatham Hall.

Mush, pure and simple: so why does it still move me so? Because I remember all those lovely girls and because there was in the Lantern Ceremony, when those words were sung, something so innocent and beautiful that only the stoniest heart could go unmoved. Chatham Hall may well have been an enclave of privilege surrounded by a countryside where poverty and discrimination prevailed; but that must not be allowed to distract us from the essential goodness of the place itself. People were happy there, they learned and grew, and they left it with fond memories that never wholly faded. One of these, an alumna of slightly later vintage, summarized the place—its charm, its girlish frenzy, its enduring influence—in a letter to Bill and Helen at the time of their retirement:

There are so many things that I remember about Chatham. Sometimes I felt we were too restricted, but now I look back and know that everything at Chatham helped me considerably. I remember "The Well" and all our gatherings there, the bell to enter the dining room, the bell that woke us each morning, trying to find a pair of stockings without too many runs in them to wear to dinner, oxford shoes, Mondays in town, the history trips, study hall and not being able to smile at anyone, the honor system, sports and our uniforms, how affected I was by the meaning of them, drying my hair in fifteen minutes under the hand dryer in the bathroom before the bell rang to be in our rooms, "A" classification, the horseshows and the riding, Brunswick stew (I had never had it) at Thanksgiving, Sunday breakfast and those delicious rolls, chapel before dinner and the race to get there on time, my first exposure to the Episcopal

Church of which I am now a confirmed member, Miss Holt and her hilarious lectures each year at assembly on table manners, the minimum requirement to eat at meals, the Tea Room after sports, three-minute phone calls home and to my boyfriends . . . so many more things too numerous to mention.

To the girls of Chatham Hall, accustomed as they were to the gentle and elderly Edmund Lee, the new rector, at thirty-seven years of age, was a revelation. "Yards," as they quickly began calling him behind his back, was "terribly good looking and very dapper," one of them recalled: "In fact it sort of seemed as though we had our own Cary Grant to be our new rector." They quickly discovered that he was a compulsive winker and that it was pointless to freight his winks with any meaning because the gesture usually was unconscious. They also soon realized that he was a bundle of energy, his mind percolating with projects to be undertaken and innovations to be made.

He was not attempting to erase the long legacy of the Lees. Quite to the contrary, he was grateful for the "orderly and quiet succession" that the Lees had engineered and he was sincere when he told the alumnae, at the time of his appointment, that he expected to make few changes in the school's operation. But there was business that needed doing, and he was eager to be about it. A primary example was the school's fire-protection system: to all intents and purposes it had none. So Bill ordered the installation of sprinklers in Pruden and Dabney and the construction of a water tower—immediately christened "Yardley's Folly"—to supply them; that tower became the most visible Chatham landmark when the town and school were viewed from White Oak Mountain, six miles to the south on U.S. 29.

Bill also felt that Dr. Lee's regulations could use a bit of loosening. He decided to let girls wear Bermuda shorts to study hall, and he permitted them to walk unescorted to town on their weekly excursion; a little later in this early period of his rectorship, he gave seniors the privilege of one weekend away from school, and he allowed the whole student body to wear lipstick on weekends, a privilege previously extended only to seniors. In these modest liberalizations he was following the same precept that he and Helen were faithful to in rearing their own children: those young people grow up strongest who are given the most freedom, who are encouraged to be self-sufficient rather than dependent. He was ever mindful that he was ultimately responsible for the health and welfare of his students, so he resisted any relaxation in the rules that would take them beyond the bounds of his supervision, but he knew that the age of Victoria was over.

Bill further knew that what we now call "image" was important to a successful headmastership, and he worked hard on his own. His manner with the girls was friendly but correct, and with faculty and staff he maintained the formalities that polite society then observed: he was "Mr. Yardley" to everyone except Helen, and everyone was "Miss" or "Mrs." to him. Finishing school or no, Chatham Hall expected its students to learn proper manners, and Bill set an example that was, if anything, hyperbolic; he was courtliness to the extreme, bowing and hand-kissing and winking—always winking!—and raising his eyebrows and otherwise elaborately putting on airs. He was almost never without a coat and tie, usually the tweeds and regimental stripes that he favored, and he customarily wore a hat, felt in winter and straw in summer; he leaped at any opportunity to put on evening dress, and when he entered the ministry he found that a whole new sartorial universe had opened to him.

His relations with the faculty were, he well knew, of utmost importance to him, and he wasted no time in cementing them. He had the good fortune to inherit a faculty that was cohesive and mutually supportive; with only one teacher, a woman whose brilliance in the classroom was matched by the volatility of her temperament, did he have trouble, and his method of solving it was to ignore it. Some things, he thought, were better left alone; he believed that this teacher's contributions to the school outweighed the bruised feelings she caused among her fellow faculty, and he kept her far longer than he should have. He had spent enough time in the classroom to have some sense of the frustrations and resentments teachers feel; he tried to ameliorate them by giving the faculty a stronger voice in the school's affairs. In the mid-fifties he established a scholarship fund that financed travel and study overseas; in 1957 he practically coerced Mary Virginia Gillam, his Latin teacher, into a summer at the American Academy in Rome, a sojourn that she ever thereafter cherished.

For the most part the faculty gave Bill little trouble, but occasionally there were exceptions. Early in his tenure a librarian was discovered to be an inebriate, hiding liquor in her room and staggering around the campus; Bill tried to be patient with her and offered medical assistance, but the poor woman declined it and reeled into the unknown, never to be heard from again. Then there was the large, amiable woman who suddenly died, leaving a husband whose grief was a most evanescent thing. After her cremation her ashes were stuck in a drawer of Bill's desk, where they remained for years; at last he concluded that the husband never would fetch them and scattered them over the campus himself, while making a helicopter inspection of it.

Bill's office was always open to the faculty, but his principal means of communicating with its members was the faculty meeting held each Tuesday evening. At first this was in Miss Holt's office, then it moved to the living room of the Rectory. "Well, we haven't much to do tonight," Miss Holt would say: and the faculty silently groaned, knowing the meeting would go on an hour or more. In the Rectory, Bill stood at one end of the long room and Helen sat on the steps at the other; by gesture and voice, she played a vital role in orchestrating the meeting, nodding approvingly when she sensed Bill was on the right track and shaking her head firmly when she thought his flamboyant streak was getting the better of him.

Customarily the faculty meeting was devoted to routine business that will be familiar to anyone who has worked in education. The academic records of individual students were reviewed, examination schedules were set, class rankings for college admissions were determined. But Bill also used these sessions as bully pulpits for his own strong views of what a school—a private school in particular—should do. There, and in letters to the alumnae, he set out what can be called, somewhat grandiosely, his philosophy of education.

"No school can be stronger than its faculty," he said. "This is a truism and like most truisms it happens to be true." What, then, is a good teacher? "*First*, the good teacher knows and loves her subject. . . . *Second*, the good teacher understands and genuinely likes young people. . . . *Third*, the truly good teacher understands the philosophy of the school she is in and is loyal to that philosophy. . . . *Fourth*, the good teacher has something on the ball professionally, she is never content to drift along in the old rut. . . . *Fifth* and last, the good teacher knows herself and her own limitations. She is a wise old bird and she knows very well that there are lots of booby traps and pitfalls for the unwary." She is "a big enough person to admit when she has been mistaken or when she doesn't know the answer," she "gets on well with all her colleagues whether they are particularly congenial or not," and she "remembers that the administration of the school is here to help her do a better job."

He spoke with real ardor of "the ancient craft of school-teaching" and the traditions out of which it developed: Jerusalem, "the fountain from which have come the moral and the ethical and the spiritual traditions of our people"; Athens, "the source of intellectual curiosity and freedom of the mind"; Rome, "the tradition of law and order, of precedent and fixed procedure, of justice and duty and the proud privilege of citizenship"; England, "the stream which is so important to us in our daily living," this being the liberating effect of the Industrial Revolution; and Virginia, where "in Jamestown was convened the first meeting of a representative body in North America and in Williamsburg were trained the men who founded our republic—where Jefferson said, 'The God who gave us life gave us liberty at the same time.'" Of the Industrial Revolution, Bill had more to say:

> America is the land in which this fourth tradition has reached its highest fulfillment. England used to be the school teacher of the world; now it is the turn of the United States to show techniques to others. We must remember the great importance of this fourth tradition but we must not let it usurp the places of the others. We cannot afford to let the tail wag the dog. We cannot let our civilization be only a material thing. We must remember that man does not live by bread alone or by synthetic fibers which may keep him warm but not happy.

He was a conservative man and he ran a conservative school, one that trained girls for the roles they reasonably could be expected to assume as women. In addressing this subject we do well to avoid the pitfalls of what historians now call "presentism": judging yesterday according to the convictions of today. In the early 1950s the bright light of feminism was nowhere to be seen—publication of *The Feminine Mystique* lay a decade ahead—and most parents who sent their daughters off to school anticipated that marriage and motherhood were the fates awaiting them. Bill, whose expectations for his own daughters were at heart the same and whose wife preferred to be addressed as Mrs. William W. Yardley, agreed; he quoted with approval the saw, "When you educate a boy you are educating only a breadwinner and a citizen, but when you educate a girl you educate a family and a home." Women, he believed, "have their own unique contribution to make and to them is often given an insight and a tender compassion which should be trained and directed."

Yet he also believed that "one of the great tragedies of American life is to see a woman's intellectual life end with marriage." Girls with good minds "have as much right as any boy to follow their interests and abilities." Further: "Our education has been dominated by the intellectual snobbery of the men's graduate schools. Women should be freed from the limitations which this snobbery implies and be free to develop their own aesthetic talents." In the end, though, he sided with the world he best knew: "A secondary school for girls must always bear in mind the future womanhood and motherhood of its students and the homes in which they will live. . . . Girls cannot develop into men, but they can develop into something just as good."

That first year at Chatham Hall was, for Bill and all of his family, one great rush of excitement and surprise and delight. We were in our new world, learning how it worked, discovering its traditions and rituals. In years to come we realized that 1949–1950 was a year like all years, that in the life of a school repetition is far more common than change, and soon enough the Yardleys settled as comfortably into Chatham Hall's routines as if they'd known them all their lives. But that first year was a journey into the unknown, a journey worth traveling one more time.

September: New students arrive on the twenty-first, old ones the following day: total enrollment, a hundred sixty. A "wild treasure hunt" is put on for the new girls, followed by a picnic and appointment of a new co-captain of the Purples. A candlelight ceremony is held for the new co-chairman of the Social Outlook Department.

October: The seniors attend their first Senior Tea at the Rectory, in white gloves. Dr. James Cleland of Duke University preaches at Sunday chapel. The twenty-nine cows in the dairy are each given names, and wooden plaques proclaiming them are mounted. A rabies scare sweeps the campus and inoculations are prescribed: "Mr. Yardley proudly becomes the first punctured and announces the campus as being off bounds to Unknown or Hungry Canines." The trustees meet. The film *I Remember Mama* is shown. The seniors, with Bill and Helen in charge, make their annual weekend trip to Williamsburg.

November: The Dramatic Club presents *Candida*. The school is taken by bus to a French movie in Danville. Dr. Van Walt, a psychologist, talks on Russia. Willis Hall is drowned in a flood of tears as *How Green Was My Valley* is shown. On Thanksgiving the Senior Quartet performs in the Meadow, followed by a Brunswick stew picnic and, in the evening, a performance of *The Devil and Daniel Webster.* The annual Gymkhana and Glee Club concert are held.

December: Sir Hubert Wilkins talks about life under the Arctic. The Dramatic Club inducts four new members. The Christmas Pageant is presented, with Karen Fagerburg "the perfect Madonna." On the sixteenth, the girls are driven to the railroad station and put aboard the various Southern Railroad trains that will take them home.

January: School resumes on the third. In chemistry class silver is manufactured and in Latin the march to Bibracte is retraced. Seniors take the Scholastic Aptitude Test. Exams begin: "Tradition marches in an unexpected manner, when Mr. Yardley appears wearing a Scotch cap!" The Lees arrive, from their retirement in Shepherdstown, West Virginia, for their first visit.

February: A "Bowl of Rice" party is held, at which "Mr. Yardley acquires and adequately demonstrates the true Chinese methods of handling chopsticks"; the next day he is auctioneer at a sale of Chinese posters. Dance Weekend is held. Charlie Eagleplume "demonstrates Indian dances and holds the school spellbound in telling the conditions of the reservations." Across town, fire sweeps through the buildings at Hargrave Military Academy. The Purples win the field-hockey game.

March: At Willis Hall, Bayley Winder presents the Arab side of the Palestine question. Spring holidays begin on the sixteenth and end on the twenty-eighth.

April: Easter brings the spring picnic, Easter eggs, and a profusion of bright new hats. Senior essays are composed. A production of the operetta *Martha* is staged, and a film, *Picturesque Poland*, is shown.

May: Final examinations. At a "quiet and very impressive service in the Chapel," the next year's Service League cabinet is installed. The Senior Banquet is held, with singing by the Senior Quartet.

June: Commencement. On Sunday the fourth the baccalaureate is preached and, in the evening, the seniors and juniors march in the Lantern Ceremony. Monday, Class Day, is occupied with the distribution and signing of yearbooks. On Tuesday Dr. Lee gives the invocation and benediction as the Commencement rites are held.

That was June 6, 1950. In a rush of trains and automobiles the girls went off for the summer, leaving the campus suddenly, eerily still; for all the years the Yardleys lived there, the quiet that descended on Chatham Hall in early June always came as a surprise. Now the campus was ours. For this first summer Bill and Helen chose to stay in Chatham, a decision that by August they realized was a mistake; they needed to get away from the school and from the heat of Southside, and beginning the next year they rented a bungalow in Middletown, Rhode Island, for two months each summer. But in 1950 Bill gave me a job working on the farm—for ten cents an hour I helped load bales of hay onto trucks and stamp down chopped corn as it poured into the silo—and devoted himself to preparing for the coming academic year.

We were fully at home there now, and quite a home it was. To all of us the Rectory seemed a palace, a grander house than any of us ever could have imagined would be ours—though of course it was not ours but the school's, a reality of which we were always dimly but somewhat uncomfortably aware. It had been built by the Lees a couple of decades before, modeled after the St. George Tucker house in Williamsburg. Of the structures that stood along the main drive through the campus, it was the only one made of wood, which was painted white. Its central section was two and a half stories high, on either side of which was a wing. As you entered the front hallway, the dining room was to the right; the kitchen wing was beyond it, with a small servant's room above. To the left of the hall was a small study, in which Helen put the desk they had purchased with the Hull house in Tuxedo Park; beyond the study was a little hall that led past a flower room (a closet, really) to the guest wing. On the second story were four bedrooms, two baths and a laundry; the attic was at that time unfinished, though later a bedroom was built there for me.

The great glory of the Rectory was the living room, which you entered by going down two steps at the end of the hall. It was approximately eighteen feet wide by twenty-five feet long and was paneled in butternut, a variety of walnut that yields a deep, rich brown wood of medium intensity. There were bookshelves in nearly every inch of wall that was not taken by windows, and in nooks beside two windows on the right side of the room. On the left side was a window seat that looked out at a bird feeder on which "Dr. Lee" had been written; Bill was much pleased when I said, "Shouldn't it be 'Mr. Yardley' now?" At the far end of the room were glass double doors that opened onto the rear porch, above which was a screened-in porch where Jane and I slept in the summer.

From the porch we stepped down to the yard, but *yard* was scarcely the word for it. Though a wooden fence surrounded what was the Rectory yard proper, the land rolled on and on, down the hill to the poultry farm; miles beyond that lay the Blue Ridge,

The Rectory, as seen from front and rear

which was indeed the color of its name and which loomed in the distance, evoking images of Daniel Boone and the West beyond. We could see the chicken house, and the Gatewoods' residence beside it, and in the distance a small dwelling or two; but otherwise all was farmland and woods, an ethereal natural prospect. There were huge, spreading trees in the yard, oaks and elms, and enough space to kick a football; eventually Bill installed a large above-ground pool, in which he cooled himself after each of his many suntanning sessions—a deep suntan being of course necessary to set off his headmasterly tweeds and silk ties.

The house wasn't ours in fact, but we made it ours in spirit; returning there is now extremely difficult for me, because nothing is stranger than going home when it no longer is home. Back in the early 1950s the staid house was filled with the shouts of children and the click of small feet, as Jane and I and our friends—and soon Sarah and hers—raced up and down the staircase, in and out of the doors. Jane and Sarah shared one of the rear bedrooms and I had the other, which came with my very own fireplace. Helen had the larger of the two in front, which was connected to Bill's room by the bathroom they shared; they chose to use separate rooms because Bill claimed to be bothered by Helen's snoring, but often in the morning we found them together in Helen's double bed, the covers pulled snugly up to their chins. It was not until years later that we deduced the significance of their modesty.

In these first years Helen was primarily a housewife. For the first time since her own childhood she had domestic service, primarily in the person of Annie Townes, a forceful and competent woman; others included Rosetta Hamm and May Lemon Devins, who finally decided she'd had enough and left a farewell note that stated, with simple eloquence, "Mrs. Yardley: I am gone." The racial dynamics of the South were utterly alien to Helen, and she had more than a little difficulty figuring out how to accommodate herself to them without being untrue to herself. She always treated her hired help with respect, and she made certain that her children did so as well; the word *nigger*, so commonly used on the streets of Chatham, was forbidden in her house, *colored* then being thought the polite term. But she was married to a man of conservative if not racist upbringing, and she was unaccustomed to encountering blacks in any except servile roles; so there is no use suggesting that on matters racial the Rectory was a citadel of enlightenment, only that it seemed so by comparison with what lay around it.

Helen and Bill's views were actually more pronounced about whites whom they considered inferior to themselves; the relationship with blacks was if nothing else clear, while that with whites was often ambiguous and, in their view, unhealthy for their children. It did not take them long to conclude that a considerable proportion of the citizenry of Pittsylvania County was made up of poor white trash, and that much of this trash could be found on the grounds of the Chatham Elementary School. Farm boys in dungarees and girls in calico, some of them barefoot, were my classmates and Jane's; we thought they were pretty neat kids, even if a bully or two teased us about our Yankee accents, but Bill and Helen ridiculed them mercilessly. When my brother, Ben, was in school he had a classmate who was called by his first initial—Q. or some such—which they considered hopelessly rustic and made mean sport of.

"How's P.D.Q.?" Bill would ask at the end of the day.

"Was A.B.C. there today?" Helen chimed in.

Mimicking the local accent, they referred to the school as "the Alimentary School," and spoke contemptuously about the teachers there, most of whom they regarded as ignorant and incompetent. In a few instances they were correct; I remember with no pleasure a homeroom teacher of stern and humorless demeanor who regarded it as her chosen mission to inflict upon her charges the doctrines of the Southern Baptist Church, which she did with a most unattractive—not to mention unconstitutional—enthusiasm. But in more cases they were wrong; these teachers were decent, hardworking women trying to shed a little light in an area where poverty and illiteracy were commonplace, and the barbs that Bill and Helen directed at them were undeserved.

Nor did they do the Yardley children much good. It is hard not to listen to one's parents talk as Bill and Helen did without being influenced by it, especially when one's parents are as intelligent, articulate and persuasive as ours were. Jane really wanted to be one of the gang, wearing blue jeans and going barefoot, but Helen decked her out in frocks from Best & Co. and sent her off looking like a little princess; she simply could not comprehend that her children were attending school in an environment utterly different from that in which she herself had, and as a result she sent us into that world at a definite social disadvantage.

Notwithstanding the aura of snobbery with which we were afflicted, I remember those grade-school years in Chatham as happy ones. Henry Hammer and I were the best of friends, and we had plenty of kids to play with—Billy White, Claude Whitehead, Johnny Motley—all of whom got a kick out of having the run of Chatham Hall's athletic fields when the girls were away. We played baseball on the lower athletic field, one boy at bat and three or four others out in the field: real country baseball, or a close approximation of it. At night I lay in the dark listening to games from St. Louis and Chicago on the Zenith table radio I'd bought with my farmhand's earnings. Often I sat at Helen's portable typewriter and tried my hand at newspapering, with results that I solemnly posted on the bulletin board in the arcade between Pruden and Dabney, for the delectation and instruction of the girls:

Buy JOHNNY YARDLEY

SPORT NEWS

There has been a talked about situation on maybe changing the American League and the National League and have just the opposit. The Yankees seem to be doing the best this year and the Indians don't seem to be doing so well , probly the yankees will play either the Cards or the Dodgers , the Red SOX don't seem to be very well either.

The Chatham Tigers finished second in the conty race.
Enter FORDS $100,000 car safety contest
win one of 700 valuable prizes

GRUBB & TERRY, inc.

Phone 480i   CHATHAN VA. . . . . .J.Y.

Helen was no baseball fan herself, but she was happy to let my mania flower. I had switched allegiance from the Yankees to the Indians—their games came in loud and clear on my radio—and was thrilled to the marrow when she returned from a trip to New York with a copy of *Player-Manager*, by the eminent Cleveland shortstop Lou Boudreau. Another trip brought biographies of Ted Williams and Jackie Robinson; the firm of A. S. Barnes, for which her sister, Minnie, was then working, annually published books about the previous season's Most Valuable Players, and these two had been the 1949 winners. One was signed, "To Johnny Yardley, Best Wishes from Ted Williams," and the other was autographed by Jackie Robinson, Duke Snider, Roy Campanella and Carl Furillo. Years later I returned to Chatham to reclaim these books, only to learn—to my horror—that Helen in one of her periodic house-cleanings had invaded my room and donated them to the Chatham Public Library. She had also thrown away my hundreds of early-1950s baseball cards.

Around or about this time Bill was called upon to fill out a form describing me, which he did as follows: "Fairly even disposition. Rather untidy. Lazy except when interested. Gets on well with boys and girls. Careless of own health. Often needs jacking up on personal cleanliness. Can be most winning and attractive. Responds warmly to friendliness. Very dogmatic in statements. Embarrassed by father's position as head of girls' school. Considers parents hopelessly old-fashioned." Snips and snails and puppy dogs' tails, that's what I was: Bill and Helen thought it high time for me to get a little polish. They sensed, correctly, that a girls' school was not the best environment for me as I screeched into puberty, and they had no reason to believe that at the Chatham public schools I could be so thoroughly educated as they had been. So in the fall of 1950 they began inquiring about boarding schools, and in the spring of the next year they settled upon one: Woodberry Forest, one hundred fifty miles to the northeast in Orange, which had been kind enough to offer me a scholarship.

In order to enter Woodberry's lowest grade, the eighth—second form, in the Anglophilic terminology of American boys' prep schools—it was necessary for me to skip the seventh grade. So in

June of 1951, en route to Rhode Island, Bill and Helen dropped me off at the house of a friend, who lived near the school and at weekend's end drove me over to Woodberry for the summer session. I was eleven years old, but thought little about being sent off at so tender an age. I had a night or two of homesickness, then entered happily into the life of the school. I had two blissful years at Woodberry and one miserable one. Bill and Helen missed me, and I them, but even though a fair amount of unhappiness awaited me before the liberation that college afforded, I know that they did what they believed was best for me and at no small sacrifice to themselves, both financial and emotional.

But I did miss life at the Rectory, for it was unfailingly interesting and surprising. As often as several nights a week the guest room was occupied, and frequently by uncommonly interesting people, because that was where the men and women who came to talk and preach and entertain at the school usually stayed. The great Irish-born novelist Elizabeth Bowen once sat in the living room before a rapt audience of a hundred girls, responding warmly to their sharp, bright questions; afterward she told Bill, "I enjoyed this afternoon more than any other visit I have made in America." A young flutist named Jean-Pierre Rampal passed through, as did the poet William Jay Smith and the British critic Colin Wilson. Jim Cleland's visits were especially cherished by Bill and Helen; the Duke chaplain had a boisterous sense of humor and a rich Scots burr that he cultivated luxuriously.

In the morning these guests were at the breakfast table, bringing the outside world to a couple who sorely missed it. For all its physical beauty and for all the camaraderie that the Chatham Hall community enjoyed, there was no getting around its isolation. Danville, eighteen miles away, was a tobacco and textiles city; eventually Bill and Helen made friends there, but Danville had no cultural life. Lynchburg was fifty miles up Route 29 and offered little except better shopping; Helen bought most of the Rectory's new furnishings there. Lynchburg also had an airport, which scheduled more flights than Danville's and thus more chances for escape to the world they knew best. It was in Lynchburg that Bill and Helen developed the "martini trick." The airport had no bar, so they provided their own. They took a flask of pre-mixed martinis with them, and on arrival put a nickel into the soft-drink machine; as soon as the cup had filled with ice they jerked it out, and poured the martini in. It made the Lynchburg airport, and flight, infinitely more tolerable.

In Chatham in those days they did not drink when school was in session. Bill's watch was in twenty-four-hour shifts seven days a week, and he feared that he might compromise himself had he alcohol on his breath or, worse, were he under its influence; further, the town of Chatham was bone dry, and he did not care to thumb his nose publicly—though God knows he did privately—at local mores. They kept the liquor they'd bought at the A.B.C. store in Danville locked away in the sideboard, but as soon as each vacation began they turned the key. Precisely at six each evening they put a nest table in front of the two easy chairs they occupied, and brought out a tray covered with cheese and crudités and crackers. They had two martinis each, and went to the dining room in mellow humor. At vacation's end Bill and I drove far out into the countryside and tossed the empties off a bridge into the stream below.

When school was in session they ate lunch and dinner at the dining room in Pruden Hall. Theirs was the rector's table; teachers and administrators had the head seats at the others, and the students rotated among them. Only on Sunday, when a light supper was served at school, and on Monday, when the weekly "Birthday Dinner" was held, did they dine at home. The latter was for eight or ten girls whose birthdays fell during that week; girls whose birthdays occurred during vacations were fit in over the course of the school year. They sat down to a dinner of fried chicken, mashed potatoes, a vegetable, ice cream and birthday cake. Then they adjourned to the living room for Sanka and "The Game," a variation on charades. The evening ended with Coca-Colas, and by nine the girls were on their way back to the dormitories. Bill and Helen did this every schooltime Monday night for twenty-two years; how they stood it, I cannot imagine.

To all intents and purposes the Rectory was a public house. Not merely were there the birthday festivities, but each Sunday there was a formal coffee for the faculty and a different group of students: one time they invited all the girls who hailed from Arkansas, who shivered the Rectory's timbers by bursting out in their state's famed Razorback cheer. Helen sat on Thomas Howe Yardley's sofa beside the fireplace, pouring coffee from a large silver urn that the school had obtained from Lizzie Gilman's estate. This may seem a tedious if not onerous duty, but the truth is that Helen thrived on it. She loved to bring out her silver and china and linens, and she firmly believed that one of her most important obligations at Chatham Hall was to set an example for the girls of how a woman—a *lady*, as in those days we called her—should look and act.

Her efforts in that direction were not limited to pouring tea. She became active as a sponsor of the Service League and the Alumnae Association, and she offered the Rectory itself as a model of what an educated woman's house should be. She and Bill had arranged the furniture themselves—their engaging the services of a decorator is inconceivable—in a style that blended formality and simplicity. By the positioning of various Yardley-Gregory chairs and sofas they broke the living room into three sitting areas; the fourth quarter was occupied by a grand piano, the only piece of school furniture in the room and one that received frequent use at student gatherings. It was a room in which white-glove receptions could be held; it was also a room in which the Yardley children could lie around in disarray, reading or doing puzzles or playing Monopoly.

There was no television set. From the day they first learned of that medium, Bill and Helen were convinced that it offered little for children except distraction from reading, schoolwork and other more edifying pursuits. They did not allow a set in the house until the assassination of President Kennedy convinced them that television could permit them to be witnesses to history; they got one in time for the 1964 presidential race between Lyndon Johnson and Barry Goldwater. But by the mid-1950s there was a set in Dabney Hall's basement recreation room; it was there, during school

Bill in his office, with two of his model ships

holidays in 1957, that I cheered for the North Carolina Tar Heels—soon to be *my* Tar Heels—as they won the intercollegiate basketball tournament.

For his part, Bill found recreation in his own room. While Helen read downstairs, Bill went to the desk he had installed in his bedroom and worked on models, at which he soon became professionally expert. He began with balsa models of antique automobiles, which he turned out at a prodigious rate; he gave them away as prizes at school events, but I fear that none of them survives. He tired of this before long and went on to ships. First he made kits—Sue and I have his superb model of the *Sea Witch*—and then he switched to original plans, which he scaled down and modeled from scratch. At these labors he was astonishingly patient, slaving happily for hours on the most minute details of rigging and deckwork; his models were his escape from the school and its cares, an escape that doubtless did much to preserve his sanity—and his family's.

That family expanded by one a couple of times each year, when Louise Yardley came to visit. At Christmas she was either in Stamford, Connecticut, with Harry and Elsie, or with us in Chatham, and in the spring she stopped over en route from Chestnut Hill to her annual stay with Woolsey relatives in Aiken, South Carolina; by tenacious frugality she had slowly built her small legacy from Tom Yardley into a comfortable cushion. The tension level at the Rectory always went up a couple of notches when she was there; she still made Bill nervous, and Helen had always been a trifle wary around her. But we children liked her just fine; she loved to play games and read aloud, and she found all of us entirely amusing.

The Gregory grandparents must have visited us in Chatham, but I have no memory of it. On the first of July, 1953, Alfred Gregory had a convulsion; we were at the bungalow we rented in Rhode Island and Helen left immediately for Maplewood, but did not get there in time to see him before he died. His widow lived almost four more years, but not happily. She had a succession of strokes, the first of them well before Alfred's death, and over the years her temperament slowly changed; in place of her characteristic good cheer, she became irritable and demanding. When she died on May 27, 1957, Helen felt more relief than sorrow. "I pray to God I'm never sick and helpless like that," she said, and when Jane started to cry she blurted out: "Don't be sorry. It's the best thing that could have happened." Soon the house in Brewster was sold—the Maplewood house had gone after Alfred's death—and an inheritance of about $25,000 was bestowed on each of the children of Alfred and Helen Gregory. The four returned to their separate lives; they remained affectionate but saw each other only rarely, to the regret of all.

Mercifully, long before Helen Ingersoll Gregory's death, new life had come to the Rectory. It was entirely accidental. One weekend in the winter of 1952 Bill and Helen had gone to the mountains for a visit with friends in Lexington. Good cheer was poured in abundance, and amorous spirits were aroused. The birth-control device was back in Chatham, but what the hell? As Bill used to say: "What do you call people who use the rhythm method? Parents." That is just what Bill and Helen became, for the fourth time, on August 16, 1953.

The two Benjamins:
Woolsey and Yardley

THEY NAMED him Benjamin, in honor of Benjamin Woolsey. This good and pious gentleman we have already met. What remains to be said of him is that as well as a faithful minister of the Lord, he was a devoted husband and father. In 1714 he married Abigail Taylor, who brought to their union a tract of land nearly one thousand acres in size on the North Shore of Long Island, in and about what is now Glen Cove; it had been purchased from the Matinicock Indians, no doubt for the proverbial string of beads, in 1668, and had passed through several owners before being conveyed to Abigail's father, John Taylor. They called this estate "Dosoris"—from the Latin *dos uxoris*, "wife's dower"—and happily lived there until Benjamin's death in 1756 and Abigail's in 1771. The land was divided between their two sons but was sold after the death of Benjamin's son and namesake; what remains in the family is the Woolsey cemetery on Lattingtown Road, a few hundred yards south of Dosoris Pond and Dosoris Island.

That Bill and Helen named their fourth child Benjamin probably had as much to do with their fondness for the name—most certainly "Benjamin Yardley" has a harmonious and dignified sound to it—as with the ancient cleric's good works. There can be no question, though, that Bill was drawn to the name because it gave his family yet another tie to the Woolseys, whom of all his ancestors he treasured most. Of Bill and Helen's children, all but Jonathan were named for Woolseys—Jane Andrews Woolsey, Sarah Chauncey Woolsey, Benjamin Woolsey—and for that matter the connection to Jonathan Edwards had been made through the Woolseys. Bill claimed to dislike his middle name, but that was nothing except false modesty; he adored it, and everything about the Woolseys. Before moving to Chatham he commissioned a portrait of his own namesake and hung it over the mantel in the Rectory, and on June 28, 1967, he wrote a memorandum to the executors of his estate that specified: "I wish cremation instead of burial. I request that the ashes be interred in the Woolsey family burial plot at Glen Cove, Long Island."

This namesake, William Walton Woolsey, was born at "Dosoris" in 1766. His was the fifth generation of Woolseys in America; the settler, George Woolsey, came from Yarmouth, his birthplace, to New Amsterdam in 1623 aboard a Dutch ship, and died in Jamaica in 1698. He and the Woolseys who followed were farmers and ministers—country people, anything except wealthy—but William Walton Woolsey was determined to be a man of commerce. As a youth he went to Manhattan; "he could not afford a candle or lamp," one of his grandsons wrote, "and by the bright moonlight he read through the British poets." He loved Shakespeare and the theater, and he was a man of strong religious and moral commitment, but neither his artistic nor his spiritual inclinations dampened his eagerness to enter the marketplace. He established himself as a merchant, and in time was elected president of the Merchant's Exchange, which position he held for three decades. His investments and business activities were widespread, as his grandson reported:

> He was a man of wise judgments, conservative, yet full of enterprise, taking a leading part in the enterprises of the times: the steamboat lines on the Sound; the first railroads, the Boston and Providence (of which he was president for several years), the New

Jersey (now the Pennsylvania) et cetera. He was one of the founders of the Jersey associates which owned Jersey City.

In 1792 William married Eliza Dwight, a connection in which Bill took excessive pride. She was the granddaughter of Jonathan Edwards and the sister of Timothy Dwight, who was noted as one of the Connecticut Wits and as president of Yale, which office he held from 1795 until his death in 1817. Dwight was a commanding figure in early-nineteenth-century American intellectual life whose influence on Yale, and thus on American higher education, was immeasurable—but he was related to the Yardleys only by marriage, and Bill's repeated efforts to represent the tie as closer always caused me slight embarrassment.

Still, it was Timothy Dwight who enabled Bill to make a public-spirited gesture in 1964, when he learned that the White House librarians, who were assembling a small collection of classic American books, had been unable to find a copy of Dwight's *Travels in New England and New York;* Bill and Helen gave their copy to the White House in memory of John F. Kennedy, which gift was recognized by—what else?—a near life-sized photograph of Lyndon B. Johnson, signed for the Yardleys by L.B.J. himself.

William and Eliza Woolsey had seven children, one of them being Bill's great-grandfather John Mumford Woolsey, but Eliza died, in 1813, before all of them were grown. Later William married Sarah Chauncey; they had no children of their own, but Sarah was beloved as a "kind, loving, large-minded stepmother." William himself was, for all his high standing in the business community, a person who loved a good scrape. Once, returning to his house on Greenwich Street late at night, he was warned by his wife that there was a prowler in the basement. He found a man inside the family safe, and quickly trapped him by sitting on the lid. He told Sarah to get the servants, but just then the burglar tried to lift the lid.

"My dear," William said, "give me first that spit." Sarah fetched the piece of iron from the wall—and William used its sharp point to jab the prowler's fingers back into the safe.

Finally, when his manservant appeared, William released his

captive. "Now, you rascal," he said, "I will give you your choice between being taken to jail or having a flogging on the spot!" The burglar chose the latter: William took off his coat, called for a heavy whip, and did the deed himself, with gusto.

On another occasion the intrepid William spotted a fellow sneaking out of his cellar with a keg of butter on his shoulder. He followed the culprit for a long distance until he put down his burden and sat to rest. William tapped him on the shoulder. "Now, my friend," he said, "you may turn about and put that keg of butter just where you found it!" The man took the measure of the hefty merchant, sighed wearily, and plodded back to the cellar. He was given the same choice as had been offered to the earlier prowler, and he chose the same punishment.

"But Papa," William's children said, "would it not be better to shut up the poor man in jail rather than to whip him?"

"No," William sensibly replied. "The flogging did him a great deal of good, and the jail would have taught him a great deal of harm."

William hoped that his son Theodore would succeed him in business, but Sarah persuaded him to let the youth follow his heart and mind. This he did at Yale, where he pursued theological studies and obtained a license to preach; he was not confident of his moral fitness for the task, however, and chose instead to study in Europe. He became an eminent classicist, in which capacity Yale appointed him professor of Greek language and literature. In 1846 he was elected president of the college; once again he questioned his fitness, but this time decided to serve. His long presidency was distinguished by improvements to the curriculum and the physical plant, including construction of the Peabody Museum of Natural History.

That Theodore Dwight Woolsey was a man of stature is beyond dispute, but his biographies give no hint of joie de vivre. For this we must turn to his sister Laura, who at the age of fifteen achieved her small place in the family's history. Her parents were planning a wedding party for one of William's cousins, and her mother was asked if she intended to invite her own cousin Aaron Burr—both were grandchildren of Jonathan Edwards—who not long before had killed Alexander Hamilton in their historic duel. "Certainly not," her mother said, "I shall never invite Mr. Burr to the house again, though should I meet him I should speak to him civilly, as he is my cousin."

But after supper the doorbell rang, and who should be admitted to the room but the contemptible Burr. Laura, who was seated beside the bride-to-be, turned to her and said in a stage whisper, "There is that horrid Mr. Burr thrusting himself in uninvited! *I* won't speak to him anyway!"

Burr made the rounds, shaking hands with all present; he "was received with entire but cold politeness." He was introduced to the bride, to whom he "made some very polite speeches." Then he turned to Laura, who sat frozen in outrage and fear. He looked at her a moment, then chucked her under the chin and said, "You saucy chit!"

It is easy to see why Bill so admired and envied the Woolseys, and so cherished his Woolsey ancestry. The Woolseys were people of position and power: not one of the famous American families, perhaps, but indisputably an eminent one. They had established themselves in education, the law, literature and commerce; their familial connections included Edwards and Dwight and Burr—a mixed bag, to be sure—and they were welcome in the best houses of the East Coast. The Woolseys had money, and they managed to hold on to it through the generations; by contrast, such small assets as the Yardleys and Gregorys may once have possessed disappeared far too soon to underwrite the establishment of even a miniature dynasty.

For a time it seemed that one might emerge within the unlikely precincts of the Ingersoll clan. By 1892 Ingersoll & Brother at 45 Fulton Street in Manhattan had expanded beyond "Novelties & Specialties" to pocket watches, which they sold as the Ingersoll Dollar Watch, "the watch that made the dollar famous." They sold, astonishingly, seventy million of them in the ensuing three decades, which permitted Robert and Charles Ingersoll to live in high style. Charles's house was not far from Maplewood, at Montclair, and Helen thought his four daughters "very glamorous"; the Ingersolls gave a Christmas party each year with "lots of favors and presents and Christmas decorations and usually a magician to entertain us." But eventually the Ingersolls overextended themselves, flooding the market with watches and collapsing into bankruptcy. Charles ended up an enthusiast for Henry George's single-tax program and devoted himself to publishing a crackpot newspaper called *Democracy.* He claimed on its masthead that Ingersoll had sold five hundred million of the Dollar Watches, surely one of the more outlandish boasts in the history of American merchandising.

Bill and Helen were amused by their connection to Rob and Charlie Ingersoll—a Dollar Watch was among the curios and mementos they displayed in the glass-topped coffee table Toimi Paarsinen had made for them in the late 1940s—but they had no illusions about them. The Ingersoll brothers were eccentrics who for a time managed to turn a novelty company into a money-making machine, but they weren't good enough at business to turn it into a going concern. The Woolseys by contrast represented rock-solid wealth and power. Woolseys had played important roles in the growth of the city of Cleveland, in the expansion of the New York mercantile system, in the evolution of one of America's great universities. The Woolseys were people who could afford to live in Tuxedo Park or send their daughters to Chatham Hall, had they thus desired: they were members of the American upper class, comfortable with their prosperity and at ease in circles of influence.

This Bill saw as his rightful inheritance; although he did not have the poor taste to say so, he believed himself an aristocrat both by birth and by training. The problem was that he had the bearing without the wherewithal. Inside his family the standing line went, "It looks as if we're rich, but we're not." This to be sure is not exactly the toughest fate that life can hand a man, but neither is it an easy one to contend with. For their entire married lives, Bill and Helen regarded the expenditure of anything more than $100 as a luxury, and for that matter they never parted lightly with $100. Yet they lived among and worked for people who casually dropped thousands, or tens of thousands: who owned two or three houses and more automobiles, who vacationed routinely in Antigua and St. Moritz, who gave their daughters charge accounts at Bonwit's and sent them off to the Madeira School with their own horses.

How it is that Bill and Helen got along with these people so well as they did is a mystery upon which I can shed little light. But they felt comfortable around old money and rarely—never, in Helen's case—gave overt evidence of feeling inferior to those who had it. Bill detested new money—in one of the more exquisite expressions of his snobbery he once said, "I'll never enroll the daughter of a dentist or a man who wears a diamond ring"—but he found something to admire in old money that has entirely eluded the appreciation of his four children. In retirement, when on occasion he preached at Emmanuel Church in Newport, he flushed with pride to see John Nicholas Brown, of *the* Rhode Island Browns, in the congregation; he knew that Brown regularly attended Trinity Church and came to Emmanuel especially to hear him, which he took as a benediction every bit as much to be treasured as one from the Lord himself.

From time to time he might talk resentfully, over martinis, about being a schoolmaster to the rich; he was all too familiar with what Louis Auchincloss, in *The Rector of Justin*, has called "that curious half paternal, half protective, almost at times half contemptuous, attitude of men of affairs for academics." But on at least one level he came to terms with it. He knew that being the schoolmaster has its own dignity, and that in the eyes of people of intellect it has far more standing than the mere possession of money; he was proud to be called rector of Chatham Hall, and to be a figure of consequence in the very small world of private education for girls. But he refused from the outset to be a member of the Chatham Hall Board of Trustees, as he had been at Tuxedo Park School—"I work for them," he said, "just like everybody else"—and he declined to offer any public pretense that he was their financial equal.

He and Helen were thrifty people who had little respect for people who were not; they thought that making ends meet without going into debt, living within one's resources, was a virtue. With amusement but sympathy, they liked to tell the story of Jane Woolsey Yardley, who saw an elderly gentleman approaching her and immediately crossed the street so as not to have to greet him; when her companion asked why, she replied, "That is Mr. Binney—he is *dipping into capital*." They prided themselves on saving and on managing their minuscule funds resourcefully; it meant a great deal to them that on this tight budget they were able to be every bit as presentable as the parents who brought their daughters to Chatham Hall, and that they could welcome these men and women to the Rectory in full confidence that they would find it elegant and comfortable.

They despised the spendthrift, and it never ceased to amaze them that in their eldest child they had spawned a ghastly example of the breed. I had been at Woodberry Forest only a few weeks when the principal subject of my letters home became the inadequacy of my weekly allowance of $1.25, which I found ways to spend immediately upon its arrival. "It is good to hear from you and have your letter of the 19th," Bill wrote on November 21, 1951, "even though the letter is taken up largely with financial problems." My plea for additional funds was brushed aside: "It does not seem to me at all necessary to have a special allowance for dry cleaning as I rarely spend as much as $1.20 a month myself. Of course I realize I am older, have more clothes, and am accustomed to hanging them up and taking care of them." For the first of more times than I can hope to count, he read me the riot act:

> I know it is tough to see other boys going off and doing things when you have already spent all your money. However, you have $1.25 a week for your allowance and you have to learn to live inside it just the way I had to learn to live within my income. Please remember that I don't own a bank or a cotton mill and that I am having heavier expenses this year than I have ever had before. You are also having a larger allowance than you have ever had before. It was less than a week ago that I sent you $2.50 and if you had really wanted to go to the E.H.S. game you could have saved $2.00 from it. . . . .
> I expect that is about enough on what must be for you a very unpleasant subject.

Indeed it was: we fought over it for years. He and Helen believed—and of course they were right—that a child had to be taught the value of money, had to understand that it was no random beneficence but the reward for hard work. Nothing angered them more than parents who lavished money and expensive gifts on their children without expecting anything in return. Once Helen came back from New York with what for her was an unusually expensive dress, a rare extravagance that had set her back a couple of hundred dollars at Peck & Peck; the following Sunday she was infuriated, and mortified, to see one of the girls wearing the same dress at chapel.

Another time a rich couple from the South drove up with a graduation present for their daughter: a Mercedes 280 SL. Bill was appalled. For weeks thereafter he raged about the extravagance of the parents, about how they were spoiling a perfectly nice child who needed to learn to earn things for herself. He was furious, but he was envious as well. Two decades later Sarah and her new husband, Don Porter, drove to Middletown in an elderly 280 SL that they were taking out to California for Don's mother. Bill looked at it for a long time, walked around it, touching and admiring it.

"That's the car I always wanted," he said quietly.

NOW WE were six. A couple of years later a seventh made ready to join us, but Helen's fifth pregnancy—which, like her third and fourth, was unintentional—miscarried. "It was," she said, "the happiest day of my life."

I think otherwise. Though Helen was relieved beyond measure to be free from the obligations of caring for yet another child, her happiest day may well have been August 16, 1953, when Ben entered her life. She loved all of her children dearly but she loved Ben best of all. In part this is because in many ways he was like her: straightforward, loyal, modest, firm but subdued in his affections. But it is also because the child who comes relatively late in a parent's life can help revive that parent's fading youth, can bring joy and companionship to a household that the older children are departing; this Ben did for Helen and Bill alike, but for Helen in particular. She was uncharacteristically open about the pride and pleasure he gave her, as she told the Chatham Hall alumnae:

> As I write this Ben is almost two months old and while he probably is just a normal average baby, we think he is a very superior article. At times he bears a startling resemblance to his father, so much so that Mme. Gagarine's first comment on seeing him was, "Why it's Mr. Yardley in a crib!"

Ben is on constant display at the Rectory where he shows a precocious interest in his lady admirers by raising his eyebrows in the approved Chatham Hall manner. We hope he will be an added attraction in bringing alumnae back to visit us.

That there is so much chronological distance between Ben and me—he is closer in age to both my sons than he is to me—is one of the larger regrets of my life. I was away in school within a few weeks of his birth, and learned of his progress primarily through Bill's regular letters:

The family are all flourishing and Ben is growing by leaps and bounds. I don't suppose you will know him when you get back. Don't forget that he will be a responsibility of yours as well as of mine. As he grows bigger you will be able to do for him a good many of the things that you probably don't remember I did for you. For instance, when you were under three, I taught you to catch and throw a ball, and you probably like baseball now because you got a very early start. We used to go on long walks together and spent many afternoons at places like the zoo in Pittsburgh.

I wish I could say that I faithfully discharged this obligation but I did not, and the fault is not entirely mine. By the time Ben was ready to toss a ball and do what few things I could teach him, the various complications of adolescent life kept me away from the house not merely during the school year but during much of the summer as well. From what I could see he was a bright, inquisitive, handsome little fellow who had inherited—as I alas had not—an enviably large measure of Bill's craftsman's gifts. He showed early promise as a model maker, and in time turned his attentions to cabinetmaking with impressive results, one handsome example of which occupies an honored place in my living room. But it was not until Ben was in college and I was well into my thirties that we began to get to know each other and to become friends.

While the infant Ben was giving his parents delight, his fourteen-year-old brother had little but trouble to offer. My honeymoon at

Woodberry Forest had ended. The boy who had been my best friend in 1952–1953 returned to school in the fall of 1953, now as my roommate, a changed fellow. It all seems unspeakably trivial now, but we quickly had a falling out over music. I had become a lover of classic jazz, and came back to school with albums by Jelly Roll Morton and King Oliver and Louis Armstrong. My roommate, by contrast, was on the cutting edge of cultural change; he returned with singles by the Drifters and the Clovers and Piano Red. "Nigger music," the young Southern aristocrats called it; the dance they did, at which my roommate was positively brilliant, was the "dirty bop." Rock and roll was here to stay, and my roommate was among its earliest apostles.

Now all of a sudden the age difference between me and my classmates began to tell; it was compounded by my being a Yankee, which in those days was still an odious thing south of the Mason-Dixon line. First by my roommate, then by his cohorts, I was subjected to teasing and bullying in forms that seem merely tiresome now—smashed phonograph records, shorted sheets, rifled bureau and desk—but were dreadfully hurtful then. Finally I requested, and was granted, transfer to another room in another dormitory. That helped, but it did not solve the problem: I had been assigned the role of pariah, and so far as I could see it would stick to me so long as I stayed there.

On the afternoon of January 26, 1954, I called Bill and Helen and pleaded with them to let me transfer. I was too proud and ashamed to give them the full story, but said that I now realized I was too young for the tenth grade and believed that I should repeat it at another school. I pointed out that if I stayed where I was I would graduate at sixteen, which would be too young for college the following autumn.

I pleaded again and again; I went to the headmaster of Woodberry and politely said that I was miserable in his school, a judgment he eventually accepted. Soon Bill and Helen consented to my plan, and began to make inquiries among their wide circle of preparatory-school connections. Applications were filled out, interviews and tours arranged, scholarship inquiries made. In time two schools accepted me. I chose Groton.

---

* * *

It is here, with my removal to Groton, that for a few pages I take center stage in Bill and Helen's story. I do so reluctantly, but out of the conviction that what happened to me at this citadel of wealth and power says something about what it is to be a member of the particular family to which I belong: not to mention about the closed world of private education in which Bill and Helen had chosen to spend their lives.

Bill was openly delighted that Groton had accepted me. The Dr. Jekyll in him—the serious educator, the loving father—was well aware of its superior academic program and of the leg up on life that a Groton diploma could give me. The Mr. Hyde—the snob— rejoiced that a Yardley was now among Roosevelts and Whitneys, Auchinclosses and Belmonts, Cushings and Higginsons, even if that Yardley was among them on scholarship. In the circles where- in the Yardleys moved, Groton was the top of the heap; one could go no higher, and there I was.

It was, as are most training grounds for the privileged, a place of great beauty. Thirty miles west-northwest of Boston, it stood in hilly country. Mount Monadnock and Mount Wachusett were on the horizon—the school's intramural teams were named for them—and their autumnal colors rivaled those of Tuxedo Park. The school's heavy redbrick buildings were in a circle, around a grassy commons; the Gothic chapel stood across from the School- house, with the dormitories on either side.

The school's motto was *Cui Servire Est Regnare*, which it trans- lated as "Whom to Serve Is Perfect Freedom." This, as a graduate pointed out not long ago in an angry letter to the alumni bulletin, is a coy evasion: a direct translation, one that reflects Groton's actual assumptions about its role, is "Whom to Serve Is to Rule." The Groton School that I entered in the fall of 1954 believed that its students were the true American aristocracy and that its obligation was to train them not to serve God but to rule mankind. Religion was much in its air, but of an oppressive variety: the "muscular Christianity" that, whether on the playing fields of Eton or those of Groton, picks up the white man's burden.

Groton's headmaster, John Crocker, was a hearty preacher of this creed. He was a decent enough man, but Groton had been most of his life and he had never learned to see beyond its walls. He had succeeded the school's founder, Endicott Peabody, who did him the quite considerable disservice of retiring to a house at the edge of the campus and hovering over Crocker's every move; it was an example that Bill Yardley had observed with horror, which explains his inordinate relief that Edmund Lee had moved away to West Virginia and had not been installed as president of Chatham Hall's trustees. But however much he may have resented Peabody's inescapable presence, Crocker was his protégé to the core: the boys he liked were the athletes, the solid citizens, the "big wheels."

I was not one of these. I was an energetic boy, just about to turn fifteen, who wanted to be accepted by his peers and to do well in his life, but I had been born—and brought up—to cut against the grain. I had spent too many hours in the company of Bill and Helen, soaking up their barbed commentary on people and institutions of the prep-school world, to take that world at face value; and I had read too much Marquand and O'Hara to stand in awe before the sons of the Boston-Manhattan nobility. I was a divided boy: part of me was eager, impressionable, vulnerable; the other part was hostile and rebellious. It was this second part that held sway.

No doubt about it: I was a royal pain, a severe case of what in places such as Groton is called "bad attitude." It did not take me long to comprehend that I was hardly the answer to Groton's prayers; my reaction was not to accommodate myself to Groton's reality, but to resist it at every turn. Part of the difficulty lay with my schoolmates. Groton was populated largely by the sons of those who fancied themselves to be America's equivalent of the British aristocracy, and who conducted themselves accordingly. The school's efforts to discourage the display of wealth were far less heartfelt than Chatham Hall's, so I was given ample opportunity for resentment and envy: at the fine clothing my schoolmates routinely wore, at the invitations they accepted to the Groton–St. Mark's Dance in New York each December, at their spring trips to Bermuda. Certainly I had friends among them, especially in my own class, but my dominant memory is of feeling, for three full years, quite thoroughly out of place.

The real culprit, though, was the school itself—or, as it prefers to be called, The School. It was a chilly, stultifying place that encouraged conformity to received behavior and attitudes and discouraged iconoclastic individuality. It was determined to be an assembly line for Back Bay and Wall Street. I was determined to be . . . well, the true object of my ambitions at that time remains a mystery, but I did not want to be a coupon clipper or a corporate lawyer or an emissary of the Episcopal Church to the privileged few. So when Groton tried to force me into its molds, I resisted with all my might.

The manifestations of my rebellion were too puerile to enumerate, though it may be worth mentioning that on a sacred Groton bench I rudely carved my own initials over those of a previous student, F.D.R.; Bill found this hugely amusing and rejected Crocker's complaint out of hand, noting that in his lifetime Franklin Roosevelt had nowhere been more roundly vilified than among the alumni of his own alma mater.

But Crocker was quite right when, in a letter dated March 15, 1955, he said of me: "At the moment he is certainly not very responsive and his relations with other boys are not always of the best." Bill responded with sorrow and bewilderment:

> Johnny is very evidently in a state of mild rebellion against me and the things I stand for and is consequently not the best adjusted boy you have at Groton. I am disappointed that he is not a little more friendly and does not reach out to people more than he seems to be doing. As a little boy, he seemed almost grown-up in his friendliness, poise, and willingness to talk with all comers. Perhaps someday he will be that sort of person again. I think you have pointed him in that direction more than you realize and that perhaps you have had more in the way of results than you are giving yourself credit for.

That was how the correspondence continued. Crocker was vexed, puzzled and critical: "At table he habitually criticizes the food which is incongruous because it happens to be quite good." Bill was hurt, embarrassed and defensive: "His mother and I are both desperately anxious about him, concerned that he seems always to be out of step with the school and under a cloud. We don't know why he is a griper and feel that in some way we ourselves have failed to help him deliver the sort of performance the school wants." By December of 1955 matters had gone so far that dismissal loomed: "Were the performance of this term to be continued we should not be able to keep him." Bill understood why, but he worried that Groton's inflexibility would have damaging effects. "I still think the boy needs a kind word and a little encouragement," he told the assistant headmaster. "He certainly is blind to his own faults, but I hate to see him becoming blind to his own virtues and losing the confidence which is so important in achieving any sort of success."

Which is precisely what was happening. Helen came to visit me in the spring of 1956 and to receive the comments, few of them favorable, of my "masters," as Groton in imitation of Mother England called its teachers. She stayed in a bare room atop the headmaster's house, where in an afternoon's conversation I poured out everything in my heart: my resentment that other boys could take expensive trips and go to prominent dances, my conviction that John Crocker loathed me, my terror of dismissal and the shame it would bring to her and Bill, my longing for a kind word in Groton's harshly masculine environment. I threw myself on the floor before her and sobbed in her lap. She cried too: out of love for me, out of sorrow for my adolescent suffering, out of fear that she had somehow failed her son and herself.

The crisis passed. On June 20 Crocker informed Bill that "Johnny has made sufficient progress to enable us to make a favorable decision as regards his return next year," though that decision was reached with reservations:

> It would be unrealistic to suppose that all his difficulties have been resolved. He is still a boy who lacks intellectual discipline. He reads a lot, but he reads superficially, and I hope very much that next year he will greatly increase his capacity to get the real substance out of a superior book. Incidentally I hope that before long he will reach a stage of maturity beyond his present strong appetite for comic books.

Mea culpa: I have no defense against the charge. In class I was bored or irritated by all but two teachers: James Waugh, from whom I learned to love contemporary poetry, and Jack Davison, who led me firmly in the general direction of intellectual self-discipline. Otherwise I resisted my instructors and was content to coast, knowing even as I did that I was putting my graduation at risk and endangering my college prospects.

My intransigence infuriated Bill. His understanding of adolescent girls was acute, but he knew less about teenaged boys; that his own son should be lurching through all these torments, and that he and Helen should be bearing the burden of them, was at times more than he could tolerate. Christmas vacation in 1956 was torture; he was short with me and critical at every turn, I was sullen and unresponsive. It especially enraged him that I had made a trade with a classmate: a madras jacket that he had bought for me with his own perfectly good money for my friend's black Stetson cowboy hat.

One afternoon during that holiday Henry Hammer and I went for a drive in the countryside. I was at the wheel of Bill and Helen's green Pontiac station wagon; I lost control on a dirt road and the car slid off to the right, crashing into and uprooting a substantial tree. We were uninjured but terrified. At a farmhouse I phoned Bill, who rushed out with Helen in the school's elephantine Dodge wagon. After they had satisfied themselves that Henry and I were all right, they packed us in the back seat and headed back to Chatham.

We drove in silence for a time. Then Bill leaned back and spoke. "Johnny," he said, "I'm not going to punish you, but there's one thing I want you to do for me."

"Yessir?" I whispered.

"Throw that God damned hat out the window!"

"Yessir!" I said. I rolled down the window and hurled the hat into a field. It landed, forlornly, on a dead cornstalk.

"Thank you, Johnny," Bill said.

My rebellion was far from over. Somehow I got it into my mind that I did not want to attend college—probably out of a fear that I would not be accepted at a good one—but instead had the notion of apprenticing myself to a radio station in Danville. The father of one of my classmates was a successful television producer who made a career in the entertainment industry seem both glamorous and enticing. I advanced this notion in a letter home in January of 1957. In his reply Bill somehow managed to contain himself. "A lot of my friends did what you are thinking about for a year or two," he told me, "or until they found themselves up against a blank wall, and went back to college for more training. One of them, Garrison Morfit, has made very good indeed and is known as Garry Moore." He went on:

> I will certainly not say a flat no to anything in reason. If you really want to go into the entertainment industry, you probably can't start too young and I can't see that a college degree would be of tremendous help. It might even be a handicap. As you know, my experience lies almost entirely outside the entertainment industry. I am not even a consumer of mass entertainment. The handful of people that get to the top in it make a great, great deal of money. The vast majority of boys and men who start in a small town or city like Danville are likely to end in the same small town or city. I suppose there is no industry in the country in which success depends to the same extent upon lucky breaks and completely fortuitous circumstances.

He professed himself unworried, but somehow he got word to Groton. Crocker's response was immediate and bizarre: he sent me to a psychiatrist. I took a train to Boston, merrily smoking contraband cigarettes—free at last!—and was received at the basement office of an odious little man who managed, in the space of less than an hour, to instill in me a prejudice against his profession that deepens and ripens with each passing year. He told Crocker what, apparently, Crocker wanted to hear: "that Jonathan not side-step going to college but try for one of the large mid-western state colleges," where I would get lost in the crowd and bring no further embarrassment to Groton.

Bill thought otherwise. He knew that I was an ambitious if addled boy and that anonymity was the last thing I wanted. He looked sixty miles to the south and saw the University of North

The graduate, 1957

Carolina. It offered a course of study in radio, television and
motion pictures, which he figured might lure me there. He was
right, though what truly lured me was Chapel Hill itself. I fell in
love the moment I saw its historic campus—the ancient, faded
brick buildings, the lawns shaded by great trees, the peaceful little
town at its edge—and I have been in love ever since. Of my four
years there it need only be said that they were happy beyond
expectation or imagination, and that much of the damage done at
Groton—damage in which I was an unwitting conspirator—was
undone. Chapel Hill saved me: it is there that my real life began.

I left Groton in June of 1957. My parents and Jane drove up for
commencement, not knowing whether I would be granted a
diploma; to their unutterable relief, I was. But when at the end of
the day we headed off to Middletown and what would be our last
full summer together as a family of six, I did not leave Groton
behind me. It stayed with me thereafter, a presence over my shoulder: a voice that said I was not good enough, that I was not cut for
success, that I was a misfit. Over and over, in silence, I raged

against that voice and against John Crocker, too, whom I saw as the embodiment of everything I despised about the cramped, self-satisfied world across which he cast so formidable a shadow.

I know now that this judgment was unkind and greatly oversimplified; however much he may have wished to, John Crocker did not cashier me, after all, and thus did not inflict upon me the ignominy attendant to dismissal. Instead he did me a favor: he gave me something against which to struggle, the proper object of revenge. This may not have been the noblest foundation upon which to construct a life, but for me it sufficed.

Some years after leaving John Crocker's school I came upon Robert Graves's masterly autobiography, *Good-bye to All That*, and its description of his miserable years at Charterhouse. He recalled a conversation in which he and a classmate expressed all their loathing for the school:

> Yet when we had said our very worst of Charterhouse, I reminded him, or he me, I forget which: "Of course, the trouble is that at any given time one always finds at least two really decent masters in the school, among the forty or fifty, and ten really decent fellows among the five or six hundred. We shall always remember them, and have Lot's feeling about not damning Sodom for the sake of ten persons. And in another twenty years' time we'll forget this conversation and think that we were mistaken, and that perhaps everybody, with a few criminal exceptions, was fairly average decent, and say: 'I was a young fool then, insisting on impossible perfection,'" and we'll send our sons to Charterhouse for sentiment's sake, and they'll go through all we did."

I took those words to heart. I did not send my sons to Groton—an empty protest, inasmuch as I could not afford to—and I paid scant attention to its affairs. I went to no reunions and lost touch with all but a handful of my classmates. Then, nearly thirty years after my graduation, I had an astonishing telephone call: Groton wished to honor me with an award, and hoped I would come to the campus in May of 1987 to receive it. I was flabbergasted, and caught wholly off guard; I could think of no polite way to refuse, and so said I would be there.

Perhaps some other occasion has aroused greater dread in me than this one, but I do not recall it. I was in a state of extreme agitation when Sue and I arrived at Groton on May 8: not merely because I was going back, but because the ceremony coincided with the thirtieth reunion of my class. My fears were unfounded: my classmates turned out to be likable men who had attached themselves to interesting women, the new presence of girls on the campus proved a blessing, and at the ceremony I was far more moved than I had expected to be. But I did not revise my prepared remarks in view of this happy atmosphere, and of this I am glad. "I hope it goes without saying that I have fond memories of friends and teachers here," I said, "but Groton as an institution served in the past thirty years primarily to nurture certain points of view and resentments that are for better or worse integral parts of whatever it is that I am today.

> By now I have come to terms with most of them, so for me this is something of an occasion for forgiveness and reconciliation, not to mention gratitude for the small miracle of being chosen for this award. I should like to say though that I hope Groton has changed in those three decades. I hope it is more sympathetic to boys and girls who are different, who do not fit comfortably into acceptable and inflexible molds. I hope it has come to understand that a school exists to serve the children who enter it, to bring out the most in *them* rather than to shape them in its own image.
>
> Of course a school exists to teach, and among the important lessons it teaches are the standards of civilized behavior. Groton has always honored high standards and for that I have always respected it. But standards are one thing, conformity is another.
>
> Chairman Mao was right: let a hundred flowers bloom and a hundred schools of thought contend.

WHILE I was away at Groton combatting the creed of muscular Christianity, Bill was in the study at the Rectory immersing himself in the liturgy of the Protestant Episcopal Church. Though no records exist as to whether entering the ministry was a specific condition of his employment by Chatham Hall, on the campus it was common knowledge from the outset of his headmastership that he would do so. He wasted little time in getting about it. One of his first acts upon reaching Chatham in the summer of 1949 was to obtain from Bishop Brown a lay reader's license "with permission to make addresses," which meant that he could read and speak from the pulpit at St. Mary's but could not administer the sacraments of the church; this was done for Chatham Hall by various ministers, including the preacher at Emmanuel Church in Chatham.

In order to qualify for this holy duty it was necessary for Bill to be ordained, which in turn meant he had to undertake the full course of theological study the church requires of all candidates for the ministry. Customarily this is done by enrolling in the seminary, but Bill had no time for that. Instead the Virginia Theological Seminary in Alexandria permitted him to "read for orders": to work his way through its rigorous curriculum by correspondence course. By the time he began to do so he was nearing his fortieth birthday, when most people's minds are unreceptive to the disciplines of academic work; not merely did Bill willingly subject himself to those disciplines, but he did so without active supervision and while overseeing the daily affairs of a school community that numbered, in toto, some three hundred people.

There is little to say about this achievement except that it was extraordinary. At the end of a demanding day in the rector's office, Bill came back to his residence and immersed himself for hours in his concordances and theological treatises. In my mind the two most vivid images of him during that period are: in his bedroom, working on a ship model, and in the study, reading for orders. The former was pleasure and the latter duty, but he pursued both with a single-minded determination that, even to the teenaged son who was busily rebelling against him, was worthy of nothing except admiration and respect.

It took five years, but by the spring of 1955 he was ready for ordination as deacon, the first step into the ministry. This ceremony took place at St. Mary's on Tuesday, April 19, with what Bill called "a veritable heavenly host" of reverend gentlemen on hand: seven ministers, including two bishops. With the congregation standing, Bill was presented by Edmund Lee to the Right Reverend George Purnell Gunn. He was asked by the bishop whether he was "inwardly moved by the Holy Ghost to take upon you this office and ministration, to serve God for the promoting of his glory and the edifying of his people," and whether he was "truly called, according to the will of our Lord Jesus Christ, and according to the canons of this church, to the ministry of the same." To these and all inquiries he responded in the affirmative, whereupon he knelt before the bishop and was welcomed into the clergy. Holy communion was celebrated, with Bill himself at the altar, and at its end the benediction was read, a prayer that "the blessing of God Almighty, the Father, the Son, and the Holy Ghost, be amongst you, and remain with you always."

Now that he was almost a minister—his final ordination came the next year, on January 25, 1956, and was an anticlimax—Bill was in heaven. "I feel like a little boy at Christmas," he told his

The newly ordained minister greets his flock

mother. Gifts were bestowed on him from all directions: Bibles, prayer books, hymnals and, most welcome of all, vestments. Miss Holt gave him a red stole, and the faculty a white one. "If you would like to give me a green or a purple one, I would love to have it though I am appalled at what they cost," he told his mother; "$28.00 seems to be standard with the minimum amount of superfluous embroidery:

If you would like to give me a rabat vest, I have two on order: a corded silk one at $18 and a plain black worsted at $12.50. No Santa Claus has shown much interest yet in the cassock at $88.00 and I suspect I will have to absorb that out of family income. Do you know that you can deduct the cost of vestments for income tax

236

purposes? They are professional expenses somewhat like a doctor's automobile.

Tax-deductible vestments: for three decades Bill had been a clotheshorse, and now the government was prepared to subsidize his wardrobe. From J. M. Hall Inc., at 14 West Fortieth Street in New York, dealer in "church embroideries, altar linens and clergy and choir vestments," he regularly ordered rabat vests—of black silk faille, preferably—and white ministerial shirts to which the traditional stiff collar was attached. "The round collar which I wear on Sundays is not as uncomfortable as it looks," he told me, "but those vests pick up every possible spot or drop of soup. The clergy really have to be very careful how they eat."

Now Bill was rector in fact as well as in name. He need no longer fret over finding a minister to perform those church offices forbidden to the lay reader, and he could fulfill a happy duty that often befalls schoolmasters who are also ministers: presiding over the nuptials of young women who once had been his students. This he did over and over, always with the greatest pleasure. Not merely was he honored to have achieved so high a place in the affections of his alumnae as to be asked to read the solemnization of matrimony for them, but he delighted in the rituals of obtaining bishops' permission to hold services in other states and dioceses. Whenever possible, he used such inquiries as opportunity to drop familial names:

I should like advice on the law in Connecticut on out-of-state clergy. I am a licensed marrying officer in Virginia and in New York. Is there any red tape similar to that in New York? I remember having to go down to City Hall, I think it was, and go through a certain amount of probably necessary red tape. Some states seem to have no regulations at all, others are rather complicated. I cannot remember for the life of me what the status is in Connecticut.

Purely incidentally, both my father and grandfather were Episcopal clergy from Connecticut. My grandfather was at the old Berkeley Divinity School when it was in Middletown. My father was ordained in Rhode Island, however, and never held a Connecticut charge. I am descended from the Reverend William Johnson who was a leading figure in the famous Yale Schism of the early eighteenth century.

"I am very glad to know of your Connecticut background," the Right Reverend Walter H. Gray replied, and left it at that, but Bill was unfazed. He pressed on, telling the bishop that the wedding—in this instance it was of his niece, Harry and Elsie's daughter, Lolly, to Robert Braunschweiger—presented manifold complications. "They do not wish a church wedding, a fact which I regret much," he noted. "Come to think of it I am being dragged into this against a number of my clerical principles, but believe that a clergyman uncle has certain responsibilities which perhaps outweigh certain of his convictions."

Of these "clerical principles" Bill cherished most those having to do with church ritual. He was low church, but among Episcopalians the absence of incense and bells hardly means a paucity of ceremony. There are right ways and wrong ways to do the business of the church, and Bill was a stickler for the former. This may seem a matter of ritualistic form over spiritual substance, but so be it; Bill's was a ministry in which for many years style predominated, but it was also one that gave great comfort to many, as has been attested to by the scores if not hundreds of Chatham Hall girls to whom Bill was the embodiment of all that a man of God should be.

As Bill's long study for the ministry ended, a new phase of his life began. It came upon him as a complete surprise, one that in time gave him as much pleasure—and certainly as much profit—as anything outside his work and his family. In the early 1950s he and Helen had bought a share of stock, for $25, in the Redwood Library in Newport, a private collection that is open to the public. They did this to express their support for an institution that had given them great pleasure during their Middletown summers; they were among the Redwood's most frequent borrowers, and they thought that buying a share of stock would be an appropriate way to say thank you.

Their loyalty was repaid one summer day in the middle of the decade. Bill and I were at the Redwood, browsing through magazines and new acquisitions, when one of the librarians came up to him. "Mr. Yardley," she said, "I know you're interested in old books, and I thought you'd like to look at some we have down in the basement. They came to us through a bequest, but they're duplicates of books we already have. If you see anything you'd like, we'll sell it to you for a reasonable price." So Bill and I descended the cellar stairs, and there it was: the Promised Land.

The bequest had come from one of the Redwood's best friends, a gentleman named Roderick Terry, who had frequently served as an officer of its board. He had amassed a private collection that many a library would envy, a collection that now sat, unwanted, in the Redwood's basement. For fifty cents a book—a dollar for folios—Bill could have whatever he wanted. As he made his first tour around the tables on which Terry's books had been dumped, Bill's heart must have pounded to the edge of seizure; he knew at once that his dream, of a book collection of his own that could compare with the one he had so admired at the Tudor and Stuart Club, was now within his grasp.

Of all the bargains he and Helen had made over the years, while at Bedford and thereafter, none compared with this. Day after day, Bill returned to the Redwood for yet another examination of Roderick Terry's gold mine, and day after day he drove back to the bungalow with further acquisitions. In all he purchased about five hundred books that summer, at a total cost of perhaps $300. These included, for fifty cents apiece, Dickens and Thackeray in original serials, and for a dollar apiece the seven volumes of the Latin classics published in the late eighteenth century by the great printer and designer of typefaces, John Baskerville. For a dollar and a half he obtained a three-volume biography of Shelley, a work of no particular distinction except that the first volume of this copy had been "extra-illustrated": it contained a holograph note by Mary Shelley, a bank draft in Shelley's own hand, and intermingled locks of hair from Southey, Coleridge and Wordsworth.

Bill financed this bonanza through his own account; from the earliest years of their marriage, he and Helen had separate accounts for their own expenditures and a joint one (requiring two signatures) for household expenses. Much to his good fortune, he had accumulated some savings in his account and had enough money to treat himself liberally at the Redwood. At summer's end he shipped the books back to Chatham and lovingly installed them in the paneled shelves in the living room. Now at last that room had the look of what in fact it was: a gentleman's library.

Among the books he brought home from Rhode Island were several first editions of the works of Anthony Trollope. He had always liked Trollope's novels, and now decided to become a serious collector of them. This, in the ensuing decade, was one of his life's chief preoccupations. By the time he auctioned off the larger part of the collection in the early 1970s it had become, as he was at pains to declare whenever the opportunity arose, "the third-best collection in private hands in the world." He accumulated it at a total cost of about $6,000 and sold it for approximately six times as much; he was proud that his collector's acumen had proved itself so profitably in the marketplace, but it was from the chase for Trollopiana that he derived greatest pleasure.

This chase was conducted through a number of dealers, mostly in New York. Chief among them was the Seven Gables Bookshop, in a couple of modest rooms on West Forty-sixth Street that were reached by a slow, tiny elevator. Its proprietors, Michael Papantonio and John S. Van E. Kohn, were legendary figures of mid-century antiquarian bookselling; they were also gentlemen, and they seem immediately to have recognized in Bill a kindred spirit. They knew that he would not bring much income to them, but they liked him personally and they could tell that he was a real bookman: not merely a collector but a man who loved rare books as much for what was within as for what was without. Bill took me to Seven Gables once, in the early 1960s when I was living in New York; he was greeted with affection and pleasure, and I always felt myself given special treatment on the subsequent occasions when I had small business with Mike and John—both, alas, now dead—and their successors.

His correspondence with them lasted a decade. Most of it is of little interest to us now, because it was businesslike and direct. He read auction catalogues and asked Mike and John to bid on certain items up to a certain ceiling: rarely higher than $50 and often much lower. He also sold books to them: as he acquired better and better copies of each Trollope title, he sent his less desirable ones to Seven Gables, which paid him on account and then resold them. "We have now had a chance to go through the four boxes of TROLLOPE duplicates you sent," Mike wrote on January 30, 1963. "We'd be willing to take them for a total price of $170." Bill replied the next day: "I was astonished to have so fine an offer for that kennel of old dogs I sent up. They are yours for $170. As I said in a recent letter, credit, not cash."

Bill loved Seven Gables; he belonged to no clubs in those Chatham days, but the bookstore—with its quiet rooms, its welcoming atmosphere, its pervasive sense of shared literary and antiquarian passions—served him better than any clubroom. Seven Gables was his home away from home, the oasis in mid-Manhattan where he was always comfortable: where more awaited him than mere business dealings involving the work of Anthony Trollope.

Indeed he did far more with that work than collect it. In the 1960s he saw a performance of Hal Holbrook's one-man Mark Twain show, whereupon it occurred to him that Trollope's work offered similar possibilities. He prowled through that work for passages lending themselves to public reading, and he acquired the garb—or the approximation thereof—of a Victorian gentleman. Thus attired, and wearing as well a false Trollopian beard and wire-rimmed glasses, he took the stage at Willis Hall to present "An Evening with Anthony Trollope"; the performance, which invariably was a miniature triumph, was repeated many times at Chatham Hall and upon occasion at other schools. He began with a brief account of Trollope's life and character—"The nice thing about him is his complete naturalness and normality"—and then launched into the great man's work. With much drama and gesticulation, he read from the novels, from the autobiography, from the travel books. He particularly favored, for its fine edge of malice, a passage from *The Eustace Diamonds*:

> Lady Linlithgow was worldly, stingy, ill-tempered, selfish, and mean. Lady Linlithgow would cheat a butcher out of a mutton-chop,

Anthony Trollope, a.k.a. Bill Yardley

or a cook out of a month's wages, if she could do so with some slant of legal wind in her favour. She would tell any number of lies to carry a point in what she believed to be social success. It was said of her that she cheated at cards. In backbiting no venomous old woman between Bond Street and Park Lane could beat her,—or, more wonderful still, no venomous old man at the clubs.

The delight that Bill took in Trollope soon found yet another outlet. It concerned him that the heat and humidity of Virginia in summer could do the books no good—the Rectory was not air-conditioned—and even more that he could not afford to have protective slipcases made for them. But soon it came to him that if he could make model ships—which hobby he had abandoned in the mid-1950s—then he could just as well make slipcases. He began doing this late in the decade and continued for five or six years, in that time acquiring a formidable collection of book-binder's tools. He did everything himself, from designing and assembling the boxes to gluing the leather on them to—this most miraculous of all—tooling the lettering and decorations on their spines. Of course he kept a ledger chronicling his labors, from which here are two characteristic entries:

THE AMERICAN SENATOR. Printed by Random House for the Trollope Society. N.Y. 1940. Limited 283–350 copies. Jerome Kern's copy, without his bookplate. Item 195 of sale of his "later" books Parke-Bernet 16 Oct. 62. Original black slip-box repaired. Enclosed in new ½ blue cloth box. Begun 20 Dec. ½ bright blue morocco. Finished 26 Dec.

DOCTOR WORTLE'S SCHOOL. London: Chapman & Hall, 1881. 2 volumes. Superb copy with Sadleir bookplate. Chemise in reddish brown bookcloth. Begun 15 August. Case ½ dark reddish brown morocco, the first of this color I have used. No labels: panels full gilt. Finished 20 August.

He was so proficient at this craft that in less than a week, working in the evening after a full day's labor, he could produce a slipcase of entirely professional quality. By the time his production had reached its peak, the living room at the Rectory positively glowed with these slipcases: the rich leather of the bindings and the bright gold of the lettering mingled with the brown butternut paneling to give the room precisely the cultured and elegant atmosphere that Bill had longed for. It may not have been the place for which Roderick Terry had intended his legacy, but his books certainly were at home there.

The Yardleys, by the same token, had by now come to feel much at home in the community whence those books had come. After three summers at the bungalow we rented in Middletown, we couldn't imagine any more agreeable summer escape. Five miles east of Newport, Middletown might as well have been in another country for all the difference between the two places. Newport was money and grandeur and show; the summer people gave themselves elaborate balls, drove their limousines along Bellevue Avenue and Ocean Drive, and sunned behind the closed gates at Bailey's Beach. Middletown by contrast was, as Saunderstown had been a generation before, quiet and unpretentious, known to few except those who owned or rented houses there. Newport was a resort, Middletown was a summer place; all the two had in common was the incandescent beauty of their rocky shorelines, the deep blue of the water, and the pristine summertime air.

Middletown had no particular business to speak of, beyond the truck farms along Green End Avenue and, overlooking the water from atop its own hill, St. George's, a boarding school for boys; it was Bill Buell, headmaster of St. George's, who had alerted the Yardleys to the bungalow's availability. Relatively few of Middletown's houses, except those on one side of Indian Avenue, had views of Rhode Island Sound or the Sakonnet River, and fewer of those houses were even remotely grand. Ted and Bobbie Sturtevant had a spectacular view of the river, but their house was a rambling white clapboard structure; Francis and Darlington Comstock owned a tiny pre-Revolutionary cottage to which they'd added a modern wing; "Lazy Lawn," where our landlords, Paul and Ilonka Rogers, lived, may once have possessed a smidgeon of grandeur, but it had long disappeared into the agreeable chaos in which the family existed.

Unlike Bailey's Beach, the beaches in Middletown were open to all. The larger and more dramatic of these was Second Beach, on the ocean side, where the waves were strong enough for surfing; this was the preferred beach for Bill and Helen and their friends, with whom they would gather to sun and chat while their various children made sand castles and swam. The other beach, Third Beach, faced the river, the waters of which were placid enough to permit small children to swim without danger; part of this was Officers' Beach, for Navy men and their families, but the rest was open to the public.

The Navy was vital to Newport's economy in those days. The War College was still in full operation; Middletown householders who returned to their permanent residences in the winter usually rented to officers attending the college's nine-month session. Sailors were all over the streets of Newport, Thames Street in particular; it was honky-tonk to the core, with the Blue Moon and other bars catering noisily to the nautical trade. Newport's central waterfront, with its seedy, slightly dangerous air, contrasted agreeably with the gold coast along Ocean Drive; as a boy I much preferred Thames Street, and Broadway nearby, sensing that here was lived something approximating real life.

All of this was years before Thames Street became a place of pricey boutiques and junky tourist traps selling America's Cup T-shirts. The bridge between Newport and Jamestown had not yet been built, allowing easy access to Aquidneck Island from Connecticut and points west, so the invasion of tourists that eventually transformed the island, destroying much of its character in the process, was still in the distant future. In those days the only direct route from the west entailed riding the ferry that ran between Jamestown and Newport; lines of cars waiting for the ferry were often long and the trip across Narragansett Bay was time-consuming, which combined to discourage many visitors and keep the island's summer population to a manageable level.

For the Yardley family the ferry was no obstacle but a welcome sign that the summer's holiday had begun. In the early years, when most of the highways were two lanes and few cities were bypassed—driving through Baltimore was a particular nightmare—the six-hundred-mile trek from Chatham to Middletown took three days, few moments of which were pleasant. There was a certain corner in Charlotte Court House, a couple of hours out of Chatham, at which I predictably and reliably became carsick, setting off a chain-reaction epidemic of nausea that quickly spread to all the other children. We were packed into the station wagon more tightly than I can now imagine: Bill and Helen in the front seat with one child, three more children in the back along with Annie and Boy; our belongings were crammed into the rear of the wagon and several suitcases were strapped to its roof.

Annie came along, at the family's expense, because Helen had gotten too accustomed to her ministrations to abandon them during what was supposed to be her vacation. In those days it was quite impossible to find public accommodations for a black person in the South, so we stayed overnight with family or friends: with Grandma Yardley in Chestnut Hill or with Francis and Alice Murray at their house on the Eastern Shore of Maryland. Once, north of Mason-Dixon, we put up at a motel along that dreadful stretch in Delaware at which every highway along the Eastern Seaboard merges into a dozen miles of sheer hell. The motel was called the Sir Francis Drake; Bill had chosen it because one of his fonder fancies was that he was in some way a kinsman of the bold seaman. But the Sir Francis proved as much a nightmare as the road next to which it sat, with uproarious parties and scandalous doings in every room except the three we occupied. "A disgrace to the family name," Bill pronounced the place, and we never went back.

We were just about as crowded in the Rogerses' bungalow as we had been in the station wagon. This strange shingle building, about half a mile from the water on Third Beach Road, had originally been erected in the glory days of "Lazy Lawn" for the presentation of amateur theatricals. What we used as the living room had been the theater, while the dining room had been the stage; the tiny kitchen was to one side of the stage and a bedroom, where Annie stayed with the smaller children, was to the other. Two additional bedrooms were at the opposite end of the one-story building; Jane and I had one of these, Bill and Helen the second. The place was furnished in the most primitive seaside style, with various pieces that had little to do with each other except propinquity, many of which were in immediate danger of collapse.

Nobody cared; we loved the bungalow, and we loved the Rogerses: Paul and Ilonka, their sons, Robin and Tim, Robin's wife, Marcia, and their amiable bulldog, Mutsa. Paul was a schoolteacher who in the summer managed the St. George's Day Camp, at which for several years I worked as a counselor; he was a passionate Boston Red Sox fan, which is to say that he had been taught all of life's hardest lessons, and a devotee of the cocktail hour. Night after night he and Ilonka strolled over to the bungalow, or Helen and Bill went to "Lazy Lawn"; over drinks and crackers they gossiped and laughed, talking about schools and politics and children and money—of which neither family had much—and whatever else touched their fancy. During this period the Rogerses were, at least for two months of each year, the friends Bill and Helen treasured most; it was a friendship such as their circumstances in Chatham denied them, and for this reason they valued it all the more.

But much though we all loved everything about "Lazy Lawn," Bill and Helen soon realized that it was inadequate to the family's summer needs; as the children grew larger the amount of room they occupied steadily shrank, which is to say that by vacation's end the bungalow seemed to them the size of a broom closet. They needed more space, but there wasn't much else available for rent in Middletown—which they much preferred to Newport, Bill's happy memories of Rhode Island Avenue to the contrary notwithstanding—and there was even less that they could afford.

Their uncertainty ended when they learned that a half-mile away, on Indian Avenue, a piece of land was for sale. It belonged to T. S. Matthews, managing editor of *Time* magazine, a leading figure in the publishing realm of Henry Luce and the husband of a former Mrs. Ernest Hemingway, Martha Gellhorn. Matthews's family had for many years owned "Boothden," a sprawling wooden house on the Sakonnet side of Indian Avenue that had been built in the 1880s by Edwin Booth, the actor, as a summer retreat. Now "Boothden" was on the market, though for a far larger sum than Bill and Helen could afford. But across the road

Matthews had an undeveloped tract of just under three acres that he was prepared to sell separately. On August 16, 1954, Bill and Helen were informed that this plot could be had for $1,500 an acre. They wasted no time in indicating their eagerness to purchase the land, and late the following winter it was theirs; the total price was $4,200, which they paid in cash. Now, for the first time in five years, they owned land; the problem, and for them it was no small problem, was that on it they had nothing except a few scraggly trees, some disagreeable bushes and a large amount of tall grass.

What they needed was a house. For a time they thought about buying from the new owners of "Boothden" the playhouse that Booth had built there, moving it across the street, and converting it into a residence, but they'd had enough of elderly theaters and wanted a real house of their own. In August of 1955 Bill advised his mother of their change in plans:

> No, we didn't buy the Edwin Booth Playhouse, after all. It was too complicated to move and might have cost much more than we have. We are, however, building a little house. Fran Comstock, the Princeton architect who lives just up the road from us, designed and will supervise the building of it. He was an angel to do it and is charging nothing for his services, merely from gratitude for what Chatham did for his two girls and out of friendship. For the time being the house will have a good-sized living room, four and one-half bedrooms and two and one-half baths. We hope to build a dining room later. The plan is quite flexible, and it is in very simple New England cottage style, no particular period and made of standard lumber and cuttings. However, we did get an old doorway with sidelights, a mantelpiece, and some moldings from a 1790 house that was being dismantled on Thames Street. We will have a lovely view and enough ground around us to be protected from the neighbors, all of whom seem to be pleasant enough.

On August 4 they signed a contract with A. & F. Construction Company to build the house for a sum of $19,000, which they were to pay in three installments. Work started at once, and before month's end Franny Comstock was able to write: "I am enclosing the well-drilling bill which must strike terror in your financial

Under construction: the house at 330 Indian Avenue

soul"—a hundred ninety-five feet drilled, at $3.50 per foot, to
obtain a flow of four and a half gallons per minute, for a total of
$682.50 minus a five-percent discount for immediate payment.
In the ensuing months correspondence flowed back and forth
between Chatham and Middletown, as Bill and Helen learned
firsthand what Mr. Blandings had gone through when he built his
famous "dream house." Finally in April Bill and Helen were able
to visit 330 Indian Avenue for themselves; I joined them on spring
holiday from Groton. We camped out in the house, as Bill reported
to the contractor:

> The Yardleys are delighted with their little house. It just about
> has everything and I think your men have done a very fine, conscien-
> tious job. The wood-working seemed to me particularly well done
> and the plaster is of very excellent quality. The furnace works nicely
> and the plumbing is all good. Even in the bitter cold weather we had
> while we were there, with high winds, we were comfortable. Best of
> all, the fireplace draws beautifully and no smoke comes into the
> living room.

In truth, Bill thought the contractor "is getting tired of our little
house and needs needling as well as flattery." Franny Comstock,
ever kind and obliging, provided this, with the result that when we
returned in June, the house was ready for us. I was the first one in,

coming down by bus from Groton with my phonograph album of a new show called *My Fair Lady,* which I played all summer long to Bill's extreme vexation and Helen's amused tolerance. A couple of days later the rest of the family arrived, and there we were: together at last, in a house that belonged to no one except ourselves.

But it was ours to occupy for only two or three months each year. For a decade and a half, from the fall of 1956 until the summer of 1971, Bill and Helen rented it to a succession of Navy families who proved, without exception, to be model tenants. Over the years the monthly rent rose from $130 to $190, which was enough to pay the taxes and upkeep on the house, but not much more; but breaking even was fine with Bill and Helen, who were relieved not to be out of pocket on the house and to have it occupied by people who cared about it.

This all of them did. Captain and Mrs. J. A. Eady, the first tenants, stayed three years—moving out in the summers when the Yardleys arrived for vacation—and when they were transferred in 1959 Bill and Helen were genuinely saddened. "We just hate to think of our house in someone else's hands next year," Bill told Margaret Eady. "You and the Captain have loved it so and taken such wonderful care of it that it has given us a fine feeling of security and comfort." Following them came a succession of Gilhooleys, Phillipses, Carvers, Cockrills and others, one of whom went so far as to draw up and mimeograph a precise floor plan. "It really is terribly well done," Bill told Commander Patten, "and makes us feel quite homesick," and later he wrote, "Mrs. Yardley and I agree without exception you are *the* outstanding tenant we have ever had in twelve years of renting 330 Indian Avenue." In that same vein, he continued:

> Every day we discover something else that was done last winter: the screen doors strengthened by corners, a light over the kitchen sink, the gate posts strengthened by metal corners, the poison ivy sprayed and definitely on the wane, the tile floors all beautifully

waxed, the grass manicured and a great many weeds killed, the flagstones lifted, filled under and raised—indeed too many improvements even to mention.

If you ever want to live in Newport again, just let me know! Anybody who improves property the way you do deserves a lower rental, not a higher one. I hope you are as comfortably situated in Norfolk and that this eventually reaches you and that you will end up your Navy career as full Admiral of the Fleet.

As he said to another tenant, "There is certainly something about the United States Navy that brings out the skillful do-it-yourself craftsman in every one of its officers whom I know." When in the summer of 1971 Bill and Helen claimed the house for themselves alone, it had been improved into a snug, comfortable dwelling that needed only regular maintenance, and no major investment, to serve them comfortably in their retirement.

If the renters gave the Yardleys satisfaction, the agent through whom they were acquired gave them delight. He was an elderly party named Francis X. A. Flannery, who had kissed the Blarney stone many a time and found it sweet. He was an ardent but whimsical Roman Catholic with whom Bill entered into a bantering correspondence.

"How goes the Ecumenistic spirit in the Southland?" Flannery inquired. "Bless us all. We are living in a great age. Hope I make Heaven and abide in the same area as you. If so, I am sure it will be because some of your spirituality rubbed off on me."

To which Bill replied, "Mr. Francis X. A. Flannery doesn't come crashing through; he makes triumphant entrance after the manner of King Louis XIV of France with consummate grace and aplomb."

Later Bill opened a missive with a paean to spring: "Lo, the daffodils are blooming and the forsythia is glorious. The redbud is budding and the dogwood is nearly full. The grass is green. Each breeze in the Virginia air is like a kiss from a maiden fair." But Flannery topped him:

Am I reading the "Faerie Queene" by the immortal Edmund Spenser of the Age of Elizabeth or possibly a masterpiece by

Geoffrey Chaucer, John Wesley or Samuel Johnson? This I was asking myself, as I dwelt on the inspirational introduction to your delightful epistle of April 10.

And did you forget the crocuses? Heavens yes and for this I will not forgive you, for currently on our lawn there are more than 400 in bloom. Purple and gold no less the classic colours of the Coliseum of Rome, in the days when Christians were martyred by the down turned thumb.

And tell me more sir, of the "kiss from a maiden fair." This to be certain, is the only way I may learn at my age, despite my anxious desires and willingness for complete and warm cooperation.

By the early 1970s Bill was addressing Flannery as "Oh Best of Real Estate Agents!" and the compliment was returned; Flannery saluted him as "Your Grace." Now they were in the midst of scriptural disputations, over the wording of certain passages in Genesis and the troubling of the waters in the Gospel according to St. John. At last Bill exclaimed:

> Between us, we certainly know those scriptures! I don't know about the young priests of your church, but I find that the young priests of my church know much more about interpersonal relationships and clinical psychology than they do about the word of God.

Bill also wrote, and meant it with all his heart, "It will be a glad day for me when I arrive and see your beaming face."

MIDDLETOWN WAS for Bill and Helen in every sense a blessing. It gave them a summer escape in which both the climate and the countryside were markedly different from Chatham, a refuge where they were surrounded by congenial friends who had grown up in their own world of the Northeast and Middle Atlantic; it gave them a house of their own, an important consideration for two proud people who were not entirely comfortable living in someone else's quarters; and it gave them a place to which they knew they could retire, if they so wished, when that distant day arrived.

But in the late 1950s retirement was distant indeed. The next several years were the high point of their private and public lives. Their children were thriving: I was at Chapel Hill; Jane was happily enrolled, as a boarding student, at Chatham Hall; Sarah was doing quite nicely at Chatham Alimentary School; and Ben was growing into a spirited, inquisitive, immensely likable little boy.

Ben joined Sarah at the public school in the fall of 1959; it is with this moment that Helen's new life began. She had emerged from the house four years earlier, assuming the job of executive secretary of the Chatham Hall Alumnae Association, but now that she had no real reason to spend most of each day in and about the Rectory, she felt free to take a more active role in the daily affairs of the school. She was a sponsor of the Dance Committee, but what really mattered was her sponsorship of the Service League. No doubt it would be easy to dismiss this organization as a toothless exercise in white-gloved do-goodery, but there was more to it than that. Whether its race-relations department really did much good in the town of Chatham certainly is questionable, but this and the league's other departments imbued in many Chatham Hall girls a sense of public service; most assuredly the league gave Helen the belief, which she had not had at Shady Side, that she was contributing to her community and doing work of value. As indeed she was: among her chief concerns during this period was a program she developed to teach reading to the numerous illiterate members of the Chatham Hall community.

But any work she did was always as the rector's wife. She earned a small salary for her alumnae work, and later it expanded along with her responsibilities, but even at its maximum of $4,200 it was barely a living wage. Though she never spoke about the subject, then or later, there is reason to believe that she harbored no small amount of bitterness at being in Bill's shadow and that this contributed to the strains in the marriage that emerged in retirement. They were not a bickering or argumentative couple in Chatham—I was never witness to what could be described as a fight between them—but Helen was a smart woman, by no means devoid of her own ambitions, who can only have been frustrated at being judged over and over not for herself but for how she reflected upon her husband, the rector of Chatham Hall.

The modern feminist movement was beginning to take shape in these years, but Helen went largely unaffected by it; she actively disliked strident rhetoric, however worthy the cause, and she was amused by such coinages as "Ms." and "chairperson." But I have little doubt that the more thoughtful feminist leaders and writers helped bring her situation into focus. She was an educated woman who, by dint of the time when she had been born and the manner in which she had been reared, accepted with only hesitant question the subordinate role into which marriage cast her. This was true of innumerable middle-class women of her generation; the difference in her case was that she was the wife of a boarding-school headmaster, living in a beautiful but isolated region that offered almost nothing to feed her intellectual appetites and her hunger for recognition.

This I think is why her children and some of her friends sensed a suppressed anger within her, a tight coil of tension that she never permitted to burst but could not entirely disguise, at least from those who knew her well. She was a power behind the throne if ever there was one, and I have no doubt that she resented it; "Oh, you and I could probably run the school," she remarked to a teacher when Bill was off on a business trip, and in a sense she was right: she could not have brought to the role Bill's headmasterly charm or his clerical dignity, but she could have kept the place running like clockwork.

She was Bill's strongest supporter, closest advisor and severest critic. Once, when a fund-raising consultant seemed to dismiss her offhandedly, Bill gave him a sharp look. "You remember one thing," he said. "That's the woman who sleeps with the rector." He ran the admissions process largely on his own, but he and Helen discussed each applicant and her judgment was often crucial; before the opening of each school year both of them took to heart every new girl's picture, and they knew all forty or fifty of them by name the day they arrived. In meetings and chapel services Helen was impatient when Bill's grandiloquence got the better of him: "He finished his sermon five minutes ago," she whispered. "Why doesn't he stop talking?" Though she and Bill were openly affectionate with each other in private, she loathed public displays. Once, while she was sitting in one of Pruden's drawing rooms with a small group of alumnae, Bill sneaked up and kissed her on the neck. She whipped around, with a look on her face as if he'd hit her. "Don't you ever do that again," she snapped.

Yet for all of that I think she was happy. She found plenty to occupy herself, and she committed herself to it wholly. She accompanied Bill on fund-raising visits to alumnae chapters, and over the years she developed strong friendships with many old Chatham girls. In 1964 she became alumnae director and editor of *The Chatham Chat;* she strengthened the school's ties to its graduates and she made the *Chat,* which appeared each fall and spring, into a first-rate publication. She loved working at the shop where it was printed, learning about layout and design; I was then spending a lot of time in the composing room of the *Daily News* in Greensboro, North Carolina, and we discovered a shared love for ink and linotypes and the craftsmen who operated them.

For a time she became infatuated with italic handwriting, after an exponent of that fine art visited the school. She and Bill both learned italic, and both did it skillfully, but it was Helen who really committed herself to it. On a school bulletin board she posted, in her own italic hand, this notice:

Italic Handwriting

If you would like to learn to write in the
Italic style join the volunteer class which
will meet Sunday afternoon at 4:00 o'clock.
You will need

> *an Osmiroid pen point*
>
> *an Estabrook pen*
>
> *a pad of bond finish paper*
>
> *Waterman's ink*

These are available at the bookstore.
We will order the "Guide to Italic Handwriting"
  about $3.95

Sign up sheet on Service League Bulletin Board

She became an apostle of Raymond Franklin Da Boll, a charismatic teacher of italic, and took a subscription to the newsletter of the Committee for Italic Handwriting. For a time letters to her children seemed to come from another person, if not another universe. The orderly if undistinctive handwriting with which we were all familiar metamorphosed, almost overnight, into a stately italic that may have said many things but did not say Helen Yardley. In time, fortunately, this interest faded away, and the script we knew and loved made its welcome reappearance.

Her life still revolved in large measure around us, but her maternal responsibilities by now had considerably diminished. By the early 1960s only Ben was still at home, Jane having gone off to Sweet Briar and Sarah following her to Chatham Hall. Helen found her children more interesting and companionable as they grew toward maturity; she talked to us as adults rather than children, and relished our company as we did hers—she was as spirited and engaging a conversationalist as anyone I ever knew. Yet something in her missed the little children and the intimacies she had with them. The last left in September of 1964, when she took Ben to the Harvey School in Katonah, New York; he was eleven years old. Back at school she went to the desk of Bill's secretary, Betty Thornton. "That was one of the hardest things I've ever done," she said, as the tears began to roll down her cheeks.

Of that same event Bill wrote, in the first of his round-robin letters to his mother and his children, "Mummy and I felt a little sorry for ourselves last night after Ben the last to go had left on the train for New York." But he wasted little time on family matters in the letter. It was not that he was unsentimental—he could, upon occasion, be mawkish—but that in this high period of his headmastership he was almost entirely preoccupied with his school. In the decade that began in the late fifties and ended, with a heart-wrenching thud, in the late sixties, Bill was at his professional peak. He had mastered his job down to its finest detail, he was in complete control of every aspect of the school's affairs, and he was having the time of his life.

Jonathan, Bill and Helen, circa 1959

Once after a dance weekend a visiting boy came to say good-bye to Bill. Grasping the headmaster's hand firmly and giving him an earnest look, the youth said: "Mr. Yardley, I want you to know that I think you have the best job in the country." Bill agreed. Though his friends and family sometimes wondered if he harbored larger ambitions—the presidency of a small liberal-arts college, perhaps, or the ministry of a prominent pulpit—he never gave evidence of wanting to be anything except what he was. As most people do, he had found his niche in the world; his was called Chatham Hall.

His routine was steady if not inflexible. He rose at seven, and breakfasted forty-five minutes later with Helen and whoever else happened to have stayed in the Rectory the previous night; the meal was cooked and served by a servant. He walked the hundred yards to his office, where his mail awaited him. Betty Thornton was there at nine, ready to take dictation, a principal preoccupation of each day. Except when conducting sensitive business he kept his door open—it faced Pruden's main hallway with its constant stream of girls, faculty and staff—and all were welcome to enter it; it amused him no end that the light immediately outside had been switched on by Dr. Lee's secretary to warn the school that the old gentleman had nodded off. He regularly played host to parents making school tours with their young daughters, and interviewed each potential applicant privately; Chatham Hall had a seller's market in those days, and only girls who were virtually certain of acceptance were encouraged to apply.

After lunch he went back to the office for more dictation. He read through incoming circulars and journals, always on the alert for something of use to Chatham Hall. In response to a flyer from Ben Silver Inc., a "manufacturer of crested blazer buttons" in New York, he wrote:

> Thank you for your form letter telling us of the very handsome blazer buttons which you manufacture.
>
> We are interested in placing an initial trial order of three dozen sets, but I think we would have to depend upon your art man to make us up a sketch for final approval. I enclose an embroidered blazer emblem as being the handiest way to show you the colors and general design of our seal.

Thus began a happy relationship between manufacturer and client. Ben Silver's buttons proved a hit, and Ben Silver himself was a courteous gentleman with whom Bill clearly enjoyed doing business. "I should like to compliment you upon the really beautiful execution of our Chatham Hall design," Bill told him. "There is great enthusiasm. Thank you so much for your careful and knowledgeable attention to our needs."

By mid-afternoon Bill was usually ready to leave the office and make his rounds. For an hour each day he functioned as Chatham Hall's head cheerleader. He might visit the Powerhouse to see how Pete Taylor's crew was getting along—one of its members, Phil Falls, was a sweet, toothless fellow whom Bill was forever bailing out of the town jail's drunk tank—or the athletic fields to watch a few minutes of lacrosse. At around five he went to the Rectory to wash up and relax, then attended chapel and ate dinner with Helen at school. He worked for a while afterward but was home by eight, unless there was a lecture or entertainment; he read *The New York Times* (they took it by mail, and got it two or three days late), or worked on a slipcase, and read himself to sleep at ten-thirty or eleven.

No detail of the school's life escaped him. At vacation time he arranged the girls' train schedules. Five nights a week he led the vespers service at St. Mary's, and on Sundays he preached. He wrote the principal copy for the school's catalogue and edited what others had written. For a girl or faculty member who was troubled he always had as much time as was needed, and his counsel invariably was wise; to a girl whose mother had suddenly died he said, as he was putting her on the train, "Don't forget that your father knew her longer than you did, and will be counting on you to help him through this hard period."

His touch with teenaged girls was unerring. I have no idea whether it was something he had learned from observing Louisa Fowler or if it had been bred in the bone, but whatever the case he was masterly with young women. The shyest applicant entered his office and within minutes was chatting animatedly about herself, laughing at his jokes and talking about what she hoped for in a school. Then, after she had left, he dictated a report on the interview that was a model of perception and empathy; these were collected in a "little black book," the mysterious disappearance of which is mourned by all who had been privileged to see it.

Bill was less comfortable with his faculty, though he got along well enough with most members of it; in the 1960s, as he began to hire married couples, he made lasting friendships with Jack Wright and Ted Bruning, whose presence on the campus came as a considerable relief to him after years with only women for adult companionship. But he was happiest when the faculty's business ran without his involvement, and unhappiest when he had to exercise an administrator's most difficult assignment; his method of firing a teacher was to leave a note in her mailbox and then go off on spring vacation, hoping that the dust would have settled by his return.

Yet where the best interests of Chatham Hall were concerned, he could be as firm as was necessary. Once he asked Bruning and another teacher to undertake an intensive examination of the admissions procedure, one that involved travel to other schools and the preparation of a detailed report. After all this had been done,

Learning how to be ladies: Sunday breakfast at the Rectory

Bill created the job of admissions director—and gave it to someone else.

Ted stormed into his office. "Why the hell after the job we did didn't you give me that job?" he demanded.

Bill looked him right in the eye. "Because I want you down there in that classroom teaching freshmen."

The arrival of men on the campus changed Chatham Hall considerably; with them came wives and small children, and an atmosphere a bit closer to life in the real world. If there was ever any hanky-panky involving male teachers and students, word of it never reached me; I know by his own testimony that the charms of his students were never a problem for Bill. But he certainly worried about this aspect of their lives; his greatest fear, which never came to pass, was that one of the girls would become pregnant. Yet when in the late 1950s I developed a massive crush on a Chatham Hall girl, and suddenly began coming home from Chapel Hill with alarming frequency, Bill turned his back as she and I sneaked off to remote—and illegal—corners of the campus to do our very innocent business; years later she said, "He must have had a romantic streak to have indulged us enough that we broke the Chatham Hall rules and got away with it!"

But then he had a goatish streak of his own. Once Betty Thornton was walking across the campus when she heard the wolf whistle to end all wolf whistles; she looked over toward the chapel and there was the rector of Chatham Hall, all innocence. Another time she went into his office and said, "Dr. Yardley, can we turn this thermostat down? I'm about to burn up."

"Oh, it's not all that hot," he said.

"Yes, but you can always take your sweater off if it gets too warm."

"Well, here's what we'll do: I'll take off my sweater if you'll take off yours."

He couldn't help joking because he was having a ball. Nothing gave him greater pleasure than the annual "Faculty Show," which was staged every other year at an unannounced time and date. The faculty and staff planned it secretly, sneaking off to the little Faculty Club, behind the garden to the rear of Pruden, to write and practice skits spoofing school life. The girls speculated madly about if and when the show would be held, but invariably were taken by surprise. They were herded into Willis Hall on one pretext or another, and suddenly there on the stage was what they had waited for all along. The teachers dashed about making fools of themselves, to the girls' screams of delight, and Bill invariably was star of the show. One year he dressed up as Mrs. Babbington of Canterbury and gave a prissy little lecture about British cathedrals, all too wickedly reminiscent of one the school had recently heard. Another year, not long after an appearance by the Bennington modern dance group, he and Virginia Holt put on tunics and tights and wigs and chased each other around the stage, leaping and prancing, to the tune of *The Rite of Spring*.

When winter holidays rolled around he was in heaven. At Thanksgiving the Brunswick stew picnic was followed in the evening by an immense traditional dinner at which many turkeys were sacrificed; the largest of these, a bird that would have intimidated a panzer tank, was carved by Bill—he had learned the art from his father, and practiced it with much waving of arms and grinding of steel—on a platform in the middle of the dining room, with elaborate ceremony and accompanying applause.

Then came Christmas. As the holiday neared, the students began a countdown, singing each evening at dinner:

> *One more week to vacation*
> *Then we go to the station*
> *Back to civilization—*
> *Away from Chatham Hall.*

To which the faculty and staff responded, with much hissing and booing as accompaniment:

> *Three weeks to the end of vacation*
> *Just picture your lack of elation*
> *January fourth for your own information—*
> *Back to Chatham Hall.*

Just before vacation the Christmas Pageant was held, with two hundred girls—for that, by the mid-1960s, was Chatham Hall's enrollment—in a crescendo of excitement and hysteria over the unveiling of the Madonna. When the great moment came it was as though St. Mary's Chapel had been struck by lightning; a bolt of electricity cracked through it, leaving the girls gasping and sobbing. Then, as Bill recalled, "they went home, leaving us drained of the Christmas spirit and like all true school people delighted to have them leave."

Now Bill could turn his attention to the Yardley family Christmas. "But then, before we could have our own family Christmas," he wrote, "we had the church Christmas in town. I wonder how many parsons and Sunday-school superintendents have pondered the traumae they have inflicted on family life over the years. With four children well spaced out, we saw our own flesh and blood as shepherds, self-conscious angels, wise men in my old bathwrapper, and even one as a friendly cow and another as a slightly bewildered Joseph."

His children didn't think it all that bad, because we knew that a Bill Yardley Christmas lay ahead. By the time Ben was old enough to appreciate such things, Bill had refined the ritual to an art. On the afternoon of Christmas Eve—never earlier, heaven forfend— the large, shapely tree was brought into the living room and placed before the double glass doors at its end. All six of us decorated the tree, but stringing the lights always was Bill's assignment, one he undertook with as much ceremony and gravity as he had devoted to the Thanksgiving turkey. When these were all in place, but not yet lit, we were allowed to hang the balls and canes and ornaments, and then to participate in the draping of the tinsel. The rule was firm: *one strand at a time*. Though we children wanted to heave tinsel onto the tree in great hasty globs, Bill insisted on meticulousness; the result, we had to admit, was a tree of exceptional beauty.

Before we could enjoy it we had, as the children of the rector of Chatham Hall, a duty to perform. While Helen stayed at home, Bill piled us into the station wagon and drove into the poorest neighborhoods of Chatham and Pittsylvania County. He waited in the car and sent us to the front doors—in many sad cases of tarpaper shacks with newspaper lining the interior walls—to call out "Merry Christmas!" and to hand to each less privileged employee of Chatham Hall an envelope in which he had put five or ten dollars. Phil Falls got a carton of Camel cigarettes rather than cash, which he would only have spent on rotgut liquor that would have led him, inexorably, to Christmas dinner in jail.

In retrospect, now that I know rather more about Southern history than I did as a child, this practice looks distressingly similar to the antebellum plantation ritual in which slaves gathered around

Massa to receive their turkeys and hams. "Chris'mas gif'," they bowed and clucked in gratitude, "Chris'mas gif'!" But though Bill's attitudes on matters racial left much to be desired, he had nothing except kindly feelings toward his employees and wished to treat them in all respects as generously as he could. He also—and to us this mattered most—wanted his children to see what Christmas was like for the less fortunate before we plunged into what was, by comparison, the extravagance of our own; it was a valuable, important and lasting lesson for all of us.

By the time we came home the sky was dark. Helen had lit the lights and the tree glowed. Its bright reds and greens and yellows were reflected softly in the brown paneling, and in the fireplace a pile of logs crackled. Bill and Helen had their drinks, while we four fidgeted in nervous anticipation. After dinner we were allowed to put the presents we had purchased or made under the tree, pathetic pile though it was; then we hung our stockings before going off to bed.

By the time I was twelve or thirteen I could no longer make it through the night. I crept down the two flights of stairs from my aerie in the attic and peered around the hall corner into the living room. Each year the sight took my breath away: an immense mountain of packages, all elaborately wrapped, often with a bicycle or tricycle standing in naked splendor. As I stole back up the stairs it was all I could do to contain myself. Later, when I was too old for a stocking, I came home from Christmas Eve revels and found on my bed a small package of Modern Library and paperback books. I still have them: *Chance*, by Joseph Conrad; *The Lonely Crowd*, by David Riesman; *The Selected Poetry of Lord Byron; Light in August*, by William Faulkner; and others too numerous to mention.

On Christmas morning we were allowed to dash downstairs, still in our nightclothes, and get our stockings. We brought them up to Helen's room, where she and Bill lay in the double bed watching us pull out our little treasures one by one, until at last each of us reached the silver dollar at the bottom. Then the hard part began: we were expected to wash and dress properly, to sit through a full-scale Yardley breakfast with maid serving—What about *her* Christmas? I sometimes silently wondered—and then to sit nervously in the living room while Bill methodically, painstakingly squeezed out a few more minutes of anxiety by doing heaven knows what in his room.

Finally, mercifully, he came downstairs. Now he was pater-familias, presiding benignly over a familial rite. One by one he handed the presents out, in whatever rotation he'd decided upon that year, beginning with those gifts likely to cause least excitement and ending with each child's moment of triumph; for years mine consisted of additions to my American Flyer train set, then of books by e. e. cummings and T. S. Eliot, then—now I was growing up, and what a letdown it was—a leather suitcase. For years Bill had great fun with Jane and Sarah. He set a package before them with a silver dollar taped to it. He flipped the coin and the girl who won got to choose: the silver dollar or the mystery package. One year Jane won and took the package: it contained a pair of electric scissors, which she thought were great. So the next year she made the same choice: the package contained a ratty old fox neckpiece with a hideous pin. One year Sarah took the pack-age: she got a plastic tablecloth decorated with a garish picture of the Last Supper.

Bill loved to wrap these packages, and spent hours on them; he sprinkled everything with glitter, which stayed in the rugs and upholstery for months. He had even more fun with the cards. No present to a child was ever from Bill and Helen or Santa Claus; instead there were gifts from the dogs—Gretchen, John Sebastian, Fifi—and from public figures, especially those whom Bill de-tested: Richard Nixon gave more presents to the Yardley children than St. Nicholas ever did.

At the end of all this we were, as families are on this happiest and most exhausting of holidays, drained. We mumbled our way through lunch, spent the afternoon napping and playing with our toys, and ended the day—by now sufficiently restored to await the prospect eagerly—gathered around the dining table before a mas-sive roast of beef.

Our Christmas was over, but Bill had one more Yuletide duty to perform. The packages had all been opened, and it was time to inform various merchants in New York and elsewhere of the inade-

Christmas 1957: Jane, Jonathan, Sarah, Helen, Ben, Bill and Boy

quacy of their efforts. "Now that the dust of Christmas must be settling even at Altman's ('The Christmas Store')," he wrote, "perhaps we can bend our attention to what went wrong *this* year with my Christmas orders." A parka for Sarah had been received, but not the one ordered:

> Then there is the matter of "the longest sweater," the one that is perfect over pants and gives the most mileage: No. 1507-106. It came through. Fortunately it fitted very nicely the object of its donation. It doesn't exactly look like the picture on Page 15 of your Christmas magazine: the cut-out beneath the turtleneck was not cut out in the one that came, nor was the belt present. As my daughter didn't realize these omissions, it didn't matter a bit, but it did make me wonder about Altman's and its descriptions of the nice presents it sends.
>
> I thought that most irritating was the substitution for the leopard skin (imitation of course) "Sahara throw": This is described as a luxurious, high-pile, cotton, measuring 60″ × 80″ and was priced at $25.00. Without any word there came a folk-knitted light-weight blanket which does not appear in the delightful Christmas magazine. Because of the lateness of the hour I gave it to another of my daughters anyway, and she seemed a bit surprised but not too disappointed. After all, when people don't know what the gift is supposed to be, they don't raise the sort of questions that the harassed donor raises. As the price tag was not included and there

was no sales slip in the Christmas wrapping box, I have no idea whether I profited or lost by this substitution—but it looks very much to me as if I must have lost because the throw which came was by no means worth $25.00. At least I would not have paid $25.00 for it knowingly.

Thereupon Bill described, in rich detail, four more instances in which Altman's had outdone itself in ineptitude; it is difficult to imagine a merchant staging a more hapless performance than this one. "I think," Bill concluded, "Altman's will be minus one reasonably good customer when next Christmas comes around as I am afraid it eventually will. I wish that your store detective or *some*one in authority would comb up these records and reimburse me for whatever must be owing due to the substitution of less expensive items for more expensive ones. You will not lose much when I don't order again, but the customer you lose is certainly not a friend anymore."

Picture him now. The time is the middle of the 1960s. He is halfway through his sixth decade and has acquired the patina of middle age; some years later a friend remarks of him, "Since he was forty years old, Bill Yardley has wanted to be an old man." He has gained a not-unbecoming amount of weight, fifteen pounds perhaps, and has a substantial look about him. His hair is gray, and his dome is bare to the sky; he is unabashed by this and speaks contemptuously of those men—Douglas MacArthur leaps again and again to his mind—who attempt to disguise their baldness by letting hair on the sides of their heads grow long and brushing it over their bald spots. On the whole his health is good, though he has the blood pressure of a man whose job has a hammerlock on him.

Beside him is Helen. She is in her early fifties and has the good fortune to be one of those women who grow ever lovelier, and ever more confident in their loveliness, with age. Her face will always be lightly freckled, but age has made her countenance softer and wiser; her smile comes more quickly, and is more sympathetic. She has discovered, after all these years, that if she cuts her hair short, it sets off her face more becomingly; there is as yet little gray in that hair. She buys her clothes from the same solid New York stores she shopped as a girl—those of them that survive, that is—and favors soft tweeds in winter, cottons in summer; she still sews skirts and knits sweaters for herself, but less often now than once she did.

They are a mature couple, easy in their ways and beginning to look for the first time to the next generation. In the spring of 1960 their eldest child had informed them that change was in the making. At Chapel Hill I had met a fellow student named Rosemary Roberts, whom I described to Bill and Helen as "an extremely attractive girl with a rather caustic sense of humor and very lively, expressive eyes." I went on to say that "I think the subject of marriage will wait for some time to come," but it reared its lovely head within a matter of weeks. By spring's end I had brought Rosemary to Chatham for the obligatory inspection, which she passed with high marks; Bill regretted that she was not a Chatham Hall girl, I think, but like Helen he responded immediately to her spirit and intelligence.

A year later we were married, by Bill, in the Baptist church of Albertville, Alabama, the small town in the northeastern part of that state where Rosemary had grown up. Bill was uneasy in the company of Southern Baptists—by this stage of her life Helen was comfortable in anybody's company—but was delighted when Rosemary's uncle steered him away from the dry wedding dinner into the wet precincts of the kitchen. Bill had cleared the way for the wedding with Bishop Charles Carpenter of the Diocese of Alabama; "I am unacquainted with the marriage laws of your state and wonder whether there is anything I must clarify legally that the marriage may be correct from every point of view," Bill had written, and the bishop had assured him that "there are no legal angles you will have to worry about." So Bill did the job on Wednesday, June 14, 1961.

Three years later, on June 18, 1964, Bill and Helen's first grandchild was born, at Mothers' Lying-In Hospital in New York. Rosemary and I named him James Barrett Yardley, in honor of his maternal grandfather, James Bailey Roberts, and my first boss,

James Barrett Reston. On January 23, 1967, the second grandchild came, at Moses Cone Hospital in Greensboro, North Carolina. He was named for the great man himself: William Woolsey Yardley II. His namesake wrote:

> It is a fearful thing to have a grandson named after one. My most solid reaction is of deep gratitude that Johnny loves me enough to want to name one of his children after me. The second reaction is to try to live up to the name so that the boy will be proud of it. My third reaction is that I have never really liked the name myself, so that I feel sorry for a little boy who carries not only it but the "second" afterwards.

This letter was written to Robert and Constance Page of Caribou, Maine, whose acquaintance Bill and Helen had only recently made. Five years earlier Bill had addressed a letter of inquiry to a friend in Fort Fairfield, Maine. "My oldest daughter, Jane, is being courted enthusiastically by a young man from your rather remote part of the world," he said, and went on to inquire about the Pages of Aroostook County and their son Rob. "From what we have seen of them," the friend responded, "they appear to be a terribly attractive family." Their son, whom the friend had met only once, "seemed very nice, very attractive—clean-cut and all that sort of thing."

Indeed he was. We all fell in love with him at first glimpse. He was of medium height, freckled, energetic, quick of foot and tongue: one of the funniest men I have known, full of laughter at the world and himself. He was a Catholic, but in time Bill shrugged this off. On February 2, 1966, he wrote to Ensign R. H. Page of the United States Navy:

> Never is permission given with more of a whole heart or enthusiasm and sureness that things are right than my approval and Mrs. Yardley's of your engagement to our daughter Jane.
>
> We are completely ready to welcome you into the family as another dear son. We hope that the months and years will speed by and that I will have the privilege either of standing up with Jane to give her away or of tying the knot which will be a permanent one.

Jane is one of the dearest people in the world with spunk and character and a lovely sense of humor and marvelous feminine qualities. You are a grand boy, too, Rob, or should I say a great young man. I am proud to have you entering the family. You have our complete blessing and a very sure feeling that you are entering a full lifetime of happiness together. I hope that the engagement will be as short as possible so that you may both enter in that marvelously fruitful life which lies ahead.

But the engagement proved longer than desired, thanks to the exigencies of the Navy and the war in Vietnam. Not until nearly a year and a half later, in June of 1967, was Rob able to obtain a leave of sufficient duration to tie the knot in proper style. He and I met for the first time a few days before the wedding, when he and Jane visited Rosemary and me in Greensboro. After an afternoon sailing together Rob and I realized we were friends for life, a conviction we reconfirmed that evening over martinis. Then Rosemary and I and our two little boys drove the sixty miles to Chatham for the wedding. Never have I attended a happier one. The Page clan was present in abundance, and Paul and Ilonka Rogers, loyal friends that they were, had come all the way from Middletown. The wedding dinner was held on the grassy terrace behind Willis Hall, under a balmy Virginia sky. Celebratory beverages were served.

June 1967:
Jane, Rob and Bill

"Paul Rogers," Ilonka said, "you're *drunk*."

"You're telling *me*!" he replied.

The next day our slightly bleary crowd gathered at St. Mary's Chapel. Jane was in a simple dress and Rob wore his lieutenant's whites. Bill did the honors, with the year-round Chatham Hall community, black and white alike, in attendance. Afterward we toasted the bride and groom, and sent them winging westward to Hawaii. Later Bill wrote to Sarah, who had come down from Montreal, where she was in college at McGill:

> Wasn't that wedding fun? To me it was a happy-sad occasion, but the happiness outweighed the sadness. I am beginning to get used to the fact that Jane doesn't belong exclusively to us anymore but that we are co-owners of her with Rob and the Pages. I can't imagine a nicer family for Jane to marry into. They are warmhearted, good people, close and loving and intelligent and outgoing. If anybody ever had a chance of things working out well, I think it is our dear Jane.

IN THIS year of their daughter's marriage and Bill's namesake's birth, all was well with him and Helen, and with Chatham Hall. In the fall of 1967 Bill cast a look backward at the dozen years since the first major construction project of his regime, the library building named in honor of Edmund and Lucy Lee, and found them good. In a report to parents and alumnae entitled "Twelve Years of Progress," he noted that 5,215 new books had been added to the library; faculty salaries had been increased 184 percent and scholarships 64 percent; the thirty-five-year-old central heating plant had been replaced; an upright piano had been purchased, the first since 1925; the infirmary had been relocated and modernized; funds had been donated for a baroque organ for St. Mary's Chapel, construction of which was near completion in Germany.

The school's physical plant had expanded considerably. A dining wing had been added to Pruden Hall, with a dormitory upstairs that was known as the Penthouse. New stables had been constructed, designed by Bill's old Baltimore friend Alexander Cochran. Where Brush House once stood was now the Virginia Holt Arts and Sciences Building, which contained a full array of laboratory equipment and a studio for the art department. Five faculty cottages had been "built, rebuilt or acquired," along with a

Mr. Chips at Chatham, with Pruden Hall in the background

new Brush House, and seven faculty apartments had been re-modeled.

Brush House was home for six faculty members, whose sentiments Bill had regularly solicited as plans for the structure took shape. It was characteristic of his involvement in the minutiae of Chatham life that he repeatedly sent them rough sketches of the design—"Herewith, a Yardley architectural floor plan of Brush House with the rooming as presently planned for 1966–67"—and sought to involve them in the deliberations. "I hope that this is as fair as possible a division of the spoils," he wrote, "according to seniority, date of asking, and possibly nebulous considerations."

Bill was keeping everybody happy in these years: faculty, staff,

alumnae, parents, students, trustees. With the latter his relationship had from the outset been cordial and smooth. It would be an
exaggeration to say that he had the trustees in his pocket, for they
never approved his decisions and requests without debate, but they
knew that a first-rate man was in charge and were most disinclined
to interfere with him. When he recommended new appointments
to the board, it was not only for whatever financial contributions
they could be expected to make to the school; he wanted a rounded
board that included people who could address questions of the
school's academic and cultural life. He also wanted a board that
would participate actively in the school's affairs, and when it did
not he was dissatisfied; he really believed that a board should be
more than a mere rubber stamp.

The full board met a couple of times each year and the executive
committee assembled quarterly. The meetings were held in the
living room of the Rectory. Years later Helen told a friend that she
always dreaded them, because she had to put on her best face for
rich people who weren't really interested in her, but if that is how
she felt she did a superb job of disguising it; and if there were
trustees for whom she could only muster the face of duty there were
also those of whom she was powerfully fond, most notably Anne
Pannell, the president of Sweet Briar, and Haddon S. Kirk, a North
Carolina businessman who served as chairman in Bill's final years.

All things considered, the trustees took good care of Bill and
Helen. By the mid-1960s Bill was earning $15,000 and Helen
$3,600, with perquisites of substantial value; in 1966 their total
income, before deductions, was $18,849.23, no grand sum for
people with responsibilities so onerous as theirs but sufficient for
their modest needs. They were anything but greedy, as had been
revealed a few years before. Jane was at Sweet Briar on a scholarship provided by Mrs. Alfred I. DuPont of Jacksonville, Florida.
On March 23, 1961, Bill wrote to her:

> You have been extremely generous and kind to my daughter, Jane,
> and the whole Yardley family is deeply grateful. At the time Jane
> entered Sweet Briar our older boy was in his sophomore year in
> college and we had several unusual expenses. Now our situation is

somewhat different. Our boy will graduate in June. My trustees have been generous to me and have raised my salary. I could not in all conscience allow you to continue your generous grant to Sweet Briar for Jane. Her mother and I and Jane herself will never forget your kindness in a time of real family need. You have our most cordial thanks and our enduring gratitude.

There are many who need the help more than I do at present. For instance I heard only the other day that my dear and close personal friend, Ronald McClintock, rector of Epiphany Church in Danville, hopes to send his daughter, Anne, to Sweet Briar. Anne's mother is an alumna; her grandfather was for many years rector of Ascension Church, Amherst, and a very dear person in Sweet Briar circles. McClintock would be mortified if he knew that I am saying anything to you about Anne. I have known her from a little girl and she is a very lovely person, intelligent, modest, and good all the way through. If somehow Anne could have what Jane now no longer needs, our cup would be full right to the brim.

"Seldom does one receive letters such as yours," Jessie Ball DuPont replied. "I shall gladly make a scholarship available for your friend's, Dr. McClintock's, little daughter, Anne, who wishes to enter Sweet Briar College. If all were as unselfish and honest as you in wishing to pass along to another the financial assistance no longer needed, it would be much easier to assist boys and girls in acquiring an education. I thank you!"

It was an exchange between two old-fashioned people: a woman, amply endowed with riches, who believed in using some of her good fortune for the benefit of others, and a man too honorable and proud to accept charity when, with sacrifices, he could meet his expenses unassisted. But though neither of them could fully perceive it, the world in which these convictions had been nurtured was slowly disappearing. Bill, with his courtly manners and devotion to the past, was becoming an anachronism.

That a new day was dawning seems first to have occurred to him late in 1967 when he learned of the death of a young woman named Linda Fitzpatrick. She had grown up rich and privileged in Connecticut—she could easily have been, though was not, a Chatham Hall girl—but had been lured to New York's hippie underworld and had been murdered in a cellar on the Lower East Side. "It could happen to anyone's daughter," Bill said, and counseled that "children need discipline as well as affection." The responsibility lay with adults: "Parents are afraid to be the only ones in the neighborhood to say 'No' when their child says, 'Susie So-and-so is going to Such-and-such for the weekend. May I go too?' Parents have to learn to say 'No' a little more often."

Still, he was sympathetic to the yearnings of the young. "You have your children in one of the more conservative schools," he told the alumnae, "yet I hope we temper our conservatism with common sense." If the girls insisted on miniskirts, so be it: "I would rather fight the good fight for high academic standards than for what may well be an out-of-date point of view about hemlines." In hopes of encouraging the students to take a greater role in the school's affairs he established a student-faculty senate, though it gave him no comfort to learn that the girls immediately began using it as a forum for grievances and demands rather than conciliation and compromise. The "nasty college riots" at first did not alarm him. To a fellow member of Alpha Delta Phi who objected to Bill's newly formed opinion that fraternities were an unhealthy influence on college life, he wrote:

> In my own talking with youngsters in college of any length of hair the ones who seem to be most in touch with the twentieth century are not the ones who sit back in fraternity houses, their attitude summarized by one of the ancient songs of our own dear fraternity: "We're the chosen few." They are the ones out there often protesting and making what looks like trouble—not the Mark Rudds but the ones asking for human relationships between themselves and the faculty and requesting usually with a degree of courtesy attention to their human needs by human beings, not computers.

Soon it became clear, though, that more was happening than Bill had bargained for. Not merely was the world outside changing, so was the world inside. In rapid succession Bill found himself confronted by demands that Chatham Hall enroll its first black students, by a noisy challenge to his own authority, and by the prospect that Chatham Hall as he had always known it would go out of existence.

The first of these was the least difficult. Over two decades Bill's feelings about blacks had changed. Some of the old condescension still remained, but the Christian in him had begun to supplant Massa; on the day of Martin Luther King, Jr.'s, funeral he gave the school's black employees a day off with pay, and later he encouraged them to use Chatham Hall station wagons and cars so that members of the Pittsylvania County NAACP could participate in racial demonstrations in Danville—no small gesture in Southside Virginia at that time. Thus he was in a receptive frame of mind when alumnae and faculty began to ask how Chatham Hall could be true to its principles and remain segregated. Early in 1968 he made the decision to admit the first black students and spent much of his time preparing himself and the community for their arrival. The two girls he chose for the task were Southerners, girls who knew what they were getting into and who would be ready for whatever Pittsylvania County might have for them.

When the decision was announced, the reaction of Chatham Hall's parents amused him. "People seem to be taking it in stride," he wrote. "The only feedback I have had has been from people who are perfectly supportive and willing to accept it but just don't want their daughters to room with them." But that was about as far as it went. The two girls matriculated in September of 1968, without notable incident; Chatham Hall was no longer a school for white girls only.

By contrast the challenge to Bill's authority was more damaging, to the school and to him. It was a direct consequence of opening the faculty and staff not merely to married men but, now, single ones as well. This had brought Chatham Hall a bit closer to the real world and had given Bill the friendship of Jack Wright and Ted Bruning, to both of whom he was mentor and exemplar, but it had also confused the natural hierarchy of things Chathamite. Bill may still have been lord of the plantation, but now he had overseers and henchmen, not all of whom offered him the blind loyalty to which he had become accustomed. A young teacher of great gifts and hot temper shocked him by shouting, behind the closed door of the rector's office, that Bill was out of touch. "You're an *old man!*" he yelled, so loudly that everyone in the hall heard him—and then he repeated the same accusation at a faculty meeting a few nights later.

What astonished everyone was that Bill absorbed the blow without significant protest. People began to wonder if he was beginning to lose his grip on the school, and they wondered all the more as an open challenge to his leadership was mounted by another man, this one married, who came to Chatham Hall in the late 1960s. Before long this interloper had decided that he could do the rector's job far better than Bill, and began making snide comments about him in formal and informal faculty meetings. Relations between the two declined rapidly, as the entire school, much to the general discomfort, could see. One morning over breakfast at the Rectory, Helen looked her husband in the eye and said, "Bill, why don't you fire that man right now? Can't you see he's after your job?" Yet Bill did nothing; he let the sniping go on for three years, until at last the man left of his own accord.

The squabble, unseemly and even puerile though it was, took a lot out of the school. Chatham Hall was no longer a happy place, at least not by comparison with only a few years before, and Bill was no longer master of all he surveyed. This may help explain why he was interested when, late in the decade, it was proposed that Chatham Hall merge with Woodberry Forest. Signs of slipping support were all about, and co-education was all the rage. "It is safe to say," Bill wrote, "that the small independent school for boys only or school for girls only is going to have an increasingly tough time. At Chatham Hall our own long-range predictions call for higher and higher tuition fees, or for shrinking the offerings and quality of the school itself."

So the two boards of trustees began their joint and separate inquiries, and a few experimental steps were taken; most notable and successful among these were week-long exchanges in which fifty Woodberry boys came to Chatham and the same number of Chatham girls went to Orange. But it was a merger for which Chatham was more enthusiastic than Woodberry, largely because Chatham's condition was potentially shakier but also because

Woodberry regarded itself, though scarcely with any good reason, as the superior of the two institutions. "Fortunately, their headmaster is young and vigorous and imaginative," Bill wrote. "Even so he is having trouble selling it to his constituency, including trustees, alumni, faculty and boys. Eventually this will take place whether they want it or not. They would be sensible to grab Chatham while we are still grabable."

But Bill proved a poor prophet. The negotiations dragged on month after month. Then Ted Bruning paid a visit to Woodberry and had tea with the headmaster, in the course of which Ted asked, "What does Woodberry expect to gain from such a merger?"

The headmaster thought a moment and then, clearly meaning to be polite, said, "Well, forty more good people for my faculty."

Ted went back to Chatham and reported the conversation to Bill.

"*His* faculty, hell," Bill said.

That did it. Bill may have been deeply worried about the future survival of Chatham Hall, but he was not about to secure that future by handing it over, lock, stock and barrel, to someone else; it might have been a school with trouble on the horizon, but it was still *his* school.

There was, in this time of uncertainty and dismay, one piece of good news—"flabbergasting" news, Bill thought. On the morning of November 24, 1967, he went to his office and found in the mail a letter from the Right Reverend Jesse M. Trotter, dean of the Protestant Episcopal Theological Seminary. "I have the pleasure of informing you," Trotter began, "that the Board of Trustees wishes to confer upon you the degree of Doctor of Divinity, honoris causa." The degree was to be awarded in Alexandria on May 22, 1968, at the seminary's commencement exercises; Bill was to treat it as "confidential information" until then.

Bill was bowled over: it was the happiest moment of his life. He was to be granted the highest honor of the world that mattered most to him; he was to become "Dr. Yardley." To Trotter he replied, "One scarcely knows what to say. Of course I wonder why on earth the seminary chooses to honor me who am not much of a

Dr. Yardley strutting his stuff

theologian and am not an alumnus though for many years a cheerful fellow-traveler. When I accept, it shall certainly be in the spirit
that Chatham Hall is the recipient of the honor and not just old Bill
Yardley the rector." Then, in a letter to Sarah, he turned to the
really important business:

> How vain can I be? On its way over from England is my new silk
> red-banded doctor's gown with full bell sleeves, the enormous hood
> of an honorary doctorate, and a velvet cap with golden tassel. Wait
> 'til you get a load of me.

Thus attired he stood, "in fear and dread and trembling and in
joy, too," as the president of the seminary's trustees read the cita-
tion. "Being true to the long line of your distinguished forebears,"
it said, "both in the church and national life, you have made an
important contribution by combining a teaching ministry with
your priestly ministrations. Performing with thoroughness and
distinction your duties as headmaster of Tuxedo Park School, and
then as rector of Chatham Hall, you have influenced, for good,
many young lives, giving them a personal desire for knowledge in
an atmosphere of practical living."

Helen was in the audience, sitting with friends. In her purse was
the telegram that had been sent the previous evening to "The Rev.
William W. Yardley, D.D.," by the students, faculty and staff of
Chatham Hall.

> Your warmth and zeal, your scholarship and love, your infinite
> patience and holy impatience are our experience. Now others recog-
> nize that which we have always known. You bring us honor, we offer
> you congratulations. Together we express our joy.

This happy day was but an interlude. The outside world that had
so afflicted Chatham Hall was now closing in on the Rectory itself,
boring right into the heart of Bill's family. His adored younger
daughter, Sarah, away in college at McGill and liberated from the
constraints of life at Chatham Hall, was discovering the thrills and
delights of freedom. In 1967 and 1968 she sent home letters
describing various student uprisings, but she was afraid to mention

the full extent of her own involvement in those activities, with the result that her letters took a slightly critical tone she did not in fact feel.

Bill thought he was corresponding with, if not a kindred spirit, at least someone who shared his own fundamental views. "It is too bad to hear about the president of McGill and his tough time with the so-called activists," he wrote in November of 1967. "Most of them are people who aren't really active in what they ought to be doing, which is to get themselves an education. Of course I speak as a member of the Establishment; after all a member of the Establishment is nothing in the world but someone who has a job or owns a little property. You, my dear, are a member by inheritance and also by ability and potential." A year later he wrote similarly: "Maybe it is my age, but I fail to understand why people who go to a university to learn something are bound they are going to tear these things down like Samson in the temple"; and when Sarah told him about a friend who was cohabiting with her boyfriend, Bill responded:

> While I am not shocked at Rita's boyfriend living in the apartment with you, I don't exactly whoop with joy. If he and she are all that nice and congenial why the dickens don't they get married? Put this down to being old-fashioned. Your mother and I, believe it or not, were both virgins when we were married. Neither of us has ever been to bed with anybody else. There is no lurking feeling in the back of our minds that there was somebody else in there.

Even as late as October of 1969 Bill was writing to a daughter whom he still thought of as innocent. "You know," he told Sarah, "we worried about you considerably when the police strike was going on in Montreal. It did sound like terror in the streets—and I wanted good old lawnorder man George Wallace up there to straighten things out." But two months later Sarah straightened *him* out, once and for all. It was time for her to tell all, she decided, and tell all is what she did. Like countless thousands of other young people of that era, she laid the whole trip on her Mummy and Daddy. In December she sent them a long, righteous letter— alas, it does not survive—in which she told them almost everything their little girl was doing. She was smoking marijuana; she

283

had been arrested at a feminist demonstration, had been jailed for several hours, and could be convicted of riotous assembly; she was active in the antiwar movement and was involved with transporting marginally illegal material—a videotape—into the United States.

The letter crashed into the Rectory like a small bomb; perhaps it is a sign of the times and her family's place that Sarah's offenses, so commonplace today, should have thundered home so traumatically. Not merely had she violated the law; she had behaved in a manner wholly contrary to her upbringing. Helen's immediate reaction is not recorded, but Bill's we have. He went to the desk in his room, trembling with anger and sorrow, and for the only time in his life at Chatham of which I am aware, began to write a letter in longhand. It is a letter that expresses his deepest fear: that as she moved into this strange new world, his daughter would now be lost to him.

"Dearest Sarah," he said, "I love you very much: let that be perfectly clear at the start of what must be an angry letter. You are making it rather harder for me to love you because your letters are conceited, egotistical, humorless, callous and bitchy. I hope you've not become all of that though you appear both out of touch with reality, and paranoid also.

> Ever since I was a little boy in Baltimore I've had the misfortune to know a large number of women (like Cousin Lizzie Gilman) who set out to change the world. They mostly have, for the worse. They lose their feminine attractiveness. They become preachy, boring, pompous, sententious and unattractive. Saddest perhaps is their deadly humorlessness; the glittering eye of the fanatic who knows she's right is not pretty, whether she's hipped on legalizing pot, minority rights, vegetable diets, or phonetic reading—or the Episcopal Church.
>
> If you're still with me, you've committed a felony (pot—and why can't you say "tried" instead of the pompous "experimented"? Where's the experiment?). You've committed a misdemeanor—on behalf of people who are not yours and in a cause which isn't any of your business. You've thrown away a good university career and rationalized your own apathy as concern for manning the barricades. Fat lot of good you'll do. You call it a "new life style" in the same way an undertaker calls himself, equally pompously, a grief

therapist. The new morality usually turns out to be doing what one wants to do when one wants to do it. The "wealthy young man" who is using his legacy on underground films sounds like an ingrate who can tear down, not reconstruct. That's generally left to the Stalins, the Napoleons, the Hitlers, and (God forfend) the Spiro Agnews. Were it not for the spoiled generation and its irresponsible, destructive paranoia we would not have to worry about such as he.

Now let me be a little egocentric. My blood pressure is at a dangerously high level. I may be obliged to retire early, or I may have a heart attack. Coincidence? Dunno, child. I haven't mentioned this before because I didn't wish to worry you. As a matter of fact I just didn't write much this fall because you kind of blocked the way for anything but anger and disapproval. Letters like this don't come naturally to me, but you asked for it. If you were seeking approval you need to look at your sensitivity level; if you were just needling you succeeded.

One final tut-tut: the complete banality, conformity and drabness of it all. I see the tedious conformity to peer-group usual in early adolescence (Yes, you're still in dear old adolescence)—the conformity of second-hand Marx, Freud, Friedan, and old Army clothes.

Well, that got quite a bit off my chest, a somewhat disappointed chest. I couldn't have written it to anyone I hated or was indifferent to. It had to be written only to someone I love. I'm sorry you'll be a day late at Xmas. If you need money for fine, lawyer, plane fare, let me know. Perhaps we may be able to talk now without rancor across that gap, crack, or chasm. I won't try to preach at you again if you won't try to preach at me . . . and if you see that sententious lady on the faculty who organized you patsies, kick her on the arse for me— was she arrested? Such are usually not. And those French don't need your help—they appear quite capable of developing their own ethnocentric paranoia and of putting bombs in mailboxes all on their own.

> With devotion, love and affection,
> Daddy

He was not finished, but added this plaintive postscript: "Sorry, Sarah, it's a horrid letter; it is meant to be. 'Experience keeps a dear school but fools will learn in no other.' Before you completely join the alienated group, will you give heed to alienating me?"

S ARAH WASN'T finished, either. A few days later she flew down for Christmas and dropped the other shoe. Helen was in bed one night when Sarah came into her room and offered to rub her back. While Helen lay there, trying to relax, Sarah told her that she was taking birth-control pills and was living with her boyfriend. Helen tensed up, but said little. Later, after Sarah had gone back to Montreal, Helen talked about the situation with a friend and worried over it for several weeks. "I didn't write sooner," she told Sarah in mid-February of 1970, "because I didn't know what to say and I still don't.

> While I may never agree with you I am probably more sympathetic to your point of view than I was. I'll just keep quiet, I guess, and will try not to worry. (I'm trying to give up worrying for Lent!) One thing which you may not appreciate is that I am caught between you and Daddy. I react to you living with Jerry emotionally and Daddy does, too, much more violently, and I have to know what he feels—and I know even if he doesn't tell me—and believe me this is shattering.

"The last six weeks have been tough," she said, "and I'm tired and discouraged myself." Not merely was she depressed by the news from Sarah, "I have also been extremely worried about Daddy's health." After years of excellent medical reports following his annual physical at Duke University Hospital, Bill had suddenly begun to show signs of decline. Previously he had been to the hospital for nothing more serious than kidney stones—the removal of which he loved to describe in lavish detail—but in October of 1969 he had surgery for an abdominal hernia: minor so far as physicians are concerned but major for Bill, who said, "It would be silly for me to pretend that I feel fine—you wouldn't believe it, and I don't."

"Daddy really had a bad case of flu," Helen wrote, "and *still* doesn't feel like himself or have any pep or oomph. I wish he could have a real rest but it looks as if one week in Florida will be all." They went to Sarasota in late March, as had been their custom in recent years, and Bill came back better in body if not in spirit. Sarah's apostasy continued to sadden and outrage him; she did not help matters when she let it be known that her little cadre might be of interest to the Central Intelligence Agency or the Federal Bureau of Investigation. The possibility that their daughter might come

Sarah, circa 1970

under inquiry, though probably never a serious one, was just about more than either Bill or Helen could take.

Sarah came to 330 Indian Avenue that summer for what proved a bizarre visit. She had by now graduated from McGill but was still in Montreal, working at part-time jobs and living in a commune. This last, to Bill, was an abomination. From the moment of Sarah's arrival he refused to speak to her, and maintained this stubborn silence until her departure several days later. It made for low comedy: sitting at the dining table with a piece of bread in his hand, he went without butter because he would have had to ask Sarah to pass it to him.

Later in the year he relented, to the extent that when Sarah passed through Chatham en route to California he offered to buy her a car; he had an extra $700 in his private account and proposed to give her a Volkswagen. She sensed that he was trying to protect her and declined the offer, but at least a small step toward reconciliation had been made. Still, it was not until 1974, when Helen visited Sarah in San Francisco, that the breach was wholly healed. By then Sarah had tired of leftist politics and, more immediately, leftist people; she had also recovered her senses of humor and of family, and had taken a responsible job driving a school bus. Helen's stay with her was happy; she liked San Francisco and Sarah's friends there, and managed to put up a good front about the way Sarah had chosen to live her life.

It was this, rather than politics, that was at the heart of the controversy with Sarah. Though Bill and Helen thought her politics rather extreme, as certainly they were, what really bothered them was *how* she lived: the sex and the drugs and the possibility of imprisonment. But on the terrible public issues of the day, they were almost entirely in agreement with her. When Bennington polled its alumnae about the war, Helen replied that "I fully share the sense of outrage that has swept across this country since the recent escalation of war in Southeast Asia." Following the announcement of the American "incursions" into Cambodia, she sent telegrams to the president and the secretary of defense expressing her "horror." She thought that "recent student action, particularly where it has been in cooperation with members of the faculty and administration as at Bennington, is one of the most positive and encouraging developments of the last few months."

But the principal subject on her mind was the health of her husband. In the fall of 1969, according to his physician, Bill "was found to have moderate elevation of his blood pressure and was put on medication for this though there was a rather wide variation in this pressure, depending on how much tension he was laboring under at the time it was taken." Bill was fifty-eight years old, but in appearance and temperament he seemed considerably older. He was stout if not fat, and moved creakily; part of this was his old-man performance, but more and more it was simple reality. His temper was shorter too; what had for years seemed amusingly curmudgeonly now had lost some of its charm, as Bill grew short with Helen and, at times, his children. There had always been a distinct difference between the side he presented in public and the one his family saw—to varying degrees all of his children harbored a feeling that he could be more loving and patient with his students than with them—but in previous years this had been something we had accepted, however grudgingly, as part of his personality; now he had less success at suppressing his rage, and his expressions of it were no longer so entertaining.

Chatham Hall, it seemed, had finally gotten the better of him; the pressure of recent years, combined with the changes in the atmosphere of the campus, had taken the fun out of the job. Too, there were signs that he was slipping. Apart from his failure to stand up vigorously against his youthful male challengers, people began to notice that his memory wasn't so keen as it had been and that his attention span had diminished.

That winter he and Helen began to talk about early retirement, and it soon became clear that she strongly supported the idea; she did not want her husband to die on the job—a possibility that by then she took extremely seriously—and she was tired of the routines and responsibilities that had been her life for more than two decades. Because their financial resources were limited they were apprehensive about losing Bill's salary and the job's many perquisites, but after weeks of discussion they decided to take the risks. They knew neither where they would live nor how they would support themselves, but early in the spring of 1970 they made a firm decision to retire, at the end of the 1970–1971 academic year.

Bill presented his plans to the trustees, who were surprised but relieved; they loved Bill Yardley but could see the warning signs as clearly as anyone else, and they did not relish the prospect of finding a way to ease him out. Instead he did the job for them. There was nothing perfunctory about their expressions of regret. "It is very difficult for the trustees to accede to Dr. Yardley's desire to be arbiter of the timing of his retirement," Haddon Kirk wrote in a letter to the school's parents, alumnae and friends. "We have great confidence in him and his continuing ability to guide Chatham Hall in the superior manner that has characterized his entire rectorate. Only in acknowledgement of what he has done for and meant to Chatham Hall do we now agree to follow his wishes."

Kirk's letter was accompanied by one from Bill. "In the middle of this recent winter I realized that the opening of the academic session of 1971–72 would put me past an interesting age," he said. With the image of Peabody of Groton firmly in mind—he once wrote that "I have seen a number of schools go down because of old men who didn't recognize when they had had it"—he noted that "there is no way for a headmaster to taper off within the school of which he is head" and that "I also have various physical things, none of them interesting to anyone but myself." He went on:

> This has been no easy decision. Helen and I love Chatham Hall. We will have served it for twenty-two years, a longer period than anyone since the founder, Dr. Pruden. We reached this decision with a degree of agony and tearing of the heartstrings. We have brought up four children in the Rectory on the hilltop. We have made literally thousands of friends. That the first daughters of the girls who were in our first graduating class are themselves to graduate in 1971 has not escaped notice. Old Mr. Chips stayed on but he wasn't a headmaster, except briefly as an acting one.
>
> Helen and I are more than grateful to the Board of Trustees for permitting us a retirement slightly ahead of schedule. They, too, realize with sympathy and affection that it is for the best of the school that "management" be changed. We don't know what we will

do. While we own a house in New England, we really think of
tapering off and spending those years which are called so nau-
seatingly now the "sunset years" somewhere in Tidewater or the
Middle South, yet far enough away from the hilltop to give our
successors a free hand and a feeling that there is no watchbird
watching them. I hope to be as kind and thoughtful as were Dr. Lee
and Mrs. Lee, our predecessors.

"I know this must shock you," Bill said to his mother, still living
at the age of ninety-two. "It doesn't really shock me at all anymore,
though I hate to give up all the authority and prestige and fun that
Chatham Hall has represented over the years." To another corre-
spondent he said, "It is delightful to have no plans. For twenty-
seven years as a headmaster I have known exactly what I was going
to be doing every day all year long. Now I don't know anything
and the relief is tremendous."

But a year remained, and in it there was business to be done.
The question of succession was of the utmost importance to Bill.
The decision rested with the trustees, but they respected his judgment and were well aware that he, more than anyone else, knew
what Chatham Hall needed. "The spectrum of specifications is
very broad," he told Lucy Lee; "we are not necessarily looking for a
clergyman or a woman or a man. We are looking for vigor and
imagination and good school experience and good supportive wife
or husband. Loving trees in my opinion is very important, and a
deep and abiding interest in rather old plumbing and roofs; above
all one must love girls and be able to see through them and forgive
them at the same time."

Bill was delighted when at the suggestion of "that wonderful
young Bishop Rose," the board of trustees decided to put a student
on the five-member screening committee; the girls themselves were
"flabbergasted." Over the months to come, just as had been the
case in 1948, the school community grew accustomed to seeing
unfamiliar faces on campus, as young couples came to Chatham to
see and be seen. Finally, in February of 1971, the trustees settled on
William Reeves, an educator and Episcopal minister with a bright,
pretty wife and three blond children; if Bill thought, as he looked

at them, that he was gazing at a twenty-two-year-old picture in his own album, who could blame him? In any event he liked them, and was pleased with the choice.

It was made at what was, for Bill and Helen, an especially depressing time. Bill was sick again, this time more disagreeably than ever before. His skin had given him trouble for years, which he did nothing to ameliorate by his prodigious sunbathing, and now it was torturing him. In January he had begun breaking out: all over his body were pigmentation, blistering, oozing and scaling. He itched everywhere, and without relief. He was diagnosed by a dermatologist in Danville as having chronic exfoliated dermatitis, and was sent to Duke for a week of treatment, where he was given prednisone and other strong medications.

Bill tried to treat the illness lightly, but it was hard. "I have deep furrows and cracks in all the calloused parts of my body like the soles of my feet and the palms of my hands," he wrote, and "my right hand is virtually crippled because there is a deep fissure between the two main callouses." Exfoliated dermatitis had taken over his life:

> The skin disease that I have is a slow one and I seem to have a stubborn case of it. While I do feel better, I feel as weak as can be, largely due to the cortisone which seems to be the basic drug. The treatments are most luxurious—three lukewarm tubs a day with some exotic bath oil and a coating of axle grease afterwards. I wear a pair of garbage pail liners on my feet by way of shoes and socks, and my basic garment is a plastic unventilated jogging suit. I wear surgeon's gloves. All of this clothing is designed to keep the grease off the furniture, which it does not succeed in doing. One would have thought I would have lost weight, but I have gained eight pounds—all of it because of the cortisone.

On the evening of April 20 Helen heard a thud upstairs and rushed to the bathroom, where she found Bill in what was later described as "a semi-stuporous, incoherent condition." She called an ambulance, which rushed him to the hospital. Then she phoned me at home in Greensboro, where I was eating dinner.

"Jon," she said, "Daddy seems to have had a stroke. He's in the hospital in Danville, and they aren't at all sure he'll live."

An hour later I was in the living room of the Rectory. Helen was agitated but collected. We fixed ourselves a glass of bourbon—alcohol policy at the Rectory had long since been liberalized—and sat down to talk.

"If your father dies," she said, "I'll have to decide what to do with myself and how to support myself."

"Do you have any ideas?"

"Well, I assume that since Chatham Hall is planning to give the two of us a pension they'd give me one, though probably it would be smaller, and of course there's Social Security. But I have abilities of my own. The idea of working doesn't scare me, in fact it appeals to me. I know I'm old to be starting out, but I know something about printing and I'm good at mathematical things."

We talked in that vein for a couple of hours—distressed about Bill but conscious that practical questions had to be addressed—and then went to bed, knowing no more about his condition than we had when I'd arrived. What we did not learn until the next day was that Bill had regained consciousness a few hours after reaching the hospital and thereafter made what his physician called "a rather dramatic recovery." By midnight he was fully awake, and trying desperately to get through to Helen so he could tell her to stop worrying. He asked nurse after nurse to bring him a telephone, but none was willing to take the time to do so. Medication finally put him to sleep, but he drifted off in an irritated state.

Early the next morning they let him call. Helen's relief was immense, though she quickly agreed that the nurses' behavior had been inexcusable and worked up a nice head of steam to match Bill's own. We ate breakfast and drove to the hospital, where we found the impatient patient looking much the worse for wear but in high humor, with splenetic words for the "God damned doctors" and the "idiotic nurses." It took a while for these angels of mercy to figure out what had gone wrong, but in the end they could find no evidence of a stroke and concluded that Bill must have suffered an extreme reaction to "large doses of medication, specifically Vitamin A, which he had been taking." They let him go after a stay of two days, and doubtless were jolly glad to be rid of him.

For the rest of his tenure as rector of Chatham Hall, Bill was confined largely to the Rectory. He sat there in his plastic suit—it

was a preposterous black thing that made him look like a superan-
nuated scuba diver—and presided over the business of the school.
"I am not pretty to look at," he told the teachers and students, "but
I don't mind having people come over to the Rectory and look at me
if only to laugh with me at the ridiculous costume I must wear in
order to keep a coating of grease from my toes all the way to my
neck. I send you my love from the drawing room of the Rectory. I
can be found there most hours of the day. The visitors-welcome
sign is usually up. Just come in and say how-do-you-do if nothing
else."

His physical discomfort was extreme, but he kept a cheerful face
for his constituency. Betty Thornton came down a couple of times
a day to bring his mail and letters for him to sign, and to take
further dictation; word of his illness had spread well beyond
Chatham Hall, and sympathetic letters were pouring in. Girls
dropped by in small groups to bring him news of the campus and
to cheer him by their mere presence; faculty members came in to
talk over business and to socialize; Haddon Kirk came up from
North Carolina to talk with him and Helen about what Chatham
Hall was prepared to do for them financially.

This was a matter of considerable urgency and uncertainty, for
Bill had never had a formal pension agreement with the school; he
had Social Security and the Church Pension Fund, but he would
not get a great deal from either and he was, in any event, still more
than two years away from his first Social Security payment. In the
spring of 1970 the trustees had studied and improved the pension
plan for teachers, but no provision had been made for Bill, so it
became necessary to improvise an arrangement. This was not
easily done; if the pension were to be based on Bill's final year's
salary of $16,000, the perquisites of his job somehow had to be
taken into account.

Bill and Helen felt, understandably, that the value of those
perquisites was high, but they soon found, as Helen put it, that
"perquisites seem more liberal when *hiring* someone than when
evaluating them for retirement!" As she listed them, they added up
to a lot: the house, plus maintenance of it and of furniture in
publicly used rooms; utilities and basic telephone service; two

part-time maids and extra help for entertaining; meals in the school dining room and food for the Rectory; fuel and basic maintenance for their automobile; fifty percent of Bill's payments for health insurance and major medical, and payment of assessments by the Church Pension Fund. They thought all of this added up to at least $10,000 a year, if not double Bill's salary, but the church fund disagreed; it set the value of the perquisites at less than $5,000 a year.

This angered and worried Bill and Helen, but there was nothing they could do about it; since they had no clear agreement with the school, they were entirely at the mercy of accountants. Fortunately they had the good offices of Haddon Kirk, whose affection and admiration for them were genuine. He rounded out the last year's perquisites and salary total to $21,000, still not what they thought it should be but an improvement, and told Bill that Chatham Hall would pay half of that, reduced only by whatever he was paid by the church fund—not by Social Security, as was the case with retired faculty members. This assured Bill and Helen of $10,500 a year and, beginning in 1973, Social Security.

They also had, thanks to the sale of the best items in the Trollope collection, what was by their standards a tidy little nest egg. By late 1970 Bill had tired of the Trollopian chase and had lost interest in the collection as an entity, if not in Trollope as an author, so he decided to sell it. He and Helen were like that: they held on to cherished items for years, such as the pedestal-base dining table, then disposed of them with scarcely a thought if they lost interest or something better came along. To handle the sale Bill chose Parke-Bernet, which in the catalogue for its sale on Tuesday, December 8, 1970, presented the first batch of them as:

THE FINE COLLECTION OF
FIRST EDITIONS OF ANTHONY TROLLOPE
Formed by
William W. Yardley, D.D.

Bill flew to New York for the great event. He came home on a cloud, for, as he told a friend, "I have a serious capital gains problem—about six hundred per cent. It all goes to show that in auctions and book collecting the whole is greater than the sum of its parts. Little books I collected here and there as sleepers on dealers' shelves or single items in auctions became important items when gathered together. I was scrupulous about collecting for condition in anything I touched." The sale gave Bill his fifteen minutes in the limelight. The Spring 1971 issue of *The Book Collector* reported, "The Parke-Bernet sale on 8 December produced no fewer than 102 lots of Trollope, an interesting complement to the Sotheby sale of Victorian fiction a month earlier. The collection was formed by the Rev. William W. Yardley, and it contained all the major first editions, and a number of unfamiliar American first editions, some of them preceding the English firsts, not always by a serious interval. . . . The biggest excitement of the sale was Dr. Yardley's particular pride, the first edition of *Ralph the Heir* 1870–1 in the original parts, one of only seven or eight copies known, which reached the fabulous price of $3,000."

The first lot fetched Bill a total of $26,585; several additional

Bill and Helen: looking to retirement

sales, the last in April of 1972, brought in an additional $9,455, for a grand total of $36,040. After Parke-Bernet's commission (twenty percent) and taxes, that left Bill and Helen with substantially more than $20,000 with which to cushion themselves in retirement. The original investment had been from Bill's private funds, but after giving himself a couple of treats he put the rest into joint investments which, along with the inheritance he eventually received from his mother's estate, gave them enough capital to produce a thousand dollars a month in income. They were certainly not to be rich in retirement, but neither were they as impecunious as they had feared.

By now they had decided that this retirement would be spent in the house at 330 Indian Avenue. They had grown accustomed to the climate of Southside Virginia and did not welcome the prospect of New England winters, so for a time they thought of moving to the Sandhills of North Carolina or the Eastern Shore of Maryland or Tidewater Virginia—all of these being of course *excellent* rural addresses—and entering into a life of genteel Episcopalian poverty. "I shall probably become a clergyman again," Bill wrote in the spring of 1970, "or wear my clergy hat and collar and take a small parish, worrying about whether the old ladies get into Heaven instead of the girls into those fearful colleges." But after another summer in Middletown they decided they could be quite happy there, all the more so since they had a house that was fully paid for: "It seems silly to sell it and move somewhere else because we couldn't reproduce it for less than $90,000. We have lots of friends there, and they say that even older people can stand the New England climate after the first year or so of getting used to it."

But before they could move, they had a ceremony to undergo and farewells to be said. Neither was easy. "Come dermatitis or high water," Bill told the school, "I aim to be with you all for the senior banquet, the athletic banquet, and for the Commencement exercises themselves—even if I have to wear my academic robe over my diver's suit. Perhaps it would add a comic note to what will be for me a very sad parting." That is precisely what he did. With his swollen feet in untied tennis shoes and his body encased in grease and the plastic suit, he pulled his robes over his head and went out, for the last time, into the center of his own small world. Just before commencement the entire community held a reception for him and Helen. Food and punch were served and presentations made. The girls gave them a set of plates, and the faculty and staff a scroll signed by every employee of Chatham Hall. "We want to give you something tangible to keep you remembering us," they said, "something easier to pack than a refrigerator, easier to keep shining than a silver service." But they couldn't decide what that something should be, so they gave a generous sum of cash instead.

Bill and Helen said their informal thanks that afternoon. The next day they made them official, with a note over both of their signatures that was posted on all the school's bulletin boards:

> We have been at Chatham Hall a long time. We suppose that the school has changed greatly during those years, though we have to stop and think about where those changes were and when they occurred and what brought them about. One thing has not changed—it is a school where friendship, affection, kindness, and loyalty, truth and honor are outstanding traits. When we look back at old yearbooks we realize that hair is cut and brushed differently now, and that the club structure is somewhat different, as is the student government. We know that the curriculum has changed vastly and that the rules, by older standards, can hardly be called petty. What has not changed is the essential goodness and kindness of the faculty and of the student body and of your acceptance of us as the inhabitants of the Rectory.
>
> Thank you for the high honor you have paid us, and the generosity of the purse which we take with us. May God bless every one of you and may Chatham Hall stand forever as a school uniquely good and uniquely fine.

The rest of Commencement passed quietly. Bill was in great discomfort, but he drew sympathetic laughs with self-deprecating remarks about "my space suit." Under a hot sun he presided over his twenty-second and last awarding of diplomas and prizes, and in St. Mary's Chapel he said his final litanies as rector of Chatham Hall. As always he had been in the past, he was out in front of

Pruden to say his good-byes to the seniors as they drove off with their parents. Then, exhausted, he went back to the Rectory; it was, for the old Virginia ham, one hell of a performance.

Now the campus was empty and the work of departure could begin in earnest. Bill removed his makeshift office from the Rectory—he was somewhat better, though far from comfortable—and set up his desk in Pruden Hall's large drawing room; Bill Reeves was on campus now, and Bill thought it proper for him to move directly into the rector's office. Day after day he dictated letter after letter to the friends who had written to say farewell, and tied up the loose ends of his long rectorship. He spent hours with Bill Reeves discussing school business, offering him advice and listening to his ideas for the future.

At the Rectory Helen was in charge of excavations. "We live surrounded by cartons," Bill told his brother Paul, "half filled or all the way filled or empty. We make little decisions every moment about what to heave ho, what to give away, and what to take." Rosemary and I drove up with a U-Haul trailer and took a couple of beds, some bureaus and chairs; this helped, but it made only a small dent. To Jane, living by now in Maine, Bill sent this plea: "There will be a big surplus of furniture when we arrive. We do hope that you and Rob will take a full share."

Finally the moving van was full and the Rectory was empty. As a parting act Bill dictated a letter to the editor of *The Pittsylvania Star Tribune*, addressed to the residents of the little town with which his relations had been something less than ideal. "Because Mrs. Yardley and I have been unable to say in person our goodbyes and our thanks to all our many friends and acquaintances in the neighborhood," he wrote, "we would like to express our gratitude and appreciation to everyone in the town of Chatham." He told them that Chatham Hall was "a real part of the community" and that "it would lack its particular charm and success were it to be located anywhere else." Now that he was leaving, he realized that Chatham was a good place: "We tear ourselves away with great reluctance but with the friendliest feeling that we have lived for a long time among warmhearted friends."

One day in late June, Helen and Ben got into the Chevrolet and off they drove: down the hill, north on Main Street, up U.S. 29 to Gretna and Altavista and points beyond. Bill stayed on to finish up his business, and came north three weeks later by air. Their means of getting there were different, but the objective was the same: after all these years, they were going home.

PART FOUR

Indian Avenue

THE CHEVROLET motored north to the accompaniment of howls, lamentations and alarums. In its back seat rode all three of the dachshunds who had been in residence at the Rectory and had terrorized the squirrels of Chatham Hall. Their names, in descending order of seniority, were John Sebastian, Anna Magdalina and Detlef Kleuker, though the last two were known, mercifully, as Fifi and Peanut. Individually and collectively, they were the bane of postmen, meter-readers and the Chatham Hall faculty; but so far as Bill was concerned, they were the greatest little guys on earth.

The first Yardley dachshund had been purchased by Helen in Newport on July 31, 1961; like all but the last of their dogs, she was short-haired and reddish-brown. She was a four-year-old bitch named Gretchen, and so far as most people were concerned *bitch* was just the word for her. Gretchen was a snappish dog whose upbringing had not been happy and who spent much of the rest of her life making the world pay for it. Bill of course adored her. She was "a spoiled child who doesn't like to leave home" and at Chatham wouldn't even walk with Bill all the way from the Rectory to the office, but that never bothered him. She had taught him that the dachshund temperament—lively, bright, neurotic, witty and fiercely loyal—was just what he loved in a dog, and he was a dachshund man for the rest of his days.

Helen was rather more reserved in her affection for the dachshunds, but like all the family she could not resist the charms of the pick of Gretchen's first litter. John Sebastian was, in the opinion of those who knew him—well, the Yardleys who knew him—the best dog in the history of dogs. Born in Danville on April 6, 1962, he worked his way into the family affections so rapidly that it seemed he had been there forever. He was a happy little fellow who soon became Charlie McCarthy to Bill's Edgar Bergen. In his office at Chatham Hall, and then during cocktail hour at 330 Indian Avenue, Bill held John Sebastian in his lap, bolt upright upon his tiny derriere, and began to croon to him. "Oooooo," Bill sang, and soon enough John Sebastian joined in: "Awooooo." Within minutes the two had a mighty racket going. "Yahooooo!" "Arf! Aoooooo!"

Wherever Bill Yardley went, John Sebastian was sure to go. They were an inseparable pair, so when in 1975 the dog died Bill felt a real loss. "Old Johann Sebastian died this spring," he told a friend, "the day after killing his last rat at the age of thirteen—the dog's age, not the rat's. He was always a mighty hunter before the Lord."

His companion, Fifi, two years younger and likewise the offspring of a Danville liaison, was "a perfectly delightful little dog with beautiful rich, red coloring and a nice nose," who promptly upon her arrival at the Rectory in February of 1965 became John Sebastian's "great friend." She was sweet—an adjective not ordinarily applied to dachshunds—with big, appealing eyes and a dear heart that nearly was broken when the only puppy of her only litter was stillborn, in the spring of 1970; Bill rushed out and bought a two-week-old puppy as surrogate. Fifi quickly became "a fiercely defensive little mother" to Detlef Kleuker, named "after the very fine German who built our organ," but called Peanut once he had been claimed by his co-owner, Jane Yardley Page, and taken off to patrol the outer precincts of New Sweden, Maine.

This canine clan was to add one more to its number, when in the summer of 1974 Peanut fathered a puppy whom Bill and Helen named Wilhelm Zweite but called Willie. Nine years later an interloper named Benny came to 330 Indian Avenue, but Benny's is another story and must be told a few pages hence.

Immediately upon arrival at Middletown, Bill took about three thousand of his Parke-Bernet dollars and made the only two really lavish purchases of his frugal lifetime: a Karmann-Ghia automobile and a tractor lawn mower. This first was described, charitably, as a sports car: beneath its sleek white exterior chugged a Volkswagen engine, so Bill did not take the curves of Aquidneck Island's roads on two wheels. The second, for which he had longed for years, was a weighty contraption upon which Bill could mow his 2.8 acres— all of which by now had been turned to lawn—in about an hour; driving the machine up and down the gentle slopes of his yard, Bill felt he was king of the world.

His immediate business, and Helen's as well, was to convert what had been a family's summer house into a retired couple's year-round residence. This involved no structural changes in the building, nor was additional winterizing necessary, but interior alterations were made: the tiny bedroom next to Bill and Helen's that originally had been Ben's was made into a walk-in closet, and the thirteen-by-thirteen bedroom at the far end of the living room became, with the addition of built-in bookshelves, Bill's study.

Into the master bedroom went the latest acquisition, a king-size bed of solid Honduran mahogany that Bill and Helen had commissioned from a cabinetmaker near Danville: they had decided to try cohabitation again, though as an insurance policy they later purchased a small convertible sofa and put it in the study. The big couch from the Hull house in Tuxedo went into the living room, facing the fireplace, with the Altman's breakfront behind it and Toimi Paarsinen's glass-topped coffee table in front. In the dining room the centerpiece was Helen Ingersoll Gregory's Sheraton table, mahogany with two leaves; before the bookshelves that ran the length of the far wall stood Thomas Howe Yardley's Empire sofa, now handsomely reupholstered in yellow damask.

Soon these pieces were joined by several from the apartment at 212 West Highland Avenue in Chestnut Hill. Eva Louise Yardley

Top: *Bill and Helen in the courtyard at 330 Indian Avenue, 1971*
Bottom: *Bill with his Karmann-Ghia and his lawn mower*

was still, in her ninety-fourth year, clinging to life with "all of the Scots-Irish-Quaker tenacity" within her, but her grip was growing ever feebler. By late 1970 Harry had moved in to care for her, though Bill thought he was "taking her for a ride": "He is very much like the sand in an oyster; it is conceivable that he will turn into a pearl, but I rather doubt it." But he acknowledged that Harry was "a great comfort" to their mother, and he told the bank officer in charge of Louise's living trust, "I really think now that the five or six bottles of Highland Dew which he consumes weekly (or is it daily?) are the tribute that Paul and I must pay as a penalty for our being so far away and so busy." Bill came to 212 West Highland Avenue shortly before leaving Chatham, and reported to Paul:

> The last time Helen and I saw mother she knew Helen briefly, but uncertainly: "You remind me of someone I used to know somewhere." She knew me only vaguely and for a few minutes. However, when we said goodbye she pulled herself together like the perfect lady she is and whispered, "Have a safe journey; and when you get home give my dear love to that precious mother of yours. I hope you find her in good health." Just who I was impersonating I shall never know. In a previous visit I had twenty lucid minutes with mother, and then her mind shifted over to you. She asked about your children and the business in Honolulu. She then went off into a tirade against President Woodrow Wilson and then I became our father, and I listened to talk about how we were going to pay Bill's tuition at the Johns Hopkins and Paul's tuition at Kent. At the end, when she was very tired, she whispered, "I want to come home and live with you in your house at Mt. Airy." At that point I must have been our Grandfather Thorne.

In her last days she was feeble and only intermittently coherent. To Harry she extended "a poor withered arm trying to give me a hug and with not enough strength to do it." For a moment she gained lucidity and said in a small, tired voice, "I hadn't known that death could be so uncomfortable and so frightening." But it came peacefully to her, on November 26, 1971, in the room where she had lived for almost forty years.

We gathered there a few days later. Bill and Helen drove down from Middletown, Paul flew in from Honolulu, and I—the only grandchild able to attend—drove up from Greensboro. It was the first time the three brothers had been together since the late 1940s, when Paul lived briefly with Harry in Connecticut and Bill was nearby in Tuxedo Park.

The paths they had traveled were markedly different. During the war, while stationed in Honolulu, Paul had fallen in love with and married a native girl, Elizabeth Maili Frost, with whom he had three children: Laura, Frost and Louli. Their postwar attempt at New England life was a failure, so they returned to Honolulu, where Paul made a considerable success for himself in the appliance business. But he had a serious interest in painting, which he had studied during a sabbatical from his company; by the time of his mother's death he had sold his share of the business and moved to Kauai, where he is now a successful painter of portraits and landscapes, and Maili a popular columnist for *The Honolulu Advertiser*.

Harry's life had gone in precisely the opposite direction. After studying under Frank Lloyd Wright at Taliesen West he seemed to have a brilliant future, but the experience went to his head. He convinced himself that he was an artist and that the world consequently owed him a living. He and Elsie lived with their two children, Lolly and Tom, in a charming little house in Stamford, but it was a hard life because Harry refused to "compromise" his "artistic principles": one evening, while Elsie was staring balefully at an enormous stack of bills, he answered the telephone and astonished her by saying, after listening for a moment, "I'm sorry, I'm not interested in building a Colonial. It's just not up my alley." Gradually he drifted into the mists of alcohol, until at last Elsie, fearing he would drag her with him, divorced him after three decades of marriage. He wandered this way and that, picking up bits of work and sponging off his mother, who loved him far too much to say no.

Her death hit all of them harder than one might think, considering her great age. "There was something ineffably sad about her death," Bill said, "not tragic but very, very sad." He thought she had let herself rot away in the dark apartment on Highland Avenue, and he wished she'd gotten "a little more enjoyment" from the substantial return that her cagey, conservative investments had earned for her. Standing before the altar at St. James the Less, holding high the small box containing her ashes, Bill could not deny the tears as he spoke her last rites:

> I am the resurrection and the life, saith the Lord: he that believeth in me, though he were dead, yet shall he live: and whosoever liveth and believeth in me, shall never die.
>
> I know that my redeemer liveth, and that he shall stand at the latter day upon the earth: and though this body be destroyed, yet shall I see God: whom I shall see for myself, and mine eyes shall behold, and not as a stranger.
>
> We brought nothing into this world, and it is certain we can carry nothing out. The Lord gave, and the Lord hath taken away; blessed be the name of the Lord.

Afterward the small funeral party drove back to Chestnut Hill for lunch with Louise's beloved cousins Martin and Betty Kneedler. I did not stay long. The division of the spoils lay ahead and I did not want to be a part of it. So I was en route to North Carolina as the three brothers began the business of apportioning the accumulated property of their mother's long life. Above all Bill had his eyes on a New England maple highboy, made in the Connecticut Valley sometime between 1740 and 1760, that stood in his mother's bedroom. He had schemed for this piece for years—Louise repeatedly had turned aside his pleas to have it earmarked for him in her will—and now had devised an elaborate plan by which to obtain it. Paul offered no resistance and Harry was foiled; Paul called it "highboy robbery."

Bill drove back up the New Jersey and Connecticut turnpikes in high glee: now he had his full share, and then some, of the relics of the familial past, and his own house in which to put them on display. As soon as the highboy arrived he and Helen brought out the steel wool, rolled up their sleeves, and went to work on it:

> This highboy had had a "Philadelphia cowl" or bonnet, which we removed, together with brass eagle and ball ornament. The whole

was covered with deep black mahogany stain, probably nineteenth century. The piece incorporates, probably original, several pieces of walnut: the molding at top of base, and three drawer-dividers in base. Refinishing involved removal of black mahogany stain and deep polishing with Butcher's wax.

That passage comes from the inventory they made in 1972 and to which they added in the years to come. They purchased a double-entry ledger, on the recto pages of which they pasted color photographs, fifty-five in all, of the house's contents; on the verso pages Bill wrote detailed accounts of each piece's provenance. The primary purpose of this remarkable accounting, which they stored in a safe-deposit box, was self-protection; burglaries were not infrequent along Indian Avenue, and fires were calamitous because of the absence of municipal water lines. But pride and a touch of vanity went into the inventory as well, along with a conviction that the children to whom these pieces eventually would descend should know something about whence, and from whom, they came:

> Bronze statue, Oedipus and the Sphinx, French, signed Emile Hebert. Presented to William H. Nielson at the conclusion of his presidency by the New York Stock Exchange, 1870. Given W.W.Y. by Lucy C. Lee after Dr. Lee's death, about 1965.

> Two Philadelphia Chippendale chairs, copies of an old one owned by Louise Thorne Yardley before her marriage in 1905: they were given by various members of the groom's (T.H.Y.) family: these are marked "Con" (Convers Woolsey) and "Grae" (Graham Sumner). Paul Yardley drew all six at the division and gave W.W.Y. three. Jonathan has the one given by John Woolsey.

> Mahogany lamp table, by Toimi Paarsinen, top inlaid with tiles by Nan Benziger, Tuxedo Park, about 1947.

Now they were settled in. "Newport is quite different from the Summer Newport we've always known," Bill told Sarah. "I'll never forget how odd it seemed to see snow on the Hanging Rocks! We're getting involved in various environmental concerns: the bay is filling up with junk, they use salt on the streets (it damages *every*thing and even, gradually, kills trees and corrodes bridge

and auto underbellies), they still burn on the open dump in Newport, etc. Contractors are still trying to cover the island with
junky houses, though there is a lack of water, sewage, schools,
police, hospitals and entertainment. The taxes of course continue
to go up."

Bill complained—he *always* complained—but the truth is that
he and Helen loved it there. From the day in July when they
arrived, they realized that retirement in Middletown was precisely
what they had needed. They were far enough from Chatham Hall
to avoid the temptation of meddling in its affairs, but close enough
to the major New England highways and airports that alumnae
and friends of the school could drop by to visit, as often they did.
They had a built-in circle of friends: some their own age, others
older or younger, all people of the genteel sort they'd known their
entire lives.

Bill missed Betty Thornton's secretarial services, but in those
first Middletown years he still kept up a lively correspondence,
mainly—though by no means exclusively—with his children.
Here is an entirely characteristic sample of it, from a letter he
wrote to me after his sixty-first birthday in September of 1972:

> You outdid yourself. The ties are superb. They glow. I wore the
> grasshoppers to the Rogers on Saturday night, and the sloops to the
> Comstocks for Sunday lunch, amid universal acclaim. Both families
> were impressed that they had the virgin wearing, and I was impres-
> sed that I got them home with no soup or martini spots. They shall
> be reserved for special occasions like the Quindecim dinner on
> Tuesday and the Headmasters Emeriti in Boston on Friday. Sorry I
> can't wear them in place of a stole with vestments.
>
> *Rambling Rose* I have read with great pleasure. Several passages I
> found pleasantly erotic—perhaps at my age I like titillation even
> better than I did when I was younger. Is there any hidden satire? Or
> is Willingham just telling a good story partly from nostalgic half-
> memories? None of the characters quite comes up to Harry, how-
> ever, in *Eternal Fire*. He is among Moby Dick and Huck Finn in the
> Pantheon.

Bill could afford Quindecim—clubby gentlemen of letters who
met monthly at dinner for martinis and mutual edification—

because he and Helen were in better financial condition than ever, thanks in large measure to Eva Louise Yardley's self-denying frugality: after federal and state taxes, each of her three sons walked away with an ample inheritance. Bill and Helen added his share to the Parke-Bernet fund and their joint savings, and put it into solid, conservative investments; at first Helen oversaw these herself, but in 1980 they turned the account over to a young investment manager whom they much liked and who did very well by them. From pensions, dividends and interest, and their own small wages, they had an annual income in retirement that began at around $20,000 and slowly climbed, with inflation and the growth of their portfolio, to about $30,000. This was not, in middle-class America, a great deal of money, but it was all they needed. Early in their retirement here is how Helen, ever practical, budgeted their expenses for a typical year:

Food, Liquor, Household, Laundry, etc.	$2,200
Utilities	1,250
Maintenance and Repair	1,000
Medical	1,400
Taxes	3,600
Insurance	500
Personal	2,000
Benjamin	4,300
Automobile	600
Financial Advice	600
Miscellaneous	1,000
	$18,450

At year's end Helen balanced actual against projected expenses and found that she'd done well: the final figure was $17,585. This budget remained remarkably consistent over the years, the medical bills rising as their health declined and the payments for Ben diminishing as he went off on his own. In their first year at Middletown he was a senior at the Brooks School, and for a time was determined to go west for college. "He's a bright and reasonably conscientious boy," Bill said, "but lacking in faith in himself and determined to remove himself from our tender and loving influence."

But in Ben the parental influence was always present, and by the summer of 1972 it had taken him in a rewarding direction. His love of the past and his talent for craftsmanship, perhaps Bill's most durable legacies to him, had drawn him to Mystic Seaport in Connecticut, at Helen's suggestion. He so loved his friends at Mystic that he decided at the last minute to forgo college—he had been headed for Chapel Hill—and stayed at Mystic for two years before heading south. This was a break from traditional patterns within the family, but Bill and Helen had already learned from Sarah that traditions were there to be broken. In the event they were happy to have him at Mystic a while longer, for it was only an hour's drive away and he often came to see them.

Not that they were sitting around pining for visitors. To the contrary, throughout the 1970s both Bill and Helen were forever on the go, together and apart, pursuing any number of mutual and separate interests. Both had part-time jobs for most of the decade, both were active in clubs, Helen did a considerable amount of long-distance traveling while Bill motored about Rhode Island and New England, and they had the most active social life they'd known together. As the 1970s wore to a close and they became less active, they also became less happy with each other, quicker to quibble and criticize and nag; but for most of that first decade in Middletown they were healthy enough to be as busy as they wished, and they were liberated from the unremitting pressures of life at the top of that hill called Chatham Hall.

They went back twice, once together and once apart. The first visit was for the dedication of Yardley Hall on April 29, 1973. The occasion was not, so far as they were concerned, quite so grand as it had been made out to be. Yardley Hall was neither a new building nor, for that matter, a building at all: it was the dining and dormitory wing that Bill himself had added to Pruden Hall a decade earlier. But they were glad for the chance to see how Chatham looked after two years' absence, and glad as well that it was alumnae weekend, which meant that dozens of their old girls—women, now, some with daughters at Chatham Hall—were there to greet them.

313

Helen made a second visit, quietly, some years later, but Bill's return, in the late 1970s, was a triumph. He was nervous about how he would be received and he dawdled on the drive down, then slipped right into the old routines as soon as he arrived. The current headmaster was away on business—following Bill Reeves's departure, the school was going through rectors at a rapid rate— and urged him to move into his old office. That is just what he did, taking on a few of the rector's chores and even dictating some correspondence to Betty Thornton. At assembly in "The Well" he pointed to his portrait on the wall and said to the girls, "That's me"—he *had* to tell them, because you'd never know it from the portrait. He held a service in the chapel, and gave a strong sermon that much impressed the students. One of them came up to him afterward and said, "Oh, Dr. Yardley, we wish we had you every day." He gave her a little hug and replied, "Honey, if you had me every day you wouldn't like me any better than what you have now."

But Chatham was yesterday; Bill and Helen let go of it as easily and finally as they'd let go of the mahogany dining table and the Trollope collection. They kept all twenty-two of their yearbooks on a shelf in Bill's study and they corresponded irregularly with many alumnae, but they had vowed not to get in their successors' way and they were good to their word. By no means was this self-sacrificial; they simply had other fish to fry.

In Middletown as in Chatham they were creatures of habit. They rose at seven, and took their time over their toilets. At eight they had breakfast. Then Bill drove a couple of miles to Marty's, a convenience store that reserved *The New York Times* for him, and both of them read it, passing its sections back and forth; Helen did the crossword puzzle, usually with dispatch and in full, always in pencil.

If Bill had ministerial duties in one of the several churches to which at various times he was attached, he went off to meet them in mid-morning; three days a week Helen reported to one of a succession of accounting jobs, not returning until mid-afternoon. If both were home at lunchtime Helen fixed it; if Bill was by himself he ate what Helen had fixed for him or rustled up something for himself—he was not good in the kitchen, to put it as charitably as possible, and was far happier when Helen was there to serve him.

In the afternoon there was always work to be done around the house and yard. Along the stone fence behind the house was a row of raspberry bushes and, for a number of years, a small garden; Helen tended these devotedly, picking the bittersweet berries with care and presiding over her rows of crisp lettuces. She planted a blueberry bush outside the dining room, and made certain to cover it with plastic mesh to keep the birds away. The boxwoods and yews in the grass courtyard between the house and garage needed regular attention, which Bill gave them, and in the summer the grass provided frequent excuse to crank up the mower and go off on a joyride.

If they weren't working, they were reading: Helen in her small armchair next to the sofa and coffee table in the living room, Bill in a similar chair in his study. In 1973 and 1974 they spent an inordinate amount of time watching daytime television, for the best show they ever had seen was on the air: Watergate. The pleasure Bill took at the humiliation of Richard Nixon was most un-Christian, but that bothered him not at all. He rubbed his hands and licked his chops as the succession of Nixonian henchmen paraded before the cameras, and when Nixon fell he was so happy he could scarcely contain himself: now he had Gerald Ford to mock and ridicule.

For a time the television set was in Bill's study, to which he and Helen repaired at cocktail time to watch the evening news. This was fine during Watergate, in which both were deeply involved, but later Helen tired of Bill's running commentary on the news and ended the custom; it is a pity that no tape-recording exists of these tirades, for they were grand shows. Suffice it to say that they consisted largely of such insults as "imbecile," "jackass," "crook," "charlatan," "pederast," "popinjay," "mountebank"—any of these, in thundering unison with "God damned," accomplished Bill's purpose.

Cocktail hour began at six and ended at seven. While Helen prepared the tray of hors d'oeuvres, Bill walked down the driveway and got *The Newport Daily News* out of its box, faithfully accom-

330 Indian Avenue: views of the living room and courtyard. Helen's chair is at the left, beside the Tuxedo Park sofa and Toimi Paarsinen's coffee table; the breakfront from Altman's is at the rear

panied by a small retinue of dachshunds. The tray was ready when he returned: a bowl of sliced green and red peppers, a homemade pâté, three or four different brands of crackers and the same number of cheeses, a bowl of black olives. Now Bill could prepare the drinks, which he did with obsessive deliberation: pouring a taste of vermouth into each glass—Noilly Prat, of course—followed by an inch of gin, dropping in a couple of olives, then adding a generous batch of ice cubes from the supply he guarded with military zeal. Over the years the gin changed to vodka, the vermouth vanished, and the olives became twists of lemon, but the routine varied not a step.

Bill sat on the sofa, Helen in her chair; the tray and drinks were on the coffee table. If they were by themselves they read: magazines, catalogues, books, the Newport paper—"the God damned *Daily News*," Bill called it, though he read every line—and commented idly to each other on what they came across. Helen was in and out of the kitchen fixing dinner, though with characteristic efficiency she had done most of the preparation beforehand, and halfway through the hour Bill came back to fix a second drink for each of them. By seven, when Helen called that dinner was ready, the snack tray had been decimated.

If they had guests the cocktail hour tended to be a tad longer and a tad wetter. Theirs was a little world in which dropping by for drinks was an accepted social ritual to which dinner need not be attached; an hour—and a mere two drinks—might not always be enough to accomplish the obligatory pleasantries. But if this meant pushing dinner back to seven-thirty, so be it; if Bill and Helen had gone out for drinks, dinner was certain to be then or even later.

It was a formal meal: not black-tie, but Helen always had on a nice dress and Bill a jacket and tie, a custom that did not begin to disappear until they had fully freed themselves from headmasterly manners. Helen set out linen table mats and napkins, and the heavy old family silver; Bill lit the two candles on either side of the white Belleek latticework porcelain flower dish that they used as a centerpiece. Grace was said, as it was at all meals, and if carving was to be done, Bill did it at table. Roasts and chops and the salt-cured hams they'd come to love in Virginia were still the order of the day, but now that Helen was her own cook again she decided to be more adventuresome than she had been in Tuxedo. That Bill didn't much like unfamiliar foods was something of a deterrent, but she decided simply to ignore it; she tried interesting recipes in cookbooks and the food magazines to which she subscribed.

The main course was always followed by dessert. It's hard to say which Bill would have had more difficulty giving up: his hors d'oeuvres or his dessert. If Helen felt uninspired she reached into the refrigerator for ice cream—he doted on concoctions like fudge ripple and chocolate chunk—but her own preference was for something healthier, fresh fruit in particular. Whatever the dessert, Bill accompanied it with cookies, which he invariably insisted upon; at lunch he ate Chips Ahoy! cookies right from the bag, but at dinner he had fancier ones on a tray. He got his little metal-and-porcelain ashtray off the heavy chest of drawers that once had belonged to Thomas Howe Yardley, lit up a cigarette, and pronounced himself satisfied.

They did the dishes together, she washing and he drying; never, never ever, did they put the family silver or the "Old Spode" china in the dishwasher. Then they went back to their reading or other diversions: for a time Bill resumed building slipcases, and Helen always had a sewing or needlepoint project under way. In the early Middletown years they stayed up until ten-thirty or eleven, but gradually—almost imperceptibly—bedtime crept forward. Depending on the condition of Bill's skin and the volume of Helen's snoring, they slept together in the big mahogany bed, or Bill went off to the foldaway in his study.

It was a quiet routine, only infrequently interrupted by small familial dramas or the unexpected appearance of strangers, and it suited Bill and Helen just fine. "Thus far we love retirement," Bill said. "It gives play to a very strong domestic strain in both Helen and me. She is a superb cook and manager. I turn out to be a passing fair painter, carpenter and groundsman."

"It's really quite remarkable," Bill wrote in 1975, "that two old crocks in their sixties can still be useful and paid—it may be because we both have skills and are willing to work and to be exploited a little." Both worked regularly for most of the decade, and there can be no question that this had much to do with the general felicity of their retirement: it got them out into the world, it gave them a sense of service, it kept them from grating excessively on each other's nerves. Not only that, but they were good at what they did; their contributions to numerous institutions were far larger than the pittances they uncomplainingly accepted as remuneration.

Before his retirement Bill had informed the Episcopal Diocese of Rhode Island that he would be moving there and would be available for ministerial work; it was not long before the church had more than enough for him to do. In the next several years he preached and held communion at a number of churches, among them St. Matthew's in Jamestown, St. Mary's in Warwick and Trinity in Newport, but the two where his service was longest and most rewarding were St. Paul's in Portsmouth and Emmanuel in Newport.

He went to St. Paul's in 1972 and spent a year as acting rector. Portsmouth was a small town on the west bank of the Sakonnet River, about ten miles north of Indian Avenue on Route 138. The church was modest in appearance and manner. "I temporarily have a little church and enjoy it," Bill wrote. "It's up-island in Portsmouth, very old but ugly; the congregation reminds me of the nice country folk in Virginia. Country folk are probably much alike the world over." Bill held services there every Sunday and during the week visited parishioners who were sick or old, or both. It was the first time he had had a congregation of his own; he discovered both that he loved the responsibility and that his therapeutic skills were as comforting to poor old people as they had been to prosperous young girls.

This is not to say that he was Mother Teresa. After church or a day of house calls he invariably came home and groused to Helen about the onerousness of his duties and the inadequacy of those who had been blessed with his presence; if he was a good Christian, he was also a carping critic. Yet I have no doubt that on balance St. Paul's was the happiest experience of his religious career, for it was there that he was a real preacher.

Later in the decade he was called to serve as assistant rector at

Emmanuel Church, at 42 Dearborn Street in Newport, only a few blocks from Trinity but miles away in social standing. Trinity, on Queen Anne Square, had been built in 1726 by the first Anglican parish of Rhode Island; it was a wooden structure, painted white, that combined the simple beauty of the New England country church with the majesty of a small cathedral, and it had a socially prominent congregation to match. Emmanuel by contrast was a much more recent stone building, of dignity but no special architectural distinction, that served a far more modest parish.

Bill might have wished for more, but Emmanuel provided what he had always needed: position and standing within the community. Just as he had been the rector of Chatham Hall, so now he was assistant rector of Emmanuel Church. He put in eight hours a week and two Sunday mornings a month, fulfilling numerous duties: assisting the rector by bringing the sacrament to persons unable to attend church; making follow-up calls to the elderly under the church's outreach program; helping the rector on communion Sundays; celebrating the Eucharist at a monthly Thursday service; and giving the rector a monthly report on his activities. For this he was paid $100 a month, $1,200 a year.

He was conscientious and enthusiastic, if privately captious, about his responsibilities. He regularly brought comfort to Roy John Doncaster at the Bellevue-Newport Health Center: "Don't bother to make a date," he reminded himself. "Go in, turn off TV, put away his cards. His roommate, a Methodist, always refuses Holy Communion, but I ask him anyway." Mrs. Anderson: "Has not wanted the intrusion of a visit—lives from day to day. Lovely person." Mrs. Aline Groff: "Will probably cry; she has lost her independence and moved to the wrong apartment house." Mrs. James Easton, at the Baptist Home: "Stone deaf. I let her read the liturgy to me, I saying only those parts reserved for the clergy. A toughie." Mrs. Charles Thomas: "I tried her in December, but she 'wasn't ready yet—try me in the spring.' It's spring now."

Bill prayed with these people, consoled them, and buried them; it was the quotidian work—the dirty work, if you will—of the ministry. He also did the more glamorous jobs, celebrating communion and preaching sermons. This latter he did from notes, as in a sermon in which he asked, "What do you answer if you were asked, 'What does Christianity say?' (1) by a sharp young Communist, (2) by a complete humanistic materialist, (3) by an indifferent, scoffing cynic, and (4) by an eager, questing pagan who approaches our faith with open mind?" No doubt, "if you're like me, you would stammer and stutter, grind to a stop, fumble for a quotation from the Bible." But if you pause to reflect, perhaps you will say something like this:

Christianity is the WAY, the path through life. On it we encounter both clear sailing and unforeseen difficulties: chance encounters, ups and downs, hills and valleys, beauty and ugliness, means and direction, opportunities and companionship, choices and blind alleys. But if we believe, "In thy light we may see the light, and in thy straight path may not stumble."

Christianity is the TRUTH, which lifts us up from the life we are living on the ground into the cosmic atmosphere. It is a reality greater than we can comprehend: our ideals, the beauty which lights our life, the answer to our questions, the clue to the meaning of existence.

Finally, Christianity is the LIFE, the mysterious energy that stirs in material substance, the force that will make those dead trees outside burgeon forth in a few short weeks, that force which makes boys grow into men and girls into women, that fills us and changes us and drives us forward. "I am come that ye may have life, and have it more abundantly."

I think I would answer the question I started with, "What does Christianity say?" by saying, Jesus is the way, the truth, the life. I would add, "There isn't any other way," or: Love is the way, caring is the way—power and force and treachery and falsehood are not the way. They are not the explanation of existence, they do not lift you up or open to you the answers you seek. They solve no problems, rather they create problems. Only Christ can do that. In him it is possible for us to have life, and to have it abundantly.

He was no theologian, and I make no claims for him as such, but he was an effective, moving preacher. He spoke to the common cares and concerns of his listeners, whom he addressed as friends and equals. His oratorical manner occasionally achieved excess, but for the most part he was calm, reasonable, compassionate. His inner soul may well have been witness to an unceasing struggle between the side of him that believed and the side that did not, but to the world he presented a figure that radiated dignity and conviction.

No such glamour or public recognition attended Helen in the duties she fulfilled in the small jobs that came her way, but this was of no moment to her. She wanted to get out of the house and to demonstrate that, however modestly, she could achieve recognition as something other than an appendage to the rector of Chatham Hall—or the assistant rector of Emmanuel Church. During the 1970s she held three jobs, none of which was unduly remunerative but all of which gave her pleasure.

The first of these was as bookkeeper for Newport Crafts, a retail operation run by the Newport Preservation Society. Its store was in the Brick Market at the foot of Washington Square, across from the Old Colony House where Rochambeau and Washington had met. The gentrification of waterfront Newport had gotten under way by then, but its full effects had yet to be discerned; Thames Street still had an agreeably raffish look. In these years Newport Crafts sold pewter and sterling reproductions, and similar pieces reminiscent of Williamsburg reproductions; these are still to be had at the store, but now it serves primarily, as does most of Thames Street, as vendor of posters and gimcracks for day-trippers.

Helen started work there in 1972, in time to rake in $326.14 for the year, but by 1975 she was up to $2,262.57; combined with $502.82 earned at Cooper Gallery, an arts-and-crafts establishment a few storefronts away from the Brick Market, this gave her a total of $2,765.39 for the year—not a grand total, to be sure, but a nice supply of pin money and, more to the point, tangible evidence that Helen Gregory Yardley was worth something all by herself.

In both of these jobs she kept the store's books and from time to time offered mature counsel to the younger people with whom she worked, who were devoted and loyal to her. She returned that loyalty, buying presents for her children from the stores at em-

ployee's discounts and steering her friends their way. She quickly
became expert in the economics of small retailing, and delighted in
this newfound knowledge; she never rattled on about life at the
store, but it was clear from the way she talked about her work that it
had opened up new dimensions for her and heightened her self-
respect.

She spoke with similar enthusiasm about St. Michael's Country
Day School, for which she became bookkeeper in the late 1970s. It
was at 180 Rhode Island Avenue, a stone's throw from the erst-
while Yardley-Woolsey compound; in 1978 it paid her $2,926,
which was about as much as she could earn without affecting the
Social Security payments that she and Bill were by then receiving.
Her work there was the same as at the stores: totting up the books,
a most undramatic occupation that nonetheless she found rewarding and challenging.

She was fit, energetic and full of projects, this despite surgery in
November of 1974 to remove her left breast, where a malignancy
had been discovered. She saw this as a token of mortality but took
it in good stride; after five years she had no further sign of cancer,
and was living a life so normal that her children rarely even recol-
lected the operation. Self-pity was not her nature; she had the
operation and got on with her life.

By the mid-1970s she had become a member of the Newport
Garden Club, and for the next several years she devoted a significant portion of her time to it. The club was an organization of
about a hundred women: summer colonists, Navy wives, Indian
Avenue residents. Membership had a certain social cachet, and
expertise at gardening was not obligatory, but it was by no means a
frivolous undertaking. Helen didn't know precisely what she could
contribute to it, but she did have one suggestion. "I'm not much of
a gardener or flower-arranger," she said, "but I'm good at figures
and if anyone ever wants me to be treasurer, I'll be happy to be."
The other members took her up on it, and soon learned that her
managerial skills were an invaluable asset. So they elected her to a
two-year term as president, and by the time she was through some
thought her the best they'd had: she was efficient, responsible,
tactful and courteous, always thanking people for assistance ren-
dered and always ready to take on trivial tasks without complaint.

The presidency gave her a treat: a trip to Seattle for the annual meeting of the Garden Club of America. She went with Gay Sheffield, the president-to-be, but she refused to share a room with her; "Bill says my snoring is disgusting," Helen said, "and that makes me uncomfortable about sleeping in the same room with somebody else." They had a wonderful time anyway: talking with other garden-club presidents, ascending the Space Needle, strolling the streets of Seattle. Gay found Helen the perfect companion: enthusiastic, curious, indefatigable, uncomplaining—always ready to make the most of an unpromising situation.

At the end of her term Helen took on the chairmanship of the club's ambitious fund-raising project: the weaving of a large needlepoint rug to be the prize in a raffle. The design was based on an Elizabethan cushion cover—in 1977, when Helen went to England and Scotland with George and Marge Wheeler, she was delighted to find the original at the Victoria and Albert Museum—and sewing it was an elaborate, painstaking process. Helen drew up a long list of instructions for her fellow members: "WASH AND DRY YOUR HANDS: Food, moisture, grease—even garden dirt—are bad for wool and canvas. Newspaper ink is *fatal*." To a woman from another club who in 1979 inquired about the project, Helen wrote:

> Because of the beauty of the design we decided to work the rug in one piece. I bought a quilt frame and have mounted the rug on this. It stands permanently (I sometimes think eternally) in my guest-room. As I have a part-time job, I set aside every Wednesday for needlepoint and the members who are working on the rug come for as much time as they can. About four can work easily at one time. We knew when we decided to work the rug in one piece that it would take a long time but it is slower than we expected. You just can't count on having every worker spend an hour or two a week on this so it is slow. But it is going to be so beautiful that we feel it is worth the extra time and trouble. We have been working eighteen months and have a long way to go but it is going faster now and everyone is enjoying the project.

In those days she enjoyed everything; she was in her early sixties, but she had the energy of a middle-aged woman who was determined to seize as much time as remained to her. Not merely did she start to cook more interesting meals, but she taught herself to bake bread and thenceforth quit buying commercial loaves; she made jellies and jams, she canned summer produce, she baked cakes and pies. In the summers she swam every day, first at Third Beach and then at a cove across the street, not far from "Boothden." She visited Jane in Maine, me in Florida—I had moved to Miami in 1974—and Sarah in San Francisco. One day after early morning tai chi classes in Chinatown, Sarah took her out for a Chinese breakfast: a rice porridge with raw chicken, and dim sum. She found it unusual, but did as she always did: cleaned her plate, and declared herself pleased. Then she laughed. "Daddy won't even believe I did this," she said.

At "Boothden" she had a new friend. In the mid-1970s Avery and Jean Seaman moved down from Providence and settled into the historic old house with its spectacular views of the Sakonnet and, on the far shore, Little Compton. Ave and Jean were about ten years younger than Bill and Helen, dedicated sailors and world travelers in whose adventures the Yardleys, Helen particularly, took vicarious pleasure. They were energetic, outspoken people whose political opinions were considerably to the right of Bill and Helen's, but on that the two couples merely agreed to disagree; they became not merely neighbors but the best of friends. The four had drinks together regularly, and every week or so Helen and Jean sat down for a chat: about the garden club, their children, neighborhood controversies—anything and everything of mutual interest. Their conversations were rarely intimate, for on the deepest matters of heart and soul Helen kept her own counsel, as did most women of her generation and upbringing; but theirs was the closest friendship of Helen's adult life, and it meant more to her than she was able to say.

But reticent though she was about her emotions, there was one qualm about which, to her children at least, she spoke openly. By the late 1970s Bill's health once again had begun to go into decline, and Helen saw before her a bleak prospect. "My greatest fear," she used to say, "is that when Daddy needs someone to care for him all the time and we don't have the money to pay for it, I'm going to have to nurse him myself. I just don't know how I can face it."

B<small>UT IT</small> was from me, not Bill, that bad news came. I had told Bill in midsummer of 1973 that there were difficulties in my marriage; in early August I sent him and Helen a letter that began, "I'm afraid that this report on my situation must be a good deal less optimistic than when Dad and I talked." As Bill stood in the living room reading the letter he quietly began to cry: he was fond of Rosemary and he cherished his grandsons, who had only recently spent two happy, playful weeks at 330 Indian Avenue. A few days later Rosemary called Helen and asked her to come to Greensboro; this she did at once, talking with the two of us separately and giving each of us practical, loving counsel.

For Bill and Helen the divorce that in time followed was painful, not merely because they cared so deeply for all four of the people most immediately affected by it but because they had believed that their family was somehow immune to marital dissolution. Harry and Elsie's divorce had saddened them, but they loved Elsie and welcomed it as a release for her from an intolerable situation. Mine was different. Mine, they suspected, was a marriage that had fallen apart largely because I had not worked hard enough to keep it together; since they had managed to overcome whatever difficulties may have arisen between themselves, they worried that they had

not passed along to me the convictions about loyalty and steadfast-
ness in which they so passionately believed.

Yet if they worried about me, in larger measure they worried for
me. I was their firstborn son; no matter what I did they would
stand by me. Bill gave me a loan of $1,000 to tide me over, and
when I decided to take a job at *The Miami Herald* they seized the
opportunity to unload some of their surplus chattels and artifacts.
They sent all of that—chairs, silverware, odds and ends—and
more. On the first day of the new year Helen wrote: "I can't
possibly tell you all that I wish for you in 1974 but I guess you can
imagine my thoughts. We'll be thinking of you so much, hoping
your new life will be happy and satisfying, that you'll find lots of
good friends and companionship in Miami and that the new job is
all you want it to be. You know how much we love you and how
proud of you we are."

A year later I came to Middletown with someone new in my life:
Sue Hartt, whom I had known professionally through her work at
the Yale University Press. She was a vivacious woman, two years
my junior; she was among other things a person of emphatic
opinions, and a match for Bill at cocktail-hour raillery. One thing
led swiftly and agreeably to another. On March 21, 1975, Bill
made one last airplane flight—by now he loathed and feared air
travel—and came to Miami with Helen for our wedding two days
later. We had not asked Bill to tie a second knot for me, but he did
agree to hold a communion service on the morning of the wedding,
in the little chapel on the campus of the University of Miami. Just
as he was about to begin the service Helen noticed that he had no
wafers, and signaled for his attention.

"Bill!" she whispered. "Psst! Bill!"

He looked at her in bewilderment. "What's the matter?" he
asked in a voice all of us could hear. "Is my fly open?"

The nuptials were read later in the day by Julian Hartt, a
Methodist minister and theologian of great distinction, who married his daughter and me at poolside in the back yard of cherished
friends. After the ceremony there was champagne and laughter;
Helen charmed everyone, and Bill winked his way into all the
ladies' hearts.

A year later they had a happy connubial day of their own. Their fortieth wedding anniversary was to be celebrated on June 20, 1976, so to honor the day they decided to throw themselves a party. It disappointed them that none of their children could come: I was in Miami, Jane in Maine, Sarah in San Francisco, Ben in Chapel Hill. But we all promised to call on the great day, and they said they would look forward to that.

They had no way of knowing that schemes were afoot. On June 16 Sarah flew to New York, stayed with a friend, and four days later took a bus to Middletown. That morning Jane left Caribou by car. At 2:10 P.M. Ben flew into Boston on American Airlines; he walked over to the Delta concourse and met my flight, which arrived at 3:18. We went out to the Logan Airport pickup line for

The fortieth anniversary: Jane, Ben, Helen, Bill, Sarah and Jon

arriving passengers, and within minutes Jane's little Subaru chugged in. We drove to Middletown; there, sitting calmly at the roadside bus stop, was Sarah. The four of us drove into 330 Indian Avenue with the horn blaring. Helen ran into the courtyard, took one look and called, "Bill! It's *my children*!"

Half an hour later, by the dozens, their friends from Middletown and Newport arrived; the four children greeted them as they walked up the driveway. A bartender served drinks in the dining room, and the elaborate buffet that Helen had prepared was set out on the dining table. Toasts were drunk and congratulations offered. At party's end we all pitched in to clean up, then improvised accommodations for ourselves in a house no longer equipped to sleep four guests without a fair degree of adjustment. The next day we did the various things that all of us liked to do in Rhode Island—we shopped on Bellevue Avenue, swam at Third Beach, ate a swordfish dinner expertly broiled by Helen—and the day following we went our separate ways.

It was five years before we were together again: in January, 1981, for the wedding of Sarah and Donald Porter. He was a tall, handsome, witty man whom only Helen and Ben had previously met but who immediately charmed us all. An unusually heavy snow fell on the wedding's eve—it was the first time I had seen snow on Indian Avenue—so the next day we pulled on our boots and tramped down the hill to St. Columba's, the intimate stone chapel where Bill from time to time had preached and where he now did the ministerial honors. Don's widowed mother was there, and a few of his and Sarah's friends; it was a family wedding, quiet and intimate and affectionate.

Jane and Rob came with their daughter, Emily, now nearly eight years old and by unanimous acclaim the family's bright new star. It was great to see Rob. I'd forgotten how much I liked talking to him, so not long after getting back to Baltimore—Sue and I had moved there in 1978—I decided to give him a call. Jane answered. When I asked to speak to him, she said, "He's not here. He's *never* here anymore." I listened in growing astonishment and dismay as she told me, sobbing, how he had inexplicably shut her out of his life and how he was now talking, emphatically and uncompromisingly, about divorce.

Three years later Rob visited Sue and me in Baltimore. Long after Sue had gone to bed he and I talked, and slowly this proud, reticent man began to tell me what had happened: how he had come to feel jealous of Jane's love for Emily, how he had curled up into a shell of his own, how he had been unable to talk to her or anyone else about what he felt and what he wanted. He was remorseful and regretful, of that there can be no doubt, but it was too late: Jane had made a new life for herself, and Rob was not to be a part of it.

But in that winter of 1981 it was Jane who was at sea, baffled by what Rob was doing to her and confused about how she should respond. Helen tried to encourage her. "I wish I knew how to say all I am feeling for you—and for Rob, too, as you must be equally unhappy. You know Daddy and I are thinking of you and praying for you. And I'm sure you know that you and Emmy can always come to us at any time you wish. I have no doubt that you can handle the situation however it develops because you have lots of strength and I think a good sense of yourself and your worth. No marriage is easy and I know I have often been unable to understand Daddy and his feelings—you never really know another person."

Helen was stunned and saddened by the news, as was Bill; there had been hints of trouble in my marriage, but this separation came as a complete surprise. Yet for all her dismay, Helen declined to let it defeat her—or Jane. She offered her love as she always had: firmly and unequivocally, but devoid of sentimentality. As she saw it Jane had a life to lead and practical difficulties to surmount, and her advice was to get on with the business at hand:

> If Rob feels your situation is "irretrievable" that sounds like a self-fulfilling prophecy with a divorce inevitable. It sounds as if he doesn't want to find any other solution. In that case I think, as does Daddy, that you should get yourself a lawyer now and not make *any* decisions without legal advice. Also *not* a Caribou lawyer but one in Bangor, Augusta or Portland. A good tough fighter who will protect

your and Emily's interests. I know you will hate doing this but you really must.

Of course you and Em can come here but I doubt if you will find Newport a place you'd want to be permanently. The job market is not good: 91 Newport teachers and 19 in Middletown have received notice they may not be rehired. Pay is low as there are so many available workers. Most young women seem to end up in real estate or as sales ladies.

I can hardly bear to think of Emily in this situation and you know how much Daddy and I would try to help you both. I'm sure that she will be all right after the first shock but it will be hard and you are right to want to get yourselves settled. But don't do it till you have had legal advice. Is your house in Rob's name or jointly? You have put a lot into acquiring it and therefore have a financial interest in it.

Rob met his obligations; it is impossible to imagine him doing otherwise, no matter what odd and troubling currents were coursing through his psyche. Jane and Emily spent the academic year 1981–1982 in Cambridge, where Jane did advanced study in education at Harvard, in a program not dissimilar to the one Bill had undertaken three and a half decades earlier. Early in her marriage she had taught at a private school in Cambridge while Rob studied law at Boston University, and with her new credentials she was approached by a number of schools. She chose Breck, in suburban Minneapolis; living in a substantial city appealed to her, and Maine had given her a decade's preparation for the Minnesota climate. She did well at Breck and in 1987 became head of its Lower School, in which four hundred students were enrolled. She bought a town house within walking distance of downtown Minneapolis, and made dozens of new friends; Helen's sense of her powers of survival had been acute.

Rob stayed in the big house in Caribou that he and Jane had purchased from his parents; he spent virtually all his time at his law practice, burying himself in its minutiae, closing out the rest of the world. Then in 1984 a malignant melanoma was removed from his stomach. He looked as healthy as ever he had, and he spoke confidently about fighting the disease, but he was also a realist.

Bravely and determinedly though he fought the disease, his was a hopeless cause. When last I saw him, in the fall of 1986, his hair had fallen out and he walked with his right arm pinched against his side, to ease the unremitting, excruciating pain in the lymph glands of his armpit; the last time we talked, in the spring of the next year, his voice was doughty but thin. On May 30, 1987, he died at his mother's house in Falmouth, Maine, at the age of forty-five.

On May 20, 1978, Bill and Helen drove to New Haven for what Bill properly regarded as a singular event in the family's recent history: Ben's graduation from Yale. He had transferred there after two years at Chapel Hill and had thrived, achieving distinguished marks and joining a wide circle of friends. Nothing had given Bill greater pleasure than dropping in on Ben during his Yale years; the way he glowed when he entered Ben's rooms left no doubt that he was thinking, "Now at last I am where I belong." His delight turned to astonishment and pride when, at ceremonies in Ben's college, it was announced that he had graduated summa cum laude: not merely had a Yardley taken the family back to its ancestral university, but he had done so in the highest academic style.

Two days after that ceremony Bill was poking along in his Karmann-Ghia when suddenly he lost consciousness. The car slid off Hanging Rock Road and into the low water standing at its side. For forty-five minutes, while police and passersby noisily but purposelessly debated what course to follow, Bill sat unattended. Finally he was removed from the car and taken to Newport Hospital, where he stayed four weeks. Doctors found that his liver was dotted with cysts; though they gave him only a fifty-fifty chance of survival, the surgery was entirely successful and within two weeks Bill and Helen were having—doctor's orders—cocktails in his hospital room. By Independence Day he was able to tell a friend, "I'm already back on my tractor and in the garden, sans pickaxe—the incision is still sore but me I'm not mad at anybody."

So far as his family could tell, his recovery was complete, though later we realized that it was the beginning of the end of his active life. Eventually he resumed his occasional trips down Interstate 95 to Westchester County—now in a small Mazda coupe, a carbon copy of one Helen had bought in 1980—where he participated to little avail in a no-smoking clinic. Perhaps the best thing the clinic did was to put him, for the first time in his life, in a community in which Jews were predominant. He was curious about their religion, and gladly accepted an invitation to a seder, which he found interesting and spiritually rewarding.

In September of 1981 he loaded up the Mazda and came all the way down I-95 to Baltimore. Sue and I had been living in his old hometown for almost three years, and he decided to pay it a visit. He was, when he alit from the car, a sight to behold: houndstooth tweed cap, herringbone tweed jacket, tartan trousers, plaid shirt and regimental tie—a sartorial cacophony such as I have not witnessed before or since.

It was, I think, one of the happiest excursions of his Middletown years. He and I drove down to Catonsville, where the incumbent rector of St. Timothy's Church kindly let Bill inspect his boyhood home: "It certainly seems small," he said of the rectory, but clearly he was touched at being there and proud to give his son a tour. We went to Fort McHenry—in all his Catonsville years this lover of historic sites had never been there—and had a martini and a crab cake at a restaurant near the Port of Baltimore. On Saturday evening his old friends Callie and Alex Cochran came for dinner; it was a joyful and affectionate reunion, and Bill was in top form. As we rose to enter the dining room after cocktails, Alex patted him on the shoulder and said, "You're a great guy, Bill Yardley"—a sentiment applauded by all, Bill not excluded.

It was his last pleasure trip. Later in the fall the exfoliated dermatitis came back with a vengeance. By early 1982 his doctors thought he needed extended treatment at Massachusetts General Hospital, so in January he drove up there with Ben. Bill managed to lose his way in the maze of highways that weave through central Boston, and after taking the wrong exit found himself in Charlestown, staring at the masts of Old Ironsides. He glared at them with exasperation, then turned to Ben and snapped, "Every time I come to Boston, I visit that God damned *Constitution!*"

He stayed at Mass General for five unhappy and dispirited

333

weeks. "Bill has had a recurrence of the skin trouble he had when we left Chatham," Helen wrote, "and has had several weeks of treatment in Boston. The skin thing covers his hands which makes them so stiff and awkward that writing is very hard for him." That is about as far as her sympathies extended; the inescapable truth is that she was glad to have him out of the house. She only once made the ninety-minute drive from Middletown to Boston during all those weeks, and the visit she paid him then was perfunctory at most.

This seems callous; it certainly seemed so to Jane, who was then in Cambridge and visited Bill frequently during his hospitalization. But Helen had good reason to rejoice at her few days of freedom; by the early 1980s Bill had become her ball and chain. He now expected her to fix his lunch daily, without fail, and he resisted all of her plans for travel. Eventually she felt obliged to quit her job at St. Michael's so as to devote herself to him full-time, but devotion is not what she felt; she was deeply resentful, because the nursemaid's role she had so feared now loomed before her and because she could see her life slipping away before she had lived it to the full.

She and Jean Seaman talked often of going to Italy together, but Helen always ended up sighing and saying, "I just don't think I can leave him alone." Once her Bennington roommate and maid of honor, now Edie Noyes Muma, called and told Helen that she and her husband were nearby; when they arrived a couple of hours later for an afternoon's visit, Helen greeted her with great joy, but also with such relief that Edie felt she must have been crying for companionship and change of scenery.

To all intents and purposes she had been grounded. Over and over she made plans to come to Baltimore; over and over she canceled them. She loved nothing more than to visit her children, and Paul and Maili in Hawaii, but by 1983 she no longer did so. She was permitted only one trip that year: a sad journey to Los Angeles, where her sister, Minnie, was dying of cancer. The next year she decided to attend a Chatham Hall reunion in Boston, which meant she would be away overnight. At breakfast Bill looked up over his applesauce and said, "Please don't go." She stared at him for a long moment, then said, "Oh, all right." She was heartbroken and angry: and all the more resentful.

It must be noted, though, that if within the bosom of her family she felt oppressed, she was a co-conspirator in that oppression. Had ever she said to Bill, "I'm going to Italy and we're going to pay to have someone come in and cook for you," he would have whimpered and complained, but he also would have acquiesced. What else could he have done? Helen was a prisoner, to be sure, but not merely of her husband: she was also a prisoner of her generation and her upbringing, both of which taught that a woman's first duty was to her husband. Helen Gregory Yardley was, above all else, a dutiful woman.

She did have one small triumph. In September of 1983 she was elected to the board of directors of the Redwood Library. Her obligations were small: she faithfully attended the board's bi-monthly meetings, though the minutes indicate that she did so quietly, and she served on its Book Committee, the real decisions of which were made by the librarians. But she enjoyed the meetings—most of the trustees were her friends—and she was quietly amused, not to mention pleased, that it was to her rather than to her notably bibliophilic husband that the board had turned.

What she did not like about the meetings was that they obliged her to drive into Newport proper—or, as she and Bill now saw it, Newport improper. Over a decade the historic old seaport and summer community had changed so drastically as to be nearly unrecognizable. Not merely had Thames Street been boutiqued to a fare-thee-well, but pedestrian and vehicular traffic was so intense that the city seemed on the edge of terminal gridlock, not merely in the high vacation season but year-round. Indian Avenue remained essentially unchanged, but elsewhere in Middletown the developers had done their dirty work, throwing up a proliferation of overpriced dwellings on what had once been potato fields and pastures. Over drinks Bill ranted and railed about the God damned developers and the God damned town council; Helen shared his sentiments if not the expression of them. The Newport they had loved was dead and their own Middletown, they feared, would soon be buried alongside it.

Helen still went about her rounds, but she rearranged them; she now shopped at a supermarket in Middletown instead of the one on Bellevue Avenue in Newport, and she took her other business to other suburban merchants. Bill went scarcely anywhere, save to Marty's for his daily *Times*; considering the confusion and inattentiveness of his mind, this was just as well for other motorists. He sat all day in his study, leafing eternally through the *Times* or picture books about British houses.

"Why don't you look at television?" Jean asked him. "You could watch the opera, if you like that, and you know they have first-rate programs on public television."

"No!" Bill shot back. "I would never look at television, never watch television!"

He preferred to slip back into the comfort of memory. When friends came for cocktails he droned on and on about Timothy Dwight and Aaron Burr and Sir George Yeardley and John Woolsey, marching out the whole panoply of relatives and connections. "Oh, Bill, come on," Helen said, "we've all heard that one before," but on and on he rambled.

His friends had been fond of him, but now many of them began to see him as a tiresome old bore. They wanted to visit Helen—for the first time in their married life she, not her husband, was the magnet that drew people into their household—but the price of doing so was getting higher and higher. They sensed, too, as at times did Bill and Helen's children, that there was more tension than affection between them now. To Jean and to Gay Sheffield, her most frequent companions in these days, Helen spoke often of her frustration that Bill seemed to be capitulating to old age. "Why can't he be active?" she asked again and again. "Why does he just sit there? I hate to see him giving up like this."

The way Bill saw it, he was merely obeying doctors' orders. Years after they should have done so, they finally told him to stay out of the sun, which was damaging his skin and exacerbating his dermatitis. So he sold his tractor, hired a lawn service, and retired to his chair. Why didn't he just say, "To hell with it! At my age I'll do whatever I damned well please," and keep right on mowing to the end? The answer almost certainly is that for all the impression he gave of quitting, of acquiescing in his debilitation, he was still hanging on to life. If the doctors told him his health would improve if he stayed out of the sun, then that is what he would do. He hated and resented their counsel, but he obeyed it because he believed it was in his best interests.

One final hurrah remained to him. On July 14, 1984, he officiated at his youngest child's wedding. Ben had graduated from the University of Michigan Law School the previous summer; while attending a cram course for the New Hampshire bar examination he had met a pert, formidably bright young woman named Carrie Green, and now was making ready to settle down with her in Manchester, New Hampshire. So once again we all came back to 330 Indian Avenue, this time with yet another addition: Colin Yardley Porter, who had been born to Sarah and Don the previous December.

July 14 was a bright, clear, balmy day: Aquidneck Island at its most incandescent. The family gathered privately at St. Columba's in the morning for Colin's baptism, then reconvened there in the afternoon for the wedding. Ben's joy was transparent and

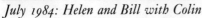

July 1984: Helen and Bill with Colin

contagious; the last of Bill and Helen's four children now had his own spouse and his own career, and all of us rejoiced with him at the love and hope with which he was suffused.

Yet as I observed and participated in these cheerful familial rites, I could not suppress a sense of anxiety and foreboding: a fear that this happy day might be our last together as a family. Bill did not seem well. While holding Colin before the baptismal font at St. Columba's, he had nearly dropped his grandson on the chapel's hard stone floor. At the wedding that afternoon he was no better. He had no baby to drop, but he repeatedly lost his way in the marital rite he had performed more often than anyone could remember. A couple of times he looked blearily out at the small congregation as if pleading for its patience. Helen was openly peevish as she stood beside her family in the front row on the groom's side. "Oh, come on, Bill," she whispered, "get it over with!"

When the wedding party had returned to the house for the reception, Bill continued in the same vein. He meant to be hospitable and avuncular, but there was a sharp edge to him. He wandered around the courtyard, trying to be friendly and amusing but succeeding only in making a small spectacle of himself. What, I wondered, did Helen think as she watched? Was she yearning for her freedom, praying that something other than nursing this pitiable old wreck remained to her?

ONE NIGHT in January of 1985 Helen went to bed with a heavy feeling in her chest; when she awoke in the morning her pain was extreme. She went immediately to her doctor, who examined her and said he did not like what he heard in her lung; she'd better go to the hospital for a more detailed diagnostic exam, he said.

She had it the next day. In the morning she went shopping, then stopped at Marge Wheeler's house for a visit; she was, if not so cheerful as usual, in good spirits and in the mood to talk. Then it was time to go to the hospital. She was tested and X-rayed, and given the news that already she had suspected: it looked as if there was a growth on her lung. Surgery would be necessary so a piece of the tumor could be removed and a biopsy made.

That was on January 14. None of her children had been told about what she was going through; she and Bill did not like to "burden" their children with bad news. But that evening Bill called me. By this point he had become terrible on the telephone; he was nearly deaf and he stubbornly refused to wear his hearing aid. It was never easy to talk with him on the phone; the state he was now in made it all the worse.

Our conversation lurched in several directions, all of them painful. What it came down to was that Bill was distraught because there was no longer someone to cook his meals and order his life.

339

His debility and self-absorption had made him, when he was at his least attractive, a selfish old man; this, not a loving and worried husband, was what came across the telephone wires that night.

I told him I would be there on Wednesday. Then I called Helen in the hospital. She sounded anxious, but certainly not hysterical. I told her that Bill seemed primarily concerned about his own well-being. "Well," she said, "that's not surprising, because I certainly have spoiled him."

On Wednesday I went straight to the hospital. Helen's relief at seeing me was transparent: she knew that at the so-called caring arts I was lamentably deficient, but here at least was a family member whose feet were more or less on the ground and who could get matters under control on Indian Avenue. About the next day's surgery she was fatalistic, and we did not labor the subject. For a time we talked about retirement communities. She had tried to persuade Bill that they should choose one and get themselves on its waiting list against the possibility of either or both of them becoming bedridden, but he had refused to discuss the subject seriously. "Nobody's going to take me to the old folks' home," he muttered, and that was that.

"Now it's probably too late," she said that afternoon. "I really doubt if we'll be able to get into a nice place in time to do ourselves any good."

Yet however resentful she may have felt toward Bill, she could not—nor did she really seem to want to—shake off the habits of all the years of watching over him. "You'd really better get out to the house, Jon," she said. "Daddy is probably sick with worry."

I arrived in time to fix his tray and pour his drink. We sat in the living room and tried to talk; it was obvious that Bill had only a dim idea of what had come to pass in his life. Quite apart from his petulant self-absorption, he was an ill man whose behavior resembled that of a person suffering from Alzheimer's disease. His mind now permitted him to see only so far as the next meal, which I went off to the kitchen to prepare; but the possibility that Helen might come back from the hospital a seriously ill woman, or that she might not come back from the hospital at all—these prospects he simply could not entertain.

After dinner he went off to his study. I did the dishes and then sat in the corner chair next to Helen's desk in the dining room. On her radio I found a jazz broadcast, which I played quietly, trying to relax after this emotionally debilitating day. After a while Bill shuffled into the kitchen for a glass of water, and suddenly things were just as they had been thirty years before. For a long moment he stared at me, then in a thin shout commanded, "Turn that God damned radio off!"

The next day's news was as bad as feared. The growth was malignant, and not susceptible to surgical removal. Radiation rather than chemotherapy was prescribed; the doctors told Helen there was a reasonable chance that the cancer would go into remission and that she could live considerably longer.

She lay in the bed, pale and drained. "Well," I said, "at least they say they can do something for you. At least there's hope that you'll get better."

"I know," she said, in a faint and colorless voice I had never before heard from her. "But I still have lung cancer."

I could think of no satisfactory reply. Bill, in the chair next to me, had nothing to add. He sat there, his jaw slack, an old man's stubble on it, looking uncomprehendingly at this woman who had been his companion for nearly half a century. He knew that all was not well with her, but even in the hospital, with its clinging medicinal smells and its pervasive aura of physical decay, the message did not come through to him. He assumed, quite simply, that she would get out of bed and come back home to cook for him.

This, incredibly, she did. Within a few days not merely was she at home, but she was back in the kitchen and at her desk, doing all the business that Bill could not—or would not—do himself. "Dear Dutch," she wrote on February 5 to Jerry Van Voorhis at Chatham Hall, "How nice it was to receive the pretty basket of spring flowers from 'Friends at Chatham Hall.' Please thank everyone for me." Then she addressed the letter's real purpose: "I hate to bother you with anything more, but, in the first few days of confusion when I went to the hospital, several days of mail disappeared—

including Bill's January check from the school. I'm sure it was thrown away so am hoping you can have a duplicate issued."

Soon the radiation treatments began. Five days a week for a month and a half she was driven to Providence, forty-five minutes to an hour each way, by Jean or Gay. As the treatments rose in number, so, too, did the pile of forms on Helen's desk, the officious computerized sheets that are, in these late years of the twentieth century, how we record the closing chapters of American lives: MAJOR MEDICAL CLAIMS EXPENSE SUMMARY, and HEALTH CARE BENEFITS SUMMARY, and YOUR EXPLANATION OF MEDICARE BENEFITS. Eventually these went into a folder called "Health Forms": in short time it was thickest of all the files in the little cabinet Toimi Paarsinen had made so many years before.

The radiation helped, though whether it added any days to Helen's life seems to me problematical. But the treatments took a lot out of her. She seemed somehow to have shrunk, to have gone just the tiniest bit out of focus, to have lost heart. She made a determined effort to be cheerful for her children, who one by one came to see her, but the effort was obvious; this was particularly evident in August, when she put her foot down and told Bill that she was going to visit Jane in Minneapolis and me in Baltimore.

Sarah flew east to baby-sit Bill, bringing Colin with her. Helen packed her little blue suitcase and went to Minneapolis. She wanted to see Jane's school and meet her friends, but her energy level was low; at a dinner for members of the administration and faculty she was charming, but had to leave early in order to go to bed. She wanted to buy a necklace for Sarah's birthday present, but after fifteen minutes of shopping she had to sit down and rest.

There and in Baltimore she left the impression that she was in greater pain than she would admit. Her breath was short, and often when she laughed she winced, though she tried to disguise it. For an hour she and I sat on the front porch with scarcely a word passing between us: she had nothing to say and I was tongue-tied, at a loss for words to say to my dying mother who wished, above all else, not to talk about her death.

The cancer was in remission, but that was the most she could hope for. It stayed that way through the holidays, which she and

Bill celebrated quietly; they had abandoned the extravagant Christmases years before and had even bought an artificial tabletop tree, but at Christmas of 1985 they barely went through the motions. Yet even in this dark time, Helen's spirit was resilient; for each of the four young women in her life—Jane and Sarah, Carrie and Sue—she knitted a sleeveless sweater vest as a Christmas gift.

Then, late in the winter, the cancer began to grow again. This time radiation offered no hope. The deathwatch had begun.

I came to Middletown in the middle of April. Helen was visibly smaller and thinner; the bones of her face had begun to show through the skin, and her shoulders were so frail that I hesitated to embrace her for fear of breaking them.

She wanted to have her hair done, so I drove her to the hairdresser's. On the way we had our only words on the subject most immediately at hand.

"I just don't know what Daddy's going to do when I die," Helen said.

"Neither do I."

"He's so dependent on me, and I can do so little for him now. I'm afraid he'll just fall apart."

I could offer nothing but a weak assent. For a mile we drove in silence, until Helen spoke again.

"Life like this just isn't much fun," she said.

Later, back at 330 Indian Avenue, I fixed drinks and snacks for them. Helen was down to a single glass of white wine, watered down, and Bill's vodka was watered too. The tray, by contrast with past glories, was a perfunctory offering: a few sliced vegetables and a couple of chunks of unappetizing cheese.

They sat in their usual places: Helen in her chair, Bill on the sofa. They hemmed and hawed, until Bill finally spoke.

"Uh, Jon," he said, "Mummy and I wonder if you and Sue would be willing to take Benny."

My jaw dropped. I looked at them in astonishment: *take Benny?* He was the last of the Yardley dachshunds; Willie had been put down only a few weeks before. For a moment my heart sank to the floor: I knew that if they were giving up on Benny, they were giving up on life.

We took him, of course: Did we really have any choice? But I was not happy about adding him to a household already ruled by an alley cat and a beagle. Our animals were placid, quiet and undemanding; Benny was neurotic, noisy and insistent. How on earth would this creature fit in?

He had been a Yardley dachshund for only three years, and he did not resemble the others in anything except height, or lack of it. From Gretchen to Willie, Bill's dogs had been short-haired and reddish; Benny was long-haired and black. He had come to Indian Avenue on an impulse of Bill's; in the summer of 1983 Bill had seen Benny's picture in the God damned *Newport Daily News:* he was "Dog of the Week," up for adoption at the Robert Potter League's animal shelter in Middletown.

Bill's heart rushed out. He drove to the league and inspected the dog, who turned out to be four years old; his American Kennel Club registration identified him as Benjamin Badger. His original owner, a woman from California, evidently had tired of his incessant demands and had dropped him out of her life. But Bill could not resist his furiously wagging tail. He made out a check for $50 to the shelter, in the lower-left corner of which he wrote, "Dachshund in a poke."

Now the dog was mine. The next morning I went to the vet's for a tranquilizer, to calm Benny's nerves and make the drive home bearable. I asked the vet, "Was it really necessary to have Willie put down?"

"No, it wasn't," he said. "He was an old dog, but he could have lived a few more years. But your father gave me no choice. He was convinced that Willie was too sick to live. I think he just didn't want to care for him anymore."

Nor did I much want to care for Benny. In Baltimore he promptly confirmed all my apprehensions. He barked at every passing cloud, he attached himself to Sue with a ferocity that confirmed his contempt for me, he whimpered whenever he was left alone.

"I can't take it," I told Sue. "That damned dog is driving me crazy. If he doesn't shape up he's going to the pound."

She counseled patience, and she was right. Over the months a funny thing happened: Benny began to work his way into my heart. Taking him for walks, I couldn't help laughing at his gait, an endearing mix of strut and waddle. In moments of high excitement he launched himself into vertical leaps, small explosions of joy. His friendliness and his loyalty—even to me—soon became irresistible; he was Bill and Helen's last gift to us.

By the middle of the spring Helen was bedridden; though she was ambulatory, she was too weak to stay on her feet for long. This proudly independent woman now depended on the kindnesses of her friends and the good offices of strangers. The financial affairs of the household had been turned over to Ben, who had power of attorney and was their trustee. More than that, it was upon Ben and Carrie that the heaviest burden of care for Bill and Helen descended. They were living in Manchester, a two-and-a-half-hour drive from Middletown; because of proximity, it fell to them to make regular visits and thus to embody, for our ailing parents, the absent love of all their children.

But the household's daily affairs were still in Helen's hands. She patched together a schedule of paid helpers who came in to cook and clean, but she was ever vulnerable to the comings and goings of others; there were days when dinner was in doubt, and times when she had to struggle into the kitchen and do the job herself.

"It's terrible," she told Jean. "I'm not able to run the house. I can't find the help to come in and Bill's no help at all."

She longed to have her children closer, but she knew that all of us worked and were tied down by other responsibilities. "I wish one of the girls would come and stay for a while," she said, but she did not press the issue with us; we came as often as we could, but no one knew better than we that it was not enough. Like all grown children who find themselves torn between their own lives and those of their parents, we were shaken by grief and guilt, yet could see no workable alternative to the unsatisfactory course we followed.

345

I returned in June. A year earlier Helen and Bill had planned to celebrate their fiftieth anniversary with the entire family, but now that it was upon them they wanted no celebration at all. No party, no champagne: in the eerie stillness of that house, they wanted no disturbance.

I came anyway. At six o'clock on the evening of June 20, 1986, I brought the drinks and snacks into the living room. Fifty years ago, to the moment, Bill and Helen had toasted each other and their future together; now they sat, measuring each breath, not speaking.

I raised my glass. What could I say? "Well, here's to fifty wonderful years." They sipped their drinks, and said nothing.

By early August, Jean had worked what seemed to Helen a miracle. She obtained, through a nursing agency in Providence, the services of what the brochure called a "Live-in Homemaker/Home Health Aide," at the cost of $95 a day. Her name was Virginia Martin. She was an immense, purposeful, good-hearted woman whose efficiency and eagerness to please seemed, to Helen, blessings from heaven. "I'm so grateful to have Virginia," she said. "Now I don't have to worry anymore."

A few days after Virginia's arrival Al Gregory flew in from California. He met Art, who lived in Massachusetts, and together they drove to Middletown. Helen greeted them in the courtyard, where she lay under the sun on a chaise longue. She was covered by a blanket, which she had drawn to her chin, hiding her emaciation. Her brothers—"the boys," as she still thought of them— stayed for less than half an hour, talking quietly; it was obvious that she was making an effort, and they did not want to tire her further.

Each day her friends came for brief visits. She hadn't the energy to talk but she wanted to listen. Gay always tried to have a funny story for her, or a juicy piece of neighborhood gossip: anything that might divert her from her pain. Her friends knew how she felt about them; these were not people who put their emotions on display. But once Helen let slip her feelings for all of them. Bobbie

Sturtevant was leaving her room at the end of a visit, and turned at the door to wave good-bye.

Helen waved back weakly. "Bobbie, I love you," she said.

Ben phoned on September 1. "The doctor says that Mummy will die before the month is out," he said. "If any of us want to see her one more time, he says we'd better do it soon."

That was Monday. I rearranged my schedule, and called first thing the next morning. I did not recognize the voice that answered.

"Virginia?" I asked.

"No, it's Jean."

"What's wrong? Why are you there so early?"

Jean started to reply when Helen lifted the receiver off the phone on her bedside table. Then she spoke.

"*Ngggh,*" she said. "*Ngggh!*"

My heart stopped.

"Ma! Is that you?"

"*Ngggh! Ngggh!*"

"Ma, I'm coming up on Thursday. I'll be there as soon as I can."

Jean broke in: "I think we'd better hang up. I'd better get to the bedroom."

There wasn't much to do except make Helen as comfortable as she could be. Bill put on his bathrobe and shuffled to the chair beside her bed; he had sat there for a while each morning since she became bedridden, silently offering what remained of his tired old love. Jean and Virginia pulled up chairs and sat beside him.

They stayed for a couple of hours, talking occasionally. Helen lay quietly, her eyes open, until at last with a small smile she closed them.

Jean took Bill's hand. "Bill, it doesn't look good," she said. For a long time he sat there, his mind slowly working, trying to comprehend what had happened. Then he spoke.

"Poor Helen," he said. "I guess she died."

———

Epilogue

S IX MONTHS later I came back to Middletown. Virginia had stayed on, caring for Bill as assiduously as she had for Helen, but this odd pair had tired of each other. Bill had become more of a handful than Virginia had bargained for. As the arteries to his brain slowly hardened, he grew ever more petulant and childish, and he was no longer continent. He needed the care that an institution best could provide.

At 330 Indian Avenue, moreover, Bill was living on borrowed time. On the last day of 1986 Ben had sold the house and property, for substantially more than ten times Bill and Helen's actual investment: what a pity it was that Helen did not live to see how healthily this investment had grown, and that Bill's mind could not entirely grasp the good fortune that had come his way. The sale meant that there was now enough money to assure Bill's well-being in a retirement community, though finding one that could admit him was another matter altogether; until we were able to do so, Ben had arranged to rent the house from the new owner.

But all efforts to obtain lodging for Bill in a "lifecare community" came to nothing. One in Massachusetts had indicated it would be able to find a room for him. Jane and Emily took him there over the Christmas holidays; he responded excitedly and with his old charm, almost winking his way into the place. But the opening never came, and on Indian Avenue time was growing short. So Ben arranged to move him into a nursing home on the outskirts of Manchester, an institution with an excellent reputation, and on March 14, 1987, I drove to Middletown to take him there.

He was in the chair in his study when I arrived. He gave me a weak welcome. I sat on his footstool and tried to tell him what was about to happen.

"Dad," I said, "Ben has found a place for you to live near him and Carrie in Manchester. He says that it's very nice and that you'll be comfortable there. Tomorrow I'm going to take you to the doctor in Providence, and then we'll go to Manchester."

He looked at me dimly; not a word had penetrated. "What's that?" he said.

Further discussion seemed pointless. I patted his thin leg. "Everything will be just fine, Dad," I said, and then I left him to his inexpressible thoughts.

The next morning Virginia and I led him to the car. He was using a walker now; it took ten minutes for him to negotiate the forty-foot trek from the front door to the driveway.

In the trunk were a suitcase with the small supply of clothing he needed for his new life, and a few mementos: a sketch of Helen as a young woman, a half-dozen novels by John P. Marquand, a few of his picture books about English houses, a photograph of three of his dachshunds. I eased him into the passenger seat, put his walker in the back, and drove away. Without a word of farewell, Bill Yardley left the little hill on Indian Avenue for the last time.

We reached the nursing home shortly before one that afternoon. "Here we are," I said, and went around the car to help Bill out. Uncomplainingly, he let me hoist him into the walker, then looked around.

"So this is where the party is," he said.

"That's right," I said, and urged him toward the door.

The decor inside was pleasant. I took Bill to the dining room. He sat there, alone, a small figure happily eating whatever was put before him, while I sneaked out to unload the car.

After lunch I moved him to the living room and gave him a *New*

York Times. In an irritated tone he asked, "Why don't you just sit down?"

"I will in a minute, Dad," I replied. "I just have a few errands to do."

Finally his room was ready. The nurse and I were steering him toward it—for some reason he had put his tattered gray tweed overcoat back on, and had a fur hat perched on his head—when an attendant pushed by with a cart on which his belongings had been piled. The picture of his dachshunds lay on top.

"Why, those are my dogs!" he said, and smiled. Then he stopped, his hands seizing the arms of the walker. With a rush, reality flooded in on him.

"No!" he shouted. "Take me away from here! Get me away from these God damned people!"

A nurse hurried up with a wheelchair. Bill struggled against us, but we eased him into it and pushed him down the hall to his room. He refused to leave the chair, but sat there pouting and swearing.

It was more than I could bear. My hands were sweating and my knees trembling. I left him and went to the nurses' station. I told the head nurse that I was exhausted, both physically and emotionally, and feared that my presence could do him no good. She agreed.

While she and I talked, Bill's curiosity got the better of him. He rose unsteadily from the chair and came down the hall, holding on to the handrail. It took several minutes, but at last he reached the nurses' station.

I put my hand on his shoulder. "Dad, I'm going over to Ben's house," I said. "I'll see you soon."

"Hmmpf!" he snorted. "That's what they all say."

I turned and walked toward the door. As I left I looked quickly back to the nurses' station. He stood there in his shabby coat and silly hat, awaiting the bidding of others. He was wholly at their mercy.

They treated him kindly and well. He was difficult at first, petulant and temperamental, but they were patient; petulant and temperamental old people were their daily business. Gradually he responded to them, and became one of their most popular patients. He was still incontinent and he did not cooperate with efforts to encourage him to exercise, but the nurses and attendants were accustomed to difficulties such as these. What they liked was that he became a sweet old man, and that he was interesting.

They never knew what was coming next. Once, apropos of nothing at all, he said, "I'm sorry that I never got my Ph.D." Another time he gazed into the hall and said, "Who *are* all those people? Why don't they leave calling cards? Why doesn't anybody leave calling cards anymore?"

He ate his three daily meals—his appetite never deserted him— and they kept a pack of cigarettes on hand for him; they pushed his chair to the smoking room when he wanted one. While he smoked he stared at the television set, and from time to time seemed interested in what he saw. This routine, punctuated by regular visits by Ben and Carrie and far less frequent ones by his more distant children, became for him a life of sorts, and all things considered he was comfortable in it.

Then, late in the winter of 1988, he had a stroke: not a powerful one, but enough to reduce the mobility of his left side. It was followed by an infection that spread to and clogged his lungs. On the evening of March 13 he lay in his bed, unconscious, gasping for each breath. The nurse attending him left briefly to check on another patient. When she returned, he was dead.

An hour later Ben and Carrie came to the nursing home. Bill lay there, still. This calmness, after so much struggle, gave them comfort.

On March 17 the children of Bill and Helen Yardley came together, for the second time in a year and a half, to say farewell to one of our parents. In September of 1986 we had met at St. Columba's Church on Indian Avenue; after that service the four of us took Helen's ashes to the rocky cove where she had so loved to swim, and scattered them in the Sakonnet River.

Now we were on Long Island, in a motel, preparing to go to the Woolsey family cemetery called Dosoris. This was as Bill had

———

wished, but we were apprehensive; none of us had been there, and we had no idea what to expect.

We drove to the cemetery: Ben and Carrie, Jane and Sarah, I and my younger son, Bill's namesake, representing the four grand-children. The moment we arrived we knew that Bill Yardley, as usually he did, had known best. The cemetery was a tranquil patch of land, a fine and quiet little place bounded on all sides by stone and brick fences. Inside we were greeted by Bill's treasured familial past. There, under a worn tombstone, lay the Reverend Benjamin Woolsey. Sarah Chauncey Woolsey rested over yonder, and Judge John Woolsey nearby.

In an ivied spot beside the wall a hole had been dug, one foot in diameter and three feet deep: so small a hole for so large a life. The minister placed the tiny box containing Bill's ashes in it, and read the brief order for the burial of the dead. A benediction was said, and the service was over.

For a while thereafter we wandered around the cemetery, look-ing at the stones and telling the family stories they brought to mind, but that was hardly an afternoon's occupation. We had a couple of hours to kill until we could claim our dinner reservations. What to do?

We decided, on the spur of the moment, to drive over to Oyster Bay, a few miles to the east, and pay a visit to Sagamore Hill, Theodore Roosevelt's treasured Long Island house. We got there at four o'clock, and for an hour had it to ourselves, this rambling old house through which the children of Teddy and Edith Roosevelt had cavorted, to which the great man had repaired to escape the cares of public life, in which he had felt closer to his deep American roots than anywhere else on earth. It was a house that still reverbe-rated with life; as I walked through it I thought not of Roosevelt lives, but of Yardley lives.

Standing in Teddy's study on the third floor, its shelves crowded with books and its walls with memorabilia, I looked out through the treetops and saw, in the near distance, a glimmer of Long Island Sound. The beauty of the scene reminded me of the beauty with which Bill and Helen had been blessed in all the places where they had lived, and the bookish clutter of the room called to mind

355

their passionate literary interests. How fitting, I thought, that an hour after my father's burial I should be in a historic site to which, some forty years before, he had taken me—hoping, no doubt, to pass along to his first son his own loyalty to his country and his abiding interest in its past.

The Roosevelts had money and fame, which Bill and Helen did not, and their names are to be found in the history books, as Bill's and Helen's are not. This is as it should be: the stories of most lives are told in private. Yet however different the paths the Roosevelts and Yardleys followed, they came from the same world: that of those Americans whose histories went back to the beginning of the country, who had through the lives of their own ancestors intimate knowledge of the traditions and convictions out of which the nation had been shaped. Theirs is a world forever lost, to be glimpsed now only in the fading relics of these vanished people who made things what they are. For all of them I recalled, in silence, the prayer that an hour earlier had been said for Bill, as a year and a half before it had been for Helen, and as in time it will be for the four children whom they brought into the world.

O Lord, support us all the day long, until the shadows lengthen, and the evening comes, and the busy world is hushed, and the fever of life is over, and our work is done. Then in thy mercy, grant us a safe lodging, and a holy rest, and peace at the last.

AMEN

Family reunion in Baltimore, June 1988: Bottom: *Sarah, Colin and Carrie.* Middle: *Jon (holding Benny), Emily, Jane and Ben.* Top: *Sue, Jim and Bill* (Photo by Larry Canner)